PRAISE FOR **SAVE THE DELI**

"Wonderful . . . both memorial and call to arms. . . . It's a trip that suggests a Proust-like mission, in which the writer, by gorging his way around the map . . . tries to recapture the joy of his first childhood meals in the storied delis of Montreal."
— *Los Angeles Times*

"Histories of delis from the Carnegie and Stage to Katz's and the Second Avenue Deli are relayed in loving detail, and it's almost impossible to come away from the book without wanting to run out for a pastrami sandwich from any one of these places."
— *Village Voice*'s Fork in the Road

"In glorious, mouth-watering detail . . . [*Save the Deli* is] part history, part travelogue and the 'Food and Yiddish Appendix' in the back is worth the price alone. . . . [Sax] captures the very essence of deli culture." — Huffington Post

"As in all great food writing, Sax describes his subject with a tantalizing vividness; his deli experiences are so well rendered that we simultaneously feel connected and estranged from the food."
— Bostonist

"A necessary, though elegiac, appreciation of the history, and the menus, and the (declining) fortunes of this culinary institution."
— *Chicago Tribune*

"A generous helping of Jewish history . . . Sax's book is a gastronomic romp." — *Jerusalem Post*

"This year's heavyweight title for world's biggest deli champion . . . goes unquestionably to David Sax." —*Tablet*

"Sax brings passion and substance to *Save the Deli*. . . . Besides providing vivid descriptions of the food he eats along the way, the author delves into the cultural history of the cuisine."
—*Barnes & Noble Review*

"Fascinating . . . A brilliantly entertaining travelogue through the world of the contemporary Jewish delicatessen. [Sax's] descriptions . . . melt in your mouth." —*Jewish Week*

"An entertaining yet often elegiac journey to chronicle an endangered cuisine . . . The detailed listing of delis in the back of the book should be laminated and kept on hand when traveling."
—Amazon's Omnivoracious

"A valued source for noshers . . . [*Save the Deli*] captures the joys, woes, and flavors of a cuisine." —*New Jersey Jewish News*

"*Save the Deli* will make you crave house-cured, smoked, steamed, and finally hand-cut pastrami—and curse the demographic changes that have caused this delicacy to disappear."
—*Winnipeg Free Press*

"David Sax might be the world's foremost delicatologist."
—*Toronto Star*

"A wistful, riotously funny paean to this quintessential slice of American Jewish history . . . A delicious romp through a fast-disappearing world."—Jewish Telegraphic Agency

"Vivid and conversational . . . This engaging book should delight anyone with an interest in culinary history and Jewish food."
—*Library Journal*

"Marvellous . . . [*Save the Deli*] is part social history, part travelogue, and a tremendous food guide." —The Commentary

"Sax is an entertaining writer, and the descriptions of the food are often mouthwatering." —*Kirkus Reviews*

"Just a few chapters in, and you'll find yourself hungry for hot pastrami sandwiches, matzo ball soup, maybe even ready to try some gribenes (chicken skin fried in chicken fat) . . . [The] chapters shine." —*Publishers Weekly*

"Sax's insightful writing is peppered with humor, and his food descriptions are, well, drool-inducing . . . To die for."
—*McGill News*

"Just the thought of a book dedicated to the history and cultural importance of Jewish Deli makes my mouth water. And who better to take on the project than passionate writer and adventurer David Sax. His knowledge and experience make him the perfect man for the job. Without a bible like this how will our next generation of eaters know the delight and pure satisfaction of biting into that perfect pastrami on rye, smothered in mustard, and accompanied by a full-sour dill pickle?"
—Gail Simmons, Judge on Bravo's *Top Chef*

"David Sax's book on delicatessens is an important work. The food is an important part of the Jewish culture. We could not have grown up without it . . . I must say that the book is a great read for anyone, from the culture conscious to the foodies."
—Fyvush Finkel, Yiddish theater legend

"A delightful tour of Jewish delicatessens across the nation and abroad, David Sax opens a necessary discussion about the very future of those beloved, yet dwindling, institutions. *Save the Deli* is a great read." —Ed Koch

"The kid knows how to eat and he knows how to write. You can't ask for more than that, although a glass of cream soda is always nice." — Alan Richman, author of *Fork It Over*

"What if they gave a pastrami on rye and nobody came? Unthinkable? That's what you think. David Sax knows better, and traces the history of the American (and Canadian. And British!) deli — its arrival, its rise, its potential fall, its possible salvation — with passion, humor, *chutzpah*, and *tam*. Enjoy."
                    — Ellis Weiner, author of *Yiddish with Dick and Jane*

"Part elegy, part lament, part rallying cry for a generation whose nitrate levels are already dangerously low, David Sax's book is an unparalleled look at the past, present, and possible future of the pastrami, corned beef, smoked meat, kishka, and cabbage rolls that have given generations the strength to kvetch and a reason to do so." — Michael Wex, author of *Born to Kvetch*

"This book is the result of an epic journey, akin to *The Odyssey* but with Rolaids. With insight, passion, and a digestive system at which one can only marvel, Sax peers between the layers of a pastrami sandwich and glimpses the evolution of Jewish community and identity." — Roger Bennett, author of *Bar Mitzvah Disco*

"A voluptuous mitzvah for schmaltzophiles, *Save the Deli* also is a singularly practical guide to the best delis from coast to coast and around the world."
                    — Jane and Michael Stern, authors of *Roadfood*

"David Sax is the M. F. K. Fisher of pickled meats. After *Save the Deli,* you'll never take a pastrami sandwich for granted again. You'll also be moved by Sax's wonderful portrayal of the folks behind the counters, and their fascinating thoughts on cultural identity, the relentless passage of time — and, of course, kreplach."
                    — A. J. Jacobs, author of *The Know-It-All*
                    and *The Guinea Pig Diaries*

SAVE THE DELI

SAVE THE DELI

IN SEARCH OF
**PERFECT PASTRAMI,
CRUSTY RYE,**
AND THE HEART OF
JEWISH DELICATESSEN

David Sax

MARINER BOOKS
HOUGHTON MIFFLIN HARCOURT
BOSTON   NEW YORK

First Mariner Books edition 2010

Copyright © 2009 by David Sax

ALL RIGHTS RESERVED

For information about permission to reproduce selections from this book,
write to Permissions, Houghton Mifflin Harcourt Publishing Company,
215 Park Avenue South, New York, New York, 10003.

www.hmhbooks.com

First published in Canada in 2009 by McClelland & Stewart Ltd.

Library of Congress Cataloging-in-Publication Data
Sax, David.
Save the deli : in search of perfect pastrami, crusty rye, and
the heart of the Jewish delicatessen / David Sax.
p. cm.
ISBN 978-0-15-101384-5
1. Restaurants — History. 2. Delicatessens — History.
3. Jewish cookery. I. Title.
TX945.4.S393 2009
647.9509 — dc22   2009013743

ISBN 978-0-547-38644-7 (pbk.)

Printed in the United States of America

DOC 10 9 8 7 6 5 4 3 2 1

Portions of the Afterword to the Paperback Edition
originally appeared in *Gourmet* magazine.

TO "POPPA" SAM SAX,
AND THE DELI-LOVING FAMILY HE RAISED

Contents

Part Three: TRAVELS IN THE DELI DIASPORA

SAVE THE DELI

"Anytime a person goes into a delicatessen and orders a pastrami on white bread, somewhere a Jew dies." —Milton Berle

Introduction

Two years before I was born, my grandfather "Poppa" Sam Sax died by way of a smoked meat sandwich from Schwartz's Hebrew Delicatessen in Montreal. Piled high with extra *speck* (paprika- and cayenne-dusted, twice-smoked slices of pickled fat), he devoured the ill-advised delicacy immediately on his release from the hospital, where he had been treated for angina. Undaunted, he indulged in the greasy treat, celebrating his vibrant life in the fullest way possible . . . by ending it in a blaze of mustard-soaked glory.

But oh, the seconds before, when the steaming, spicy smoked meat melted the white fat between those rye slices, combining into a flavor explosion that no Jewish man of his generation could possibly resist. Did he feel the tightening of his chest after the first few bites? Did he chalk it up to that momentary high that comes from eating a truly great deli sandwich, when the senses are heightened and the body shuts down to savor the pleasure? Who knows? All that matters is that he died as he lived—in love with Jewish delicatessen. I never met "Poppa" Sam, but his legacy has slowly pickled my soul with a craving for salt, garlic, and secret spices. It is the continuation of a flavor-bound tradition that worships fatty sandwiches in brightly lit temples of abusive service and clanging dishware. Some bloodlines pass down intelligence, wealth, or physical strength. Not mine. My birthright was an unconditional love of deli.

This is a book about Jewish delicatessen, about deli's history and characters, its greatest triumphs, spectacular failures, and ultimately the very future of its existence. This book is a look deep into the world of the Jewish deli, told through the histories and experiences of those who keep it alive. It is the tale of the immigrant counterman, the no-nonsense supplier, the kvetching customer, and the fourth-generation deli owner, all of whom are balancing the tastes of tradition with the necessities of a business. It is a book about the economics of a nineteenth-century trade in the modern world and the pressures delicatessens face, financial and otherwise, that have caused many to disappear.

Foremost, this book is about the meats one finds in a Jewish delicatessen: aromatic corned beef, peppery pastrami, braised brisket, garlicky salami, and silken tongue. But it is also about steaming bowls of chicken soup with fluffy *matzo* balls, and Yiddish-named dishes that start with K: *knishes*, *kishke*, *kasha varnishkes*, *kreplach*, *kugel*. It is about rye bread, garlic-soaked pickles, and mustard—whether yellow or brown, but always mustard, because butter and mayonnaise do not belong in this book.

When "authentic New York" pastrami is served shrink-wrapped between stale slices of white bread in Nebraska gas stations, the longing for Jewish delicatessen—real Jewish deli—sticks in your gut like a half-digested *knish*. The delis that inspired this book are worthy institutions: temples of worn Formica and chipped dishware fronted by a Jewish surname in the possessive: Steinberg's, Dale's, Malach's, Sax's.

That these places are the last of a dying breed is the sad truth driving my crusade to save the deli. Across North America, and in select cities of the Diaspora, Jewish delicatessens are disappearing faster than chicken fingers at a bar mitzvah buffet. People have been decrying deli's demise for decades. "Mom and Pop labored long and hard in their corner deli, but they no longer prevail," wrote Kevin Leonard in the obscure 1976 book *The Dilly Deli Guide and Cookbook*. Though his book was mostly a travel guide, his sense of the deli business's perilous state was dead on: "Except for a fortunate few, many now simply endure." Three decades later, it is telling that fewer than a dozen of all the delicatessens listed in Leonard's book remain in business.

In many cities delis simply no longer exist. In others, one or two holdouts are barely hanging on. Traditional products are disappearing from menus and shelves because they don't fit into the bottom line. As have gone the Jews, so too have gone their nearby delis. So in many ways, this is a book about the Jewish experience, told via Jews' most recognized contribution to the American table.

But the situation is not without hope. Delis do their best against tremendous odds. Places like Katz's Delicatessen in New York or Shapiro's in Indianapolis are some of the oldest restaurants in North America. Jewish deli clearly has the ability to endure. But can it thrive, and how?

I have spent the past three years searching out an answer, embarking on an obsessive quest to save the Jewish deli. I have ingested mountains of cured meats, rivers of mustard, and lakes of chicken soup in sixteen states, two provinces, and six countries. In these pages I hope to open your hearts to the same unrestrained love of Jewish delicatessen that I feel . . . and then subsequently fill those hearts with cholesterol. So head over to your favorite Jewish deli, pick up a pound of pastrami, another of corned beef, a loaf of rye, some full sour pickles, a jar of mustard, and a case of Dr. Brown's. Don't forget the *matzo* ball soup. Because this is a book about Jewish food, and it would be a shame to read it on an empty stomach.

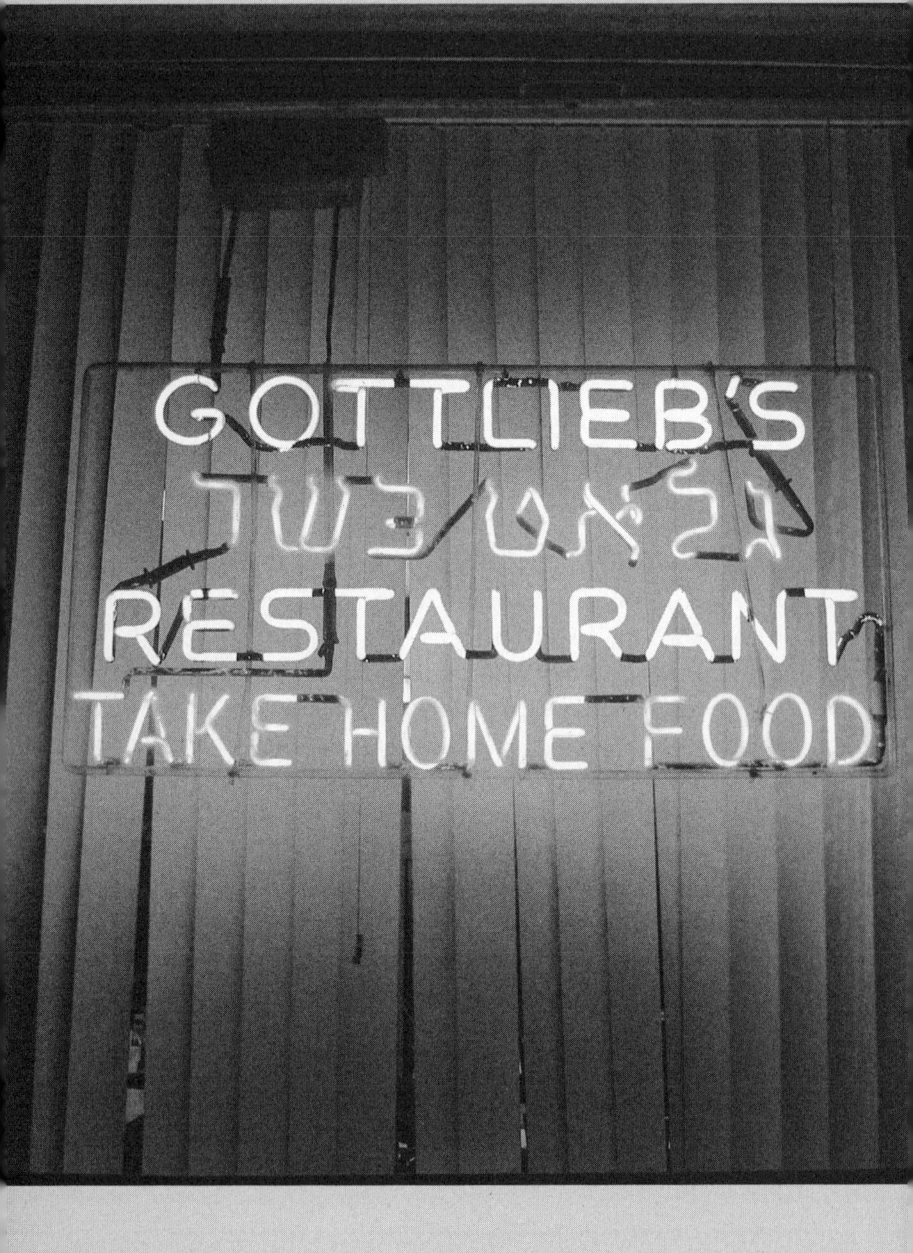
GOTTLIEB'S
RESTAURANT
TAKE HOME FOOD

NEW YORK, NU?

New York is the de facto world capital of Jewish delicatessen. Amid its canyons of skyscrapers and endless
stretch of satellite cities and suburbs, one finds more
Jewish delicatessens than anywhere else on earth. The delicatessen
as we know it today is every bit as much a product of New York as
it is of Yiddish European culture. The sights, sounds, and tastes that
tell us we are inside a Jewish delicatessen were all formed over the
past century and a half as the delicatessen emerged and evolved in
New York City. And yet, just as New York City was the place where
our concept of the Jewish deli came into being, so it is in New York
where the deli is facing its greatest challenge. Make no mistake.
What happens in New York will affect delis the world over.

Next! Behind the Counter at Katz's Delicatessen

3:14 P.M.: Basic Training

Charlie held out a white kitchen apron and a brand-new red Katz's Delicatessen baseball hat. I tied the apron on and slipped the hat onto my head.

"Okay," Charlie said, "follow me."

We walked two-thirds of the way down Katz's massive counter, squeezing into a narrow opening. Charlie called one of the counter-men over.

"Yo John," Charlie said. "This is David. He's going to start cutting tonight." John nodded and looked at me with more than a hint of suspicion. "Just show him how it's done, okay?" John okayed in approval. Charlie looked at me, smiled, and sang the words "Good luck."

John had no time to waste. "Yo man, here's what you do." He swung his body around 180 degrees, grabbing the hot handle of the steam box. Big as an office desk, the array of large metal steam boxes are the final home for Katz's pastrami and corned beef. As John opened one of the lids, a blast of steam shot out, blanketing our bodies in the perfume of garlic, salt, and sweating meat that had been seasoning countermen here for generations. He pulled his head back for a second. Then he dove in.

Using a two-pronged carving fork, John sorted through a hot treasure chest of meat, stabbing and flipping until he found a pastrami that caught his eye. After he hauled out the meat, John and I stepped back to the wooden cutting board. Repositioning the pastrami so the leaner tip pointed to his right and the fatter end was directly in front of his belly, John raised his fork and sunk it about two and a half inches from the tip. "Okay man, watch carefully," he said. "You wanna hold your knife on an angle, and use the fork to help control it." Resting the back of the knife's edge against the fork on a 45-degree angle, he drew back his arm and *sskt-sskt-sskt-sskt-sskt-sskt-sskt* perfect slices of pastrami rhythmically came away.

John now raised the knife and *THWACK* came down, splitting the ribbons of pastrami into two even piles. He then delicately slid the blade underneath one half of the meat and lifted it neatly on top of the other half. Grabbing two slices of rye from beneath the counter, John took a wooden spoon out of a bucket of spicy brown mustard and painted the bread. He placed the meat on the rye and closed it, cutting the sandwich in half. He once again slipped the knife beneath and lifted the whole thing onto a waiting plate. John pulled the blade back and voilà, the sandwich rested there perfectly.

Next, we squeezed by other cutters and grabbed three pickles from two buckets. John lined them up side by side, held them in place with his hand, and with three quick slashes he sliced the pickles in half, tossing them onto another plate. "That's it, man. You got it?" I nodded. John stepped out of the way, raised his hand, and flicked a "come here" wave to the crowd, shouting "*Next!*" Within seconds customers started to line up in front of me, yelling orders.

"Katz's has to exist because if it didn't no one else would have any standard by which to be judged."

Having co-owned Katz's Delicatessen since 1988, Fred Austin seemed to be a tailor-made figurehead for the bad-ass deli. Goateed and bald, he stood well over six feet tall and boasted a substantial girth, which, given his image in the yellowing photos, had been steadily compounding over the years. "You can tell how long a person's worked here by how much weight he's put on," Austin once joked to a reporter. He was raised in the Lower East Side of the 1950s and 60s, and deli was tied into the very fabric of his life. "There were delicatessens *literally* on every block," Austin said, including two (Brother's and Henry's) on the very same stretch of Houston Street as Katz's. "You couldn't walk a block without tripping over one. Now, we're the only one left."

It is sadly fitting that the last original Jewish delicatessen on the Lower East Side also happens to be the oldest, not only in New York, but worldwide. The business was established in 1888 by the Lustig family, who sold to the German-born Eisland brothers in 1902, at a site directly across Ludlow. They were bought out in 1916 by Benny and Harry Katz (also German), who changed the name to Katz's and moved the deli across the street. In 1950, the Katz brothers doubled the deli in size, moving the entrance to the current location at the corner of Houston and Ludlow.

Over two decades ago, Fred Austin's brother-in-law, Alan Dell, told him that Katz's Delicatessen was for sale. Katz's had been on the market for a number of years, and Austin and Dell, businessmen with no deli experience, scooped it up from the Katz family. "I remember this huge feeling of nostalgia came over me when I walked in the door the first time and nothing had changed," Austin said. Their honeymoon was brief.

"It was rough going," Austin recalled. "There used to be crack addicts hanging out on the median strip on Houston Street. . . . New York was a deadly place for a long time. It was prominently highlighted as an example of a city that was going to be abandoned in twenty years." Austin and Dell reduced their salaries, shortened business hours, refinanced the mortgage, and cut back on staff. Katz's just squeezed by until the 1990s, when momentum shifted. "Ever since then things have been good," Austin said. "The city has rebounded with a joy and a vengeance that no one had expected."

The Lower East Side is now one of the most dynamic areas of Manhattan. Where tenements and warehouses once stood, condos rise in their place. Where salamis and pickles were once sold from pushcarts, today they can be bought at the nearby Whole Foods. Fashion boutiques are quickly replacing shops hawking schmattes, while butchers have been converted into clubs and bars. The junkies are long gone and tourism has now become the base of Katz's clientele. During the week, Austin estimates, half the deli's sandwiches are sold to tourists. On the weekend, that number jumps to 75 per cent. To cater to them, Austin and Dell have expanded the menu, adding cooked items such as blintzes, soups, and even Philly cheese steaks. Where people once stayed away from the deli after dark, Katz's recently expanded its weekend hours to 3 a.m., to accommodate the after-bar crowds. Late night was becoming as important as the lunch rush.

"You have to come in at night," Austin told me.

I asked him if I would be able to go behind the counter and interview the cutters.

"You can cut sandwiches if you want to."

Was he serious? How could I possibly pass this up?

"Show up this Saturday around five o'clock. We'll put you to work," Austin said, adding, "Just don't lose any fingers," without even the hint of a smile.

8:20 P.M.: The First Slice Is the Sweetest

"Are you open?" asked a man in rumpled sports jacket.

I stared past him blankly.

"Hey, umm, can I, like, get a sandwich?" he asked again.

Wait. Did they seriously expect me to step up and start making sandwiches?

"Uhhh, yeah, sure, what'll ya have?" I asked.

"Gimme a pastrami on rye."

Easy enough. I wheeled around to retrieve a pastrami from the steam box and stepped right into the path of one of the other cutters, nearly smacking my face into a scalding hunk of corned beef hanging off his sharp fork. "*Cuidado!*" he snarled in Spanish. The steam blinded me momentarily, clearing to reveal twenty pastramis piled in a shallow pool of bubbling black water. I stabbed and flipped a few, but couldn't really discern any difference. I picked up a random hunk, turned back to the counter, and ceremoniously slapped the meat down onto the worn wood. Let's see, what did John do?

First, leaner tip to the right and sink your fork in. Good.

Knife on an angle against the fork. Good.

The knife was sharp and the meat cut easily.

"Yo man! Yo yo yo! Whatchu doin'????"

I looked up to my right to see one of the busboys, the youngest staff behind the counter, running over as if I were carving up his cat. "Man, first you gotta give the guy a taste," he said. The customer looked a little puzzled but eagerly plopped the meat in his mouth and promptly deposited a rolled-up bill into the tip cup. The busboy handed me back the knife and I resumed cutting, instantly bringing out another cry of "No, no, no, no, man, look!"

He took the knife and cut gracefully, his slices falling more evenly than mine and also thinner. He handed me back the knife and, with the look of a disappointed teacher, went back to hauling plates. I could understand why. Busboys weren't even allowed to touch knives; they had to earn their way up to the cutting board via the broom, and here was some fool who walked in off the street and started butchering sandwiches.

I cut the slices in half, piled them up, grabbed the bread, slathered the rye with mustard, slid the meat onto the bread, and closed the sandwich. Not bad. Then I went to cut the sandwich and my hand went through the bread. The cutting board was now a mess of pastrami slices, torn rye, and mustard. Shit. I grabbed more bread and tried to reconstruct the sandwich as best I could. What emerged was neither pretty nor proper, though it was entirely edible, which I assured the customer with a knowing smile.

"Pickles?" he asked.

Squeezing the pickles between my fingers, as John had shown me, I rapidly drew the knife across each, taking out a chunk of cumbersome rubber glove in the process, though, thankfully, no fingers. I handed over the pickles and sighed with relief.

"Do you want my ticket?" the customer asked.

I realized then that I had no idea how much any of this cost.

"Umm hey," I asked the counterman on my left, "how much for pastrami?"

"Thirteen forty-five."

"Do I just write that on the ticket?" I asked again. "Is there a code or something?"

"Yeah, man, just write it on," he replied. "Jeez."

I put the ticket on the cutting board, where it quickly soaked up all the meat's grease and became transparent. I scrawled as best I could and left the cashier to figure it out. Customer No. 1 just walked away dazed. One sandwich down and I was already exhausted, dejected, and in way over my head.

9:00 P.M.: The Steady Hours

Each sandwich I made was progressively better. I cut more quickly and more evenly, chopping and stacking the meat in one clean motion. The cutter to my left, Freddo, gave me tips as I went along:

—Don't scrape the board with the edge of the knife. It dulls the blade.

—Cut leaner meat from the tip and fatter from the back.

—If you don't have a lineup, put the meat back into the steam box so it stays moist.

—Dig the pastramis out from the bottom of the steam box. Those have been steaming the longest.

Though Katz's pastrami is smoked by an outside purveyor, it is dry cured. This gives Katz's pastrami its signature dark red color and also a less salty flavor, which many claim is the finest in New York, if not anywhere. A traditionally made product has its nuances. Like snowflakes (if snow came from cattle), no two pastramis are exactly alike. Sometimes the flesh would be buttery soft, with very few sinews to impede my carving, but often I'd cut into one that was tough and fibrous, and I'd find myself battling through a maze of tissue. Pros would call this "butchering," which a growing pile of wasted scraps attested to. Whenever I hit a tough piece, Freddo did his best to teach me how to carve it properly, slicing along the fatty center of the pastrami, a highway of sorts, until it split in two, and then watching as he trimmed the "shit" out—those thin, tough, yellow membranes that ruin a sandwich. I soon learned to admit a sort of failure. If a pastrami was too tough, I'd bring it back to the steam box to tenderize longer and get another. This is the same way experienced Katz's customers order their sandwiches.

"The pastrami is unmatched at Katz's," famed defense lawyer Alan Dershowitz told me. Raised on kosher delis in Brooklyn, Dershowitz has his Katz's ordering down to a science. "You have to stand in front of the counterman with three or four dollars in your hand, and you have to taste three or four different pastramis before you accept one. It's like a wine in France. It's either too lean or too fat. I remember when I was trying to be healthy once, I ordered a lean pastrami at Katz's and it was a disaster. It was inedible, and we had to order one that was more marbled. We realized the idea is not to have *less fat* pastrami, but to have less *fat pastrami*."

The crowd arrived in waves. Everything would be quiet for twenty minutes, and then they'd appear in front of me, holding out tickets and barking orders like Wall Street traders. For half an hour I'd work in a daze until the lineup just disappeared and I could take a moment to wipe my board down, regroup, and talk with the other cutters.

A nineteen-year-old Dominican-born counterman who had started at Katz's three years before, Freddo's real name was Alfredo Fernandez. He certainly looked older, with a pencil-thin beard and compact frame, but his impish grin, and the fact that he occupied the far end of the counter, betrayed his youth. Like Freddo, most of the countermen at Katz's are either Dominican or Puerto Rican. The night shift is largely in the hands of the younger generation. Charlie, the night manager, who was in his late twenties, had started at Katz's in his teens, but studied hospitality in college, and was now high up in the deli's management. Though he worked some days, it was the late shift that Charlie loved most. "In the day you got a lot more older people and a lot more orders to go," he said. Lunch lineups can snake out the door, which is astounding considering the place can seat up to 355 diners. If a tour bus happens to disgorge its passengers, up to a dozen cutters will face lineups seven-deep.

Nights were also when the cutters let loose, teasing each other constantly. The narrow space between the counters became a gauntlet of doom, as hip checks and arm grapples met brazen countermen who dared walk into another man's space. At one point, Beni, one of the most senior cutters, grabbed me by the arm and started twisting, taunting me in Spanish, calling me a pussy, slowly jabbing his carving fork into my side. I froze. Beni then looked up and realized he had the wrong guy. "Hey, sorry, I thought you were someone else," he said, patting me on the back, "but now you're one of us, okay?"

During the night shift, the walnut-skinned Beni (whose full name is Bienvenido Quiros) was the alpha-cutter, occupying the far end of the line, right down by the window. Katz's was Beni's latest (and he hoped last) home in a life of New York delis. When he came over from Puerto Rico in the 1960s, he began working as a butcher at Cookie's, in Long Island. From there his résumé reads straight from the obituary pages of New York Jewish delicatessens: 1st Jewish Deli, 6th Avenue Deli, Broadway Deli, Wolf's Deli. Beni learned to hand-cut meat at the legendary Lou G. Siegel, where they called him "Beni the Surgeon." He then went on to stints at the Stage Deli, Carnegie Deli, Sarge's Deli, and the legendary Schmulka Bernstein's on Essex. Finally, he wound up at Katz's. "This is the best deli by far," Beni said, effortlessly disassembling a corned beef. "The merchandise is so good because when you slice by hand the juice stays in the meat. With a machine, it draws the flavor out." Beni was best known for asking whether customers wanted their pastrami "lean and mean" or "juicy like Lucy."

Of seventy-three employees, only a handful were Jewish, including Austin, Dell, head chef Kenny Kohn, and a Ukrainian-born cutter named Pyotr Okmyansky, known simply as Peter, the oldest, and last, Jewish counterman at Katz's. Peter was born in Kiev, Ukraine, in 1933, as Stalin's famine was ending. He learned a little Yiddish from his mother, though the food served at Katz's was not something he ate back home. By the late 1970s, Peter was working part-time as a mechanic and played professional trombone in the national music conservatory. When his mother got the chance to come to the United States, Peter went with her, followed a year later by his wife and daughter. They moved to Brooklyn, where Peter worked at a gas station, and in 1985 a friend offered him a job at Katz's. Because the counterman's position came with medical insurance, he took it.

Most of the cutters back then were Soviet Jews, who in just four days taught Peter the art of carving a sandwich. After years working in the Soviet system, he fell in love with the job. Aside from putting his daughter through medical school, it afforded Peter unthinkable opportunities. He has served debutantes and movie stars, as well as President Clinton. "He come to counter, yes, Clinton, big man, he like a lot to eat," Peter recalled. "He order two or three hot dogs, pastrami sandwich, and something else."

As we spoke in the back of the deli, Peter rubbed his thick, calloused hands together. His full mane of white hair was hidden underneath the black Katz's baseball cap he always wore (most of the countermen wore paper hats). "I feel I can work steady here," Peter said. "Nobody can push you here, business is really business, you understand?" Physically, age didn't seem to be a factor, though co-workers often complained of Peter's moodiness and an obsessive need to organize the cutting stations. He boasted that he could sharpen fifteen knives a night, including all those at the start of his shift and the shift after him. It was a duty he took on because he felt he did it better than anyone. "I can't stay home. I feel sick, I feel tired. Here [Katz's] give me more physical energy," he said, flexing his biceps. "I feel more young working here."

12:00 A.M.: Prime Time

Somewhere after the twentieth pastrami sandwich, I somehow forgot that I was researching a book. Customers approached me and I was no longer nervous. "What are ya havin,' honey?" I'd say, or "What can I get you, bud?" I'd jostle and joke with the ladies— "Take a taste of this, sweetheart, I made it myself"—and I'd bust the chops of the lads—"C'mon, big guy, you don't think you can handle the club roll?"

The highlight of my night came when a tourist turned to his wife and said, "Guys like him have been here for decades. They're the real New York Deli Men. Hey buddy," he asked me, "how long you been working here?"

"Four hours," I answered.

He burst into laughter. "See, honey? He even has that famous Katz's sarcasm."

Still, anything other than a straight-up pastrami, corned beef, or turkey sandwich was a curve ball. Reubens, which were very popular, required a series of steps that involved slicing the corned beef, placing it onto a plate, microwaving Swiss cheese onto the meat, sliding it neatly onto bread, slathering on Russian dressing, and closing it with as little mess as possible. Mine looked like they'd been dropped off buildings. Likewise, the damn rubber gloves, prescribed by the health department, cause the hands to sweat, and they didn't fit properly. Each time I tried to wrap a takeout order, I'd catch a fingertip under a fold of paper and wrap half a glove up with the customer's sandwich.

The big Saturday night rush started trickling in after midnight, when bar hoppers migrated from the funky lounges of the East Village to the Lower East Side to end their evenings in innumerable basement bars and clubs. My lineup expanded seven-deep, and I served the following characters over the course of the next few hours:

—A Russian mobster with appropriately leopard-print-clad, large-breasted, bottle-blond companion. She wanted: "Meat. No bread, just meat. To go." He tipped twenty dollars.

—A nebbish Jewish man with his black fiancée. "She's converting for me," he said with a beaming smile, "so I brought her here." Brisket on rye.

—A guy from Boston who ordered his pastrami on white with lettuce, tomato, and mayonnaise. I subtly recommended it on rye with mustard. He preferred his way. I restrained myself from slashing his throat.

—A coked-out blond model with her two gay friends, all in skinny jeans. "Hey honey," she said, glassy-eyed, "oh you're so cute, mmmmm I want a meat sandwich, honey, *hahahaha*, I want tongue with potato salad and cream cheese."

——A pair of six-foot-plus, thick-as-trees, combat-boot-wearing bikers in bomber jackets. They looked like skinheads crossbred with Hells Angels. "One pastrami, please, and one Reuben." Polite and genteel as Queen Elizabeth.

In addition to this there were Mexican tourists, wealthy debutantes, the Bridge and Tunnel club crowd, sarcastic cops, bleary-eyed immigrant workers, Upper East Side preppies, and a few hardscrabble East Village Jews. In short, it was a cross-section of anything the streets of New York could throw my way.

"I use the term organic to describe this place," said Fred Austin, "not to mean we serve organic products, but in the sense that it's alive. For many years Katz's was essentially a community room for the neighborhood." But as million-dollar condominium suites replaced the co-ops where Austin had grown up, where was that neighborhood heading and, with it, Katz's deli? Real estate values had risen 1600 per cent since Austin had taken over. "If I had to pay rent here, it would be fifty to sixty thousand dollars a month," he said. "[People] complain about the price of a pastrami sandwich now, but I'd have to charge forty dollars with those costs."

Part of him may have been nostalgic for the Lower East Side of yore, but Austin knew better than to stand in the way of progress. "Manhattan is exciting and electric and hard because things keep changing. Our original architecture and decor is here and I don't want it all replaced with steel and concrete, but I'd hate for someone to come along and say 'You can't paint here without a permit.'"

Offers to purchase Katz's Delicatessen come to Austin and Dell almost weekly, reportedly as high as $21 million. "Not that Katz's is a charity or social welfare experiment in any extent, but I've got seventy-five families who depend on Katz's and thousands of people who come here daily for fun and food," Austin said. "I have so much fun here I would not want it to change in my lifetime. It's very tempting to get that type of money, but what would I do with it? Buy another deli?"

Was he saying he'd never sell?

"Well, 'never' is a long time," he replied. "It's my goal not to sell. I can't imagine the circumstances where I would need to sell. If it's worth $5 million today it'll be worth $10 million tomorrow."

This was in November 2006. Three months later, I began to hear rumors from others in the delicatessen business that Katz's was quietly being put up for sale. Their asking price was supposedly north of $30 million with rumors flying as high as $50 million. Though they denied the rumors at every opportunity, Alan Dell later admitted to me that they were trying to figure out a way for developers to build on top of the deli, without having to close it down. Though the recession killed that plan by late 2008, most in the deli business, and in New York, agree that some transaction for Katz's is only a matter of time.

"It seems against human nature for anybody to resist the millions of dollars co-owners Fred Austin and Alan Dell are certainly being offered," *New York Magazine*'s Grub Street blog wrote. "Other men have sold atomic secrets for less."

2:15 A.M.: Last Call.

"TAKEOUUUT!" Charlie hollered at the top of his lungs, eliciting a unified chorus of "TAKEOUUUUUUUT!" along the counter.

The cleanup crew immediately started stacking chairs and clearing plates. The countermen on my end closed up shop. I looked down at the floor and beheld a trash mountain pooled around my ankles: torn hunks of bread, little bits of fat and gristle, the ripped white paper that held rye loaves, splotches of mustard and Russian dressing, rubber gloves galore, and a thick bed of sawdust. My shoes were coated so densely with peppercorns that I could have tossed them into the steam box and sliced them into sandwiches. My pants were stained transparent with grease. Every inch of me emanated pastrami musk. I handed Charlie back my apron. It was the greatest night of my life.

From Pushcarts to $15 Sandwiches: A Nosh of New York Deli History

The air is thick with the warm vapor of boiling chickens. A gentle clamor fills the ears; the clang of cutlery, a few gulps of liquid, the sizzle of fat on a hot surface. Conversation—loud, passionate Yiddish punctuated by a marionette's thrust of hands and fingers—fills the foreground. It is interrupted by loud vocalizations of a meal: the pleasantly high-pitched *ahhhhh*, uttered in surprise when the food arrives; deep inhalations, as shallow bowls of golden chicken soup with *matzo* balls are brought under the nose;

a cacophony of crunching and slurping and sucking and lip smacking as a platter of stewed chicken fricassee is passionately devoured; the barely audible squish as hot, thin slices of garlicky tongue are pressed by teeth into an onion bun.

When done, the diners—who are all large bearded men dressed in skullcaps, long coats of thick black wool, and stained white button-down shirts—fold their hands atop formidable bellies, lean back in their chairs, and recite *Birkat Hamazon*, the traditional grace uttered after meals. They rise to pay the son of the owner, a man in his late twenties with wire-rimmed glasses and a reddish beard. When his father, a stern man whose life knew only hardship before coming to America, is in the deli, there are rules to be followed, but he has retired early tonight, so the shy son can *kibitz* a bit with the customers. Having paid, the men will don their elaborate black fur hats and walk into the encroaching darkness, destined for synagogue.

Though the scene could have been plucked from the turn of the century, when New York's delicatessens were the gathering place for the men of the city's vast Jewish community, the above took place one November evening in 2006, at a family-owned delicatessen called Gottlieb's in Williamsburg, Brooklyn. Set on the most prominent corner of the Satmar Hasidic community (the most insular and strictly Orthodox of Brooklyn's religious Jewish communities), Gottlieb's is one of the few places in New York where you can experience the feel of a deli as it was more than a century ago. Inside, Yiddish is the lingua franca. English, spoken only to non-Jewish goyim (including modern Jews such as myself), is pronounced with a thick accent.

Gottlieb's hums along in the same way that it has since the day it opened in 1962. Menashe Gottlieb, like his father, Joseph, and grandfather Shloime Zalke, stands behind the counter with cousins and employees, all male, all Jewish, all bearded and with curly peyos of varying lengths dangling from their temples.

"*Ve* don't *vant* to change it all *de vay* around," Menashe Gottlieb told me. "People like *de* old style, especially *dese* days."

First off, let's get one thing straight. New York City did not invent the Jewish delicatessen.

Wait. . . . Stop. . . . Put the gun down.

It's true.

The word *delicatessen* is a mix of French and German, vaguely meaning "delicious things to eat" or "delicacies." The foods that we associate today with "Jewish deli" or "New York deli" are the culinary legacy of the Ashkenazi Jews, a population that lived in, and was kicked out of, seemingly every corner of Europe over the course of the past millennium and a half. When the Romans exiled the Jewish people from the land of Israel in 70 CE, the exiles spent much of the next few centuries bouncing around the Mediterranean. After the French king Charlemagne granted Jews rights around 800, many began moving to Europe, with large numbers settling in present-day Germany. The word *Ashkenaz* meant *Germany* in medieval Hebrew, a language that soon mixed with German to form Yiddish (literally "Jew-ish"), still heard in places like Gottlieb's.

Ashkenazi Jews ate by the dietary guidelines laid out in the biblical kosher laws, principally the avoidance of pork, which was a staple of the European diet, and the mixture of meat and dairy. Anything deemed unkosher, from shellfish to meat not killed and butchered according to kosher laws, is labeled *treyf*. When the Jews arrived in a new territory, they took a look at the local food and improvised. In Poland, the pig's blood and buckwheat breakfast sausage called *kishka*, was adapted by Jews, who substituted beef intestines, chicken fat, and *matzo* meal. The German medieval practice of pickling meat to preserve it gave way to pickled tongue and corned beef. Almost every single dish we know as Jewish, with the possible exception of bagels, *matzo*, and *gefilte* fish, can be traced back to another country's table.

Local tastes shaped the palate of different Ashkenazi populations over time. Those living in Polish areas favored sweeter dishes. Those in Hungary relied heavily on paprika for seasoning. The Romanian Jews were fiends for spice and smoke. All the Ashkenazi communities had a proclivity for garlic and onions, and a reverential worship of *schmaltz*, or rendered fat, most often made by boiling the fat of geese, duck, or chickens. It was a diet forged out of necessity, characterized by poverty, and dictated by the word of God. Some say it was the original fusion cuisine, a taste of forced globalization. With each move to a different land, the Ashkenazi Jews combined a bit of the old with the new. When Ashkenazi Jews became more urbanized after the Enlightenment, their food supply went from what was homemade to bought: bread from the baker, meat from the butcher, and cured meats from the delicatessen, which made kosher-preserved meats and sausages in the local style.

So no, New York didn't invent Jewish deli. But New York provided the perfect incubator for the Jewish delicatessen to blossom into a vibrant symbol of Ashkenazi cookery and an outlet for the melding of Jewish food and American culture. The first New York delicatessens were likely German (Aryan, blond-haired German), which sold specialties such as sausages, sauerkraut, meatloaf, frankfurters, liverwurst, and pretzels. In the post–Civil War era, Germans were the largest immigrant group in New York. Of the estimated six million Germans that arrived in America during that period, a significant percentage were Jewish.

The first big name in American Jewish deli was that of Isaac Gellis, a Berlin-born sausage maker who came to New York in 1871 at the age of twenty and quickly established himself in the Lower East Side. Gellis soon became the premier kosher meat magnate in America, building up an empire from sales of German-style kosher hot dogs, sausages, salamis, and cold cuts. Later there would be corporate-owned stores, larger factories, and signature Isaac Gellis delicatessens, but in the beginning it was just a whole lot of tube steak. Gellis's wealth financed the construction of the first downtown Orthodox synagogue, on Eldridge Street. This was the first to be built by Eastern European immigrants, who began to arrive toward the end of the nineteenth century. Their appearance in New York would completely alter the face of that city and transform the Jewish delicatessen into a New York institution.

Between 1880 and 1920, some two million Jews from the Russian empire, the bedrock of the Yiddish world, sailed to America, fleeing czarist persecution. Hundreds of thousands of refugees from other countries such as Romania (which was in the Austro-Hungarian empire) joined them. Most arrived in New York and settled on the Lower East Side. New York's Jewish population exploded as a result of this exodus. It was as though all the *shtetls* of Europe had emptied into several square miles in Manhattan. Compared to their urbane and now prosperous German-American Jewish counterparts, these immigrants were poor, uneducated, and religious, and most found work plying the few trades that were accessible in the old country: tailoring, peddling wares, collecting scrap, and food preparation.

Suddenly, the foods of a people dispersed for nearly two thousand years came together in one corner of Manhattan. Romanians tasted the dishes of Poles and Litvaks, Russians cooked for Ukrainians and Germans. Early on, the preferred vehicle for Yiddish food was the pushcart. In many cases, the wife would pickle, bake, or cook in the cramped tenement apartment at night, and the husband would sell the food all day. Soon, enterprising shopkeepers and suppliers began making bulk amounts of foods in their stores, selling them to armies of pushcart peddlers to distribute around the neighborhood. Foods needed to be cheap, preserved (because there wasn't refrigeration), and easily eaten by hand. Most customers were garment workers, who ate at their sewing machines or on the street. The most popular items were *knishes*, black breads, ryes and bagels, pickled herring (wrapped in newspaper), salamis, other cold cured meats, and pickles. Hot foods, like pastrami, soups, and briskets, had no way of staying warm on most pushcarts and were sold at shops or made in the home.

By the turn of the century, pushcarts were fading from New York's landscape. In an effort to control the unsanitary conditions of the Lower East Side that many middle-class New Yorkers abhorred, the mayor's office imposed strict regulations in 1906. Licenses were issued to a limited number of vendors, who were soon required to remain stationary, in locations designated by officials. As the pushcarts disappeared, they were increasingly replaced by what would become the delicatessens we know today.

Pastrami came to New York by way of Romanian Jews, who were a relatively small minority. In Romania, pastrami is not so much a food as a method of preparation that involves a heavy dry rub of salt and spices to cure and season the meat, and later smoking to cook it fully. Its origins, which may date back as far as Byzantium, can be found in Turkey, where *basturma* was a form of pressing spiced meat. In some North African countries, one can even eat camel pastrami, though the Moroccan market for a hump on rye has yet to take off. Jews who lived in Romania and Bessarabia adapted the food to kosher norms, most often spicing and smoking duck or geese.

No records exist of who first made pastrami in New York. Likely, the initial New York pastrami was made with fowl, which was the main protein of the Ashkenazi Jewish diet in Europe, where beef was a seldom-eaten luxury. But Manhattan was an excessively difficult place to raise geese, and they were soon replaced by inexpensive cuts of kosher beef raised out on the vast American plains. The turning point for Jewish delicatessen, which catapulted it from an obscure immigrant food to an American cuisine, was the marriage of this cookery with the simultaneously emerging American obsession with the sandwich.

Patricia Volk, a writer in New York, claims that her great-grandfather, a Lithuanian butcher named Sussman Volk, was the first to sell a pastrami sandwich in that city. His tale is certainly demonstrative of how the deli evolved out of necessity and chance. Volk came to New York in 1887 and set up a small kosher butcher shop on Delancey Street. One day, a Romanian friend stopped by and asked Volk if he could hold on to his suitcase while he returned to Romania. In exchange, he gave Volk his recipe for pastrami, which soon became a hit with nearby garment workers. One enterprising customer asked for his meat between slices of rye bread and a legend was born. Whether or not Volk made the first pastrami sandwich, what he did in Sussman Volk's Delicatessen lit a small fire in the belly of New York. The delicatessen, previously a takeout counter of prepared foods, had been transformed into a sit-down restaurant. The *shtetl* kitchen met the emerging New York lunch counter, and the foods of the old country were being served in the preferred manner of the new. It was no longer just Jewish, or Yiddish, but American.

Other delicatessens followed suit: Katz's, Jacob Bronfman's, Theodore Kranin's, Schmulka Bernstein's on Essex, each growing larger and more lavish than their predecessors. The delis at the turn of the century followed a simple formula; they were largely on the Lower East Side, were almost uniformly kosher, and served a limited selection of foods. Chief among these were the holy trio of corned beef, pastrami, and pickled tongue, followed closely by roast brisket, beef salami, and beef baloney. Lox, bagels, cream cheese and other dairy specialties were found in dairy "appetizing" stores, which sold smoked fish and dairy exclusively and never sold meat because of kosher laws. Portions grew enormous. After the routine starvation of *shtetl* life, a full stomach was the greatest pleasure one could imagine. A Jewish restaurant review consisted of two key questions: "How much does it cost?" and "How much food do they give you?"

Several companies, such as Isaac Gellis, got into the business of supplying meat and other products to delis that wanted to save labor and material costs by outsourcing production. Other established food companies found a niche in the deli business. Gulden's Spicy Brown Mustard became the perfect accoutrement to deli meats. Dr. Brown's sodas quickly became the elixir of choice, particularly the strange Cel-Ray tonic, a bright green celery-flavored beverage. In 1906, *Butcher's Journal and Delicatessen Magazine* launched, while unions began organizing behind deli counters and owners reacted with their own trade associations.

By the 1910s and early 1920s, the character of the Lower East Side was changing. The Bronx and Brooklyn offered cooperative apartments, subsidized housing, and even the slight possibility of owning a little green stamp of yard, and much of the Lower East Side's residents fled to the outer boroughs. By the mid-1920s, the U.S. government greatly curtailed Jewish immigration until well after World War II. In the span of less than forty years, some two and a half million European Jews had come to the United States, largely to New York. Theirs was the delicatessen generation, and the halt in arrivals of new Jewish immigrants marked one of the key turning points in the evolution of the deli. Before it had been a European undertaking created and molded by immigrants. From then on, it would be increasingly American in character.

By the 1930s, almost 80 per cent of the south Bronx was Jewish. In Brooklyn, nearly a million Jews made up half the population of the massive borough. Delis could be found from Williamsburg to the far stretches of Coney Island. As the fortunes of the second-generation New York Jews improved, the once humble delicatessen began splitting off into several different incarnations. The most numerous was the kosher delicatessen, the most common breed of deli before World War II. The kosher delicatessen served hot meats and cold cuts, sandwiches, soups, stewed or braised meat dishes, and baked goods. There were counters and tables and, in some instances, grumpy, scowling waiters.

A 1931 report put out by the City of New York's Department of Public Markets found 1,550 kosher delicatessen stores in the city's boroughs (in comparison to only 150 kosher dairy restaurants at the time). "Since most of the delicatessens in that era were kosher ones," said Ted Merwin, a professor of religion and Judaic studies at Dickinson College who has done the most extensive academic research on the history of the New York Jewish delicatessen, "I think you could safely say that there were a total of around two thousand delicatessens in the city as a whole during that decade."

Though kosher eating was the de facto diet for the Eastern European immigrants when they first arrived, the business of kosher soon evolved into something far more complex. In the *shtetls* of Europe, each town had perhaps one rabbi and a *shochet* (slaughterer), who deemed what was kosher and what was *treyf* without much fuss. But kosher eaters in New York had innumerable competing kosher authorities claiming their particular seal of supervision was the holiest. By 1934, the kosher industry was supplying over $200 million a year in food to New York alone (that's over $3 billion adjusted for inflation). During the first half of the twentieth century, prices for kosher meat soared, leading to several violent meat riots. During these, delicatessens and butcher stores closed to protest the slaughterhouse prices, while organized mobs of angry housewives took to the streets, banging pots and assaulting the police. In one 1910 riot, gangs of women roamed Jewish neighborhoods, and if anyone was selling or carrying kosher meat, the meat would be stripped from their hands and tossed into the gutter or doused in kerosene. It all makes today's *kvetching* at the cash register seem rather civilized by comparison.

State laws governing who could sell kosher and how it could be labeled had been on the books for years, but enforcement wasn't centralized, and many passed off *treyf* meat as kosher, pocketing the profit. "The difference in prices between kosher and non-kosher products is a source of great temptation to substitute non-kosher for kosher articles," wrote the mayor's Kashruth Committee in 1932, after incidents of kosher fraud became a matter of public concern. "The struggle to rid the Jewish community of the kosher food cheat is, as a matter of fact, one of the hardest tasks now confronting New York Jewry." There were fierce battles over territory between various rabbis and kosher authorities.

The results were twofold: first, the New York kosher world began to split, with the most religious orthodox followers becoming more and more stringent. Eventually, the ultra-orthodox would adopt the mark of glatt kosher as their new, supposedly higher standard. Glatt kosher emerged with the immigration following the Holocaust of ultra-orthodox Hasidim, who saw the kosher standards of the large Orthodox Union as too lax. Apart from several rules over the inspection of the cow's lungs for lesions, the difference between glatt kosher and what I'll call regular kosher is the degree of rabbinical supervision and observance. Kosher delicatessens will be certified by a particular kosher authority, who inspects the premises regularly, but a glatt kosher deli must have a supervising *mashgiach* working on site at all times (more on him later). Glatt kosher delis close on the Sabbath, as well as most of the Jewish holidays, major and minor. Kosher delis will stay open on every day except Rosh Hashanah, Yom Kippur, and Passover. With the influx and growth of Hasidic communities across America, and their refusal to accept the kosher standard of others, glatt kosher has become the de facto standard of the entire orthodox community. Until recently most glatt kosher meat in America came from the giant Rubashkin slaughterhouse complex in Postville, Iowa. The company's stranglehold on the market was so complete that when the Postville plant closed in October 2008 (after Rubashkin filed for bankruptcy following the largest immigration raid in U.S. history), beef practically disappeared from American kosher supermarkets.

The flipside of all this was the birth of the delicatessen we find most commonly today: the kosher-style deli, a.k.a. the Jewish deli or New York deli. Even within this realm, there is a spectrum of what owners are willing to serve and what they won't. Originally a kosher-style deli indicated a place that adhered to kosher principles (not mixing milk and meat, no pork or shellfish), though it was unlikely they used kosher meat, and almost certainly had no rabbinic supervision. They were modern kosher, refusing cheese on a sandwich, declining to even offer cream for the coffee.

Though kosher Jews will say, with unwavering conviction, that the only true Jewish delicatessen is a kosher delicatessen, what predominate in New York today are Jewish-owned, Jewish-operated, Jewish-patronized, non-kosher delicatessens. Among them are some of New York's best-known delis, including Junior's, Katz's, Carnegie, and the Stage. Some kosher-style delis may have stopped being kosher for economic reasons; some were simply never kosher. They were opened by those who wanted no part of the complicated, expensive, and often hypocritical world of kosher certification.

As non-kosher delis grew in number, so too did they expand in size. They were big. They boasted everything under the sun: a full kitchen, deli counter, appetizing section (which sold dairy items like cream cheese and smoked fish), and in-house bakery. Abundance was the name of the game, and each worked to have the whole Ashkenazi food chain wrapped up under one roof. Many delis became famous for specialty items. Both Lindy's on Broadway and Junior's of Brooklyn started as delis, but quickly evolved into places devoted almost exclusively to rich cheesecakes thick as a car's tire. As the Jewish delicatessen gained a tremendous foothold around Midtown Manhattan, close to the heart of Broadway and America's entertainment industry, the comedians embraced the deli like a mother's bosom, drawing from the rich trove of *shtick* within its walls:

"For this record to have the proper flavor, you have to rub a little corned beef fat on top. It'll be tough, you need those little *gree-be-knees*, you know, those little Jewish popcorn, eh Max?"

The above is from the comedian Jack E. Leonard. It's sometime early in the 1960s, and the legendary Stage Delicatessen is packed with the usual roster of Broadway luminaries. At the center of it, Stage's gravelly voiced Russian-born owner, the hefty, horse-betting Max Asnas, is walking around with a microphone strapped to his body.

The scene exists on a rare vinyl recording dubbed *Max Asnas: The Corned Beef Confucius*, which offers a time capsule into Midtown's deli heyday. Already, the place would have been known for towering combination sandwiches named after local customers such as Walter Winchell, Joe DiMaggio and Marilyn Monroe, Jack Benny, George Burns and Gracie Allen or Milton Berle. Back then, the Stage was where "celebrities go to look at people," and in the clubhouse atmosphere of the narrow room, one-liners cut quick as the blade of the slicing machine:

Morey Amsterdam: "I was sitting in here and a fellow was eating with his hat on. A fellow called out and said, 'Hymie, I need mustard!' and a big glob of mustard fell on this man's hat."

Max Asnas: "I offered to clean his hat, and he got mad. He said, 'Dis is a very expensive hat,' I said, 'What do you think we use here, cheap mustard?'"

Morey Amsterdam: "A woman was complaining that cold water was dripping on her. Max said, 'For these prices, what do you expect, hot water?'"

The equally famous Carnegie Delicatessen was where television writers from Brooklyn and the Bronx—Sid Caesar, Mel Brooks, and Carl Reiner—met and joked around with the hot acts of the Catskills—Jackie Mason, Gene Baylos, Henny Youngman, and the legendary Freddie Roman. "I remember they started building the Americana Hotel, right across from the deli," recalled Roman, now the dean of the Friar's Club. "So Gene [Baylos] waits for the first day of construction, when they bring in the big earth movers, and he runs across the street and starts yelling, 'Where's the foreman?' and the foreman comes up and Gene yells, 'You schmuck! I told you 43rd Street, not 53rd Street!'"

Jewish talent often brought gentile friends for an introduction to the world of Jewish food. No longer was Max Asnas cracking in his native Yiddish to exclusively Jewish clientele. Instead, he served them sandwiches of corned beef with cheese on top and, if they so wanted it, a tall glass of milk. Many New York delis were known for flagrantly *treyf* foods. Take the Reuben sandwich, probably the most famous deli combination sandwich ever. Invented at Reuben's Delicatessen on 58th Street, it combined hot corned beef, sauerkraut, and Russian dressing on grilled dark rye with a layer of melted Swiss cheese. It was the sacrifice many New York delicatessens felt they needed to make to gain a foothold in the mouths of gentile America. Few were going to put up a fuss if a little sacrilege was required to gain a level of acceptance and appreciation for their food and culture that Jews had never known before.

Through the Great Depression, many delis were able to survive by promoting their thrift. At a deli, cash-strapped workers could usually afford at least soup, a small hot dog, or a *knish*. The hard nubs of salami were placed in a bowl on the deli counter and sold for a "nickel a *shtikl*." Once World War II broke out, the sons of deli owners went off to fight, and delis sold bonds to support them. A waiter named Louis Schwartz, who worked at the Sixth Avenue Delicatessen (between 55th and 56th streets), sold an astonishing nine million dollars in war bonds, mostly to customers. His efforts paid for 66 P-47 Thunderbird fighter planes, each of which sported the name Louis the Waiter as they sped into battle. Schwartz's key sales pitch was a little rhyme that urged patrons to "Send a Salami to Your Boy in the Army." Sixth Avenue Delicatessen shipped salamis overseas to troops, and soon other delis around the city were following the practice, especially Katz's, which many people attribute as the originator of the slogan. Katz's still ships salamis to U.S. troops stationed anywhere in the world.

When World War II ended, it triggered a significant shift for American Jews. No, they couldn't quite yet join the country clubs, but many Jewish Americans were no longer regarded as outsiders. The 1944 GI Bill helped level the economic playing field, paving the way for American Jews to earn college degrees, buy cars or homes, and start businesses. As their parents had moved from the

Lower East Side to the Bronx and Brooklyn, now those who grew up in those boroughs hopped bridges and settled the wilds of Long Island, New Jersey, Staten Island, and Westchester, where new pre-built subdivisions like Levittown kicked off America's suburbanization. Delicatessens followed, opening in new strip malls and shopping plazas. It was the start of the golden era of American Jewry, and people reveled in the success of excess.

However, the postwar years held a bitter edge for America's Jews, and precipitated the decline of the deli just as it reached its zenith. One only had to visit the long counter at Katz's Delicatessen to see them . . . the survivors. They gazed ahead with distant eyes, slicing meat with forearms marked by smudged blue numbers. By 1945, the Nazis had accomplished what centuries of pogroms and royal decrees had not. They had rid Eastern and Central Europe of its Jews. Those who survived fled abroad, went to Israel, or were swallowed behind Stalin's Iron Curtain. By the 1950s, there would be no more waves of Eastern European Jews moving to New York and opening delicatessens. From that moment on, the deli was severed from the land and tradition of the old country forever, and the Jewish delicatessen in New York would never grow again. While the postwar era was a boom time for American Jews, for the New York Jewish deli, it marked the beginning of the end.

The first blow came with the rise of the supermarket, which consolidated separate errands to the baker, delicatessen, butcher, and grocer. Those in Jewish areas set up large deli counters, with cheaper, mass-produced meats. So what if the corned beef tasted like SPAM? You could just pair it with a Gabilla frozen *knish*, which came in little oven-ready squares. In fact, by the late 1950s, a housewife on Long Island could fill her cart with prepared, preserved, frozen, or canned kosher Jewish foods ranging from Crisco vegetable shortening (eliminating the need for *schmaltz*), to Manischewitz bottled *gefilte* fish and powdered *matzo* ball soup mix (eliminating the need to cook). American Jewish households began replacing fresh breads and stewed meats with reconstituted variations of cornstarch and other artificial colors and flavors. Jews were less interested in tradition than they were in convenience. As postwar America's flavors became more homogenized, so too did the deli's.

Jewish food became more palatable to gentiles as well, with advertising campaigns that reached out beyond the Jewish community. The two most famous were the Hebrew National slogan "We Answer to a Higher Authority," which sold the image that their hot dogs were cleaner than the gentile competition because they were kosher. The other summed up the new reality perfectly: the Brooklyn Commercial Bakery changed its product name to Levy's Jewish Rye and promptly posted advertisements all over the subways, declaring, "You don't have to be Jewish to love Levy's."

Today, the glatt kosher market, which follows the regular kosher market by a decade or so in product innovation, is at this point. When I went to New York's Kosherfest, the world's largest kosher food trade show, there were kosher gummi bears; kosher barbecue sauce; kosher non-dairy ice cream; kosher frozen pizzas; kosher beef jerky; kosher mock bacon; and kosher mock shrimp, crab, and other pseudo-shellfish. There were giant booths devoted to the new flavors of glatt kosher cold cuts, but the focus was on mesquite chicken and Thai turkey, rather than pastrami or corned beef, all of it heavily processed.

Among such offerings there was very little food you would find in a delicatessen: a pickle guy, a few black and white cookies, some hot dogs, and a bored representative from the Gold's horseradish family. The glatt kosher restaurant world is no different. Delicatessens such as Gottlieb's, or the Noah's Ark chain from New Jersey, are vastly outnumbered by glatt kosher Middle Eastern, French, Japanese, and Chinese restaurants.

The second change of the postwar era took shape as New York City began to decline economically. The Big Apple's population peaked in 1950, when the effects of suburbanization began to alter the makeup of the city. Television began its migration to Hollywood. This had the effect of emptying the once-packed celebrity delicatessens around 7th Avenue of their famous faces. Ordinary people flocked to these delis to look at the pictures of celebrities who used to sit at the counter. Times Square became a haven for prostitution and porn as Broadway lost its crowds to suburban movie theaters.

The situation in the outer boroughs wasn't much better. Both Brooklyn and the Bronx can mark their nadirs by events in baseball. For Brooklyn, the date was September 25, 1957, when the beloved Brooklyn Dodgers left for Los Angeles. For the Bronx, the low point came during the 1977 World Series. When the ABC blimp panned past Yankee Stadium to focus on a large fire raging out of control, sportscaster Howard Cosell famously remarked, "There it is, ladies and gentlemen, the Bronx is burning." Following that summer's violent blackout, Cosell's quip seemed to confirm that New York was a Dante-worthy hellhole. New York City was nearly bankrupt. Though the 1980s offered some upswing in the economy, crime continued to rise, as did homelessness. The Lower East Side and the East Village were no-go zones at night, home to junkies and street gangs. Riding the subway was perceived as a genuine threat to your health. In neighborhoods that were once thriving with Jewish life, slums plagued by violence and poverty became the norm. This was no easy place for a delicatessen to survive.

It wasn't until midway through Rudy Giuliani's term as mayor in the mid-1990s that things began to turn around significantly. Through a mixture of increased policing and economic factors beyond Giuliani's control, the city rebounded to new heights, revitalizing much of Manhattan. Tourism returned to Midtown, and Brooklyn once again became a desirable place to live. Not even the al-Qaeda attack on the World Trade Center could dent New York's rise. But for the Jewish deli, the damage was irreversible.

Delicatessens had begun declining drastically with the move to the suburbs. According to the historian Ted Merwin, there were only 150 kosher delicatessens listed in the five boroughs by 1960.

Even if non-kosher delicatessens, which were increasingly domi-
nating the market, were factored in, the number was no higher than
three hundred or so, a decline of roughly 85 per cent in just three
decades. Today, there are but a few dozen Jewish delis scattered
around New York City, perhaps a dozen or so in all of Manhattan,
two in the Bronx, two in Queens, and five or six in Brooklyn. Those
in Manhattan cater mostly to tourists, and elsewhere the rest are
barely hanging on. In less than a century and a half, the Jewish
delicatessen came to New York, multiplied like crazy, and died off
even faster. In fifty years' time, it is possible that no delis will exist
at all in New York City.

Formica Philosophy: Why New York Needs Its Jewish Delicatessen

Ask a friend about his or her first trip to New York, and most likely it will include a story about a delicatessen. On my first visit to Manhattan at sixteen, my parents whisked me directly from the airport to dinner at the Carnegie Deli. We could have eaten anywhere, but they wanted to take me someplace special. Though I've enjoyed great meals at a number of New York restaurants, from obscure Brooklyn bistros to the linen-covered tables of Daniel Boulud, those tend to fade from my memory rather quickly. I certainly recall the experience: the wait in the opulent lobby, the pearly smile of the hostess, the bejeweled diners, but if you ask me what I ate, I couldn't possibly tell you.

But not deli. I have met hundreds of people who can recall with precise detail a salami sandwich they had half a century ago. Deli is one of the few restaurant experiences on par with home-cooked meals, a realm of warmth so sensually rewarding that it remains with us throughout our lives. Why is this? What differentiates the Jewish delicatessen from other restaurants, and what purpose does the Jewish delicatessen fulfill in our lives? Why does delicatessen food resonate so deeply with us, and what type of relationship do we have to the delicatessen? If the Jewish deli indeed is in decline, what will New York be losing if it disappears?

"Delis are big, vibrant places where people eat enormous portions of big salty meats. Where fat is prized . . . revered."

So said Ruth Reichl, the editor of *Gourmet* magazine and the former restaurant critic of the *New York Times*. Playing with a set of metal pickup sticks in her office, Ms. Reichl was recalling a particular deli sandwich she had eaten as a child—"I wasn't just eating this wonderfully delicious, fatty sandwich. I was eating my own history. . . . It's sort of everything that as human beings we're trained to like; it's fat and salt and sweet at the same time"— adding in a hushed tone, "How could you not like it?"

And how couldn't you? I have introduced enough first-time delicatessen eaters to the joys of corned beef to know it's a slam-dunk almost every time. I know macrobiotic health nuts who will leave the fat on a brisket out of respect for the taste, and more than a few vegetarians who have returned to the carnivorous world by way of a pastrami sandwich—reviving their kale-deadened taste buds, bite by greasy bite. A lot of foods taste great, including the delicatessens of other cultures. But much as I love veal sandwiches, burgers, falafels, and tacos al pastor, none of those foods transmit the caloric embrace of a Jewish deli.

In delis, people see life. They see hope. They smell comfort. Each of the delicatessens I visited in New York had stories from the weeks after the 9/11 attacks, when regular customers came by in droves. The world they'd known was literally tumbling down, and their first reaction was to seek out the comforting certainty of *matzo* ball soup and cabbage rolls. In delis, New Yorkers taste love. Love for food, love for friends, and occasionally, aphrodisiacal moments of pure, physical passion, like Meg Ryan's "I'll have what she's having" orgasm in *When Harry Met Sally,* or George Costanza's "I find the pastrami to be the most sensual of all the salted cured meats."

There is also a certain restorative property to deli. "It's the idea of that old-world food," said my friend Gail Simmons, an editor at *Food and Wine* magazine, and a judge on the hit reality cooking show *Top Chef.* Carving up an overflowing open-faced brisket Reuben at Artie's Delicatessen on the Upper West Side, she extolled the virtues of such survivalist cuisine: "This was the food of Eastern European firebreathers. It is pure comfort food, preserved and pickled to outlast anything." When New Yorkers are sick, they'll fight their seasonal ailments with jars of soup, containers of chopped liver, and dense kugels. As a form of health care, it's cheaper than most every other option, and the side effects from a combination of *kasha* and *knish* are virtually nil.

In some instances, deli can actually save lives. Take the case of Harris Salat, a food writer who fought off cancer a few years back. "I didn't really plan on doing it, but the first time I came back in the taxi from chemotherapy I spotted the Katz's sign like a beacon and I just had to stop there." Salat would go by Katz's after every treatment, loading up on pastrami sandwiches, which would sustain him for days. Amazingly, while most chemotherapy patients shed weight, Salat gained thirty pounds. "I didn't go to

Katz's with some grand ideas in mind. It just felt right and felt good. I'd be weak and I'd buy a big bag of food there and I'd munch on it. It was like a Jewish power bar."

Even in death, deli is there. A steaming sandwich snuck in past watchful nurses conveys an immeasurable gesture of love. Sadly, this is not something reserved for elderly Jews. While staying with my friend Christopher Farber in Brooklyn, I met Drew Goren. A talented young photographer, Goren was in the terminal stages of cancer in November 2006. Rail thin, he could hardly move without inducing some form of pain and his appetite was almost nonexistent. But we talked for hours about New York's deli-catessens. Weeks later, as he lay dying in the hospital, Farber brought him a large order of Sammy's Romanian Steakhouse's famous *schmaltz*-heavy chopped liver, loaded with fried onions and shredded radish. Goren devoured it with gusto, a content smile beaming across his face in what was undoubtedly the last, and best, deli meal of his life.

Though Jewish weddings and *bar mitzvahs* are now more likely to feature sushi bars than a tray of cold cuts, the one event where delicatessen food is almost always present is the *shiva*. When a Jew dies, the immediate family is obliged to host a mourning period over the course of a week. Friends will send meals, quite often from a local deli. Catharsis in a platter of sliced tongue may seem like a cheap way to cope with death, but it is surprisingly effective. Ben's, a chain of kosher delis based in Long Island, even has a separate Condolence Catering and Coordinated Shiva Service department. The *shiva* catering options at Ben's lean toward the hearty—soups, roast chicken, stuffed cabbage, brisket, Hungarian goulash, cold cuts, and heavy noodle puddings.

I asked Ben's owner, Ronnie Dragoon, why these foods tended to dominate *shivas*, even if the deceased were not deli eaters. "Because that's when they feel most attached to the tradition," he said. "Rites of passage typically make that bond stronger." It is fitting, then, that the other rite of passage where delicatessen food dominates in the Jewish life cycle happens to be at the *bris* (circumcision) or baby-naming ceremonies. From birth to death, enshrined in deli. What other restaurant offers cradle-to-grave service?

Over the past century, the setting of the New York Jewish deli has been finely crafted, complete with its characters, rituals, and symbols. How delis look and smell, who works there, and how they treat you are the key elements delineating a Jewish delicatessen from any other sandwich shop. They are decorated in what one owner called "utilitarian chic," and everything serves a purpose. Formica tables and sturdy metal or wooden chairs are favored because they are nearly indestructible. Tablecloths are pointless, as deli is a meal of spills. Cutlery should be slightly bent. The occasional chipped dish establishes credibility. Deli tables are almost always square and packed together tightly. Lights should burn so brightly that the difference between night and day cannot be discerned. Floors are best made up of black and white tiles laid in a checkerboard pattern. Walls can be decorated with old photographs of the deli owner's family, or faded celebrities, or both, as well as nostalgic posters of New York.

Like blue jeans, delicatessens need to straddle a fine line between comfortably haggard and respectable. Jewish delicatessens that gleam too brightly are suspect. "I can't eat in that place," deli customers will say of the sterile specimen, "it feels like a hospital cafeteria." They want a deli to feel lived in. They want an institution. A certain amount of *schmutz,* the Yiddish word literally meaning dirt, is highly prized; perhaps a few scraps of meat around the cutting machine, or a little grime trimming the ceiling tiles, but never too much, because delis can overdo the *schmutz,* and many in New York regularly do, sentenced forever by an avalanche of complaints. "You want to eat at Sax's?" they'll question in astonishment. "I'd never set foot in that place, even if I was forcibly dragged there by Hezbollah. It's filthy!" If the toilets dare exhibit a level of sanitation any less than a Japanese nuclear plant, no Jew will ever eat there. Period.

The most important thing to fill the physical space of a Jewish delicatessen, besides the food, is its people:

The Owner/Manager: When Sandy Levine walks around the tables at the Carnegie Delicatessen, everyone gets a greeting, a hand-shake, and a dose of shtick. "Where ya from?" he'll say, working the crowds of tourists. If someone says Hawaii, he'll joke about surfing. If it's Ireland, he'll drop the name of a famous bar there. He'll laugh with the roar of an elephant and play with a giant plastic pickle. "Rosie!" Levine will yell, and a diminutive Chinese waitress runs over. "I'm doing a picture, comb my hair." Levine will whip a worn plastic comb out of his pocket and, bending his six-foot-plus frame, he'll present his head to five-foot-minus Rosie, who will comb the half dozen strands over the shiny dome of Levine's scalp to the roar of the crowd. When they return to Omaha or Osaka, they will surely talk about the crazy owner of the Carnegie Delicatessen and make a note to return the next time they are in New York.

Where the clientele is more local, owners nurture an inherent familiarity with customers. Up in Riverdale, the leafy enclave of the west Bronx, Yuval Dekel continues the tradition of his late father at Liebman's, a small, cozy kosher delicatessen that serves incredible homemade stuffed cabbage and "hush puppies," which are mini-hot dogs wrapped in *knish* dough. With a largely local and elderly cus-tomer base, Dekel will deliver meals to their houses on Friday nights, and when they fail to come in, he will call to check up on their health. It's not his job, strictly speaking, but in a way, it is his duty.

The Counterman: Here is the field sergeant in the daily battles of a deli's existence. Though he appears in the guise of an employee, decked out in grease-stained fatigues, the counterman is the single most important person in a delicatessen. He's generally a no-nonsense man (I've yet to meet a counter-woman), whose deft ability with steaming meat and sharp blades is a source of wonder. Slim and harried, he'll speak in short sentences drowning in sarcasm. The rarest of breeds is the owner/counterman. One of the few I've encountered was Freddy Loeser, the owner of Loeser's Kosher Delicatessen in the West Bronx, a person who epitomizes what old-school New Yorkers once called a Deli Man, literally someone whose existence is wholly delicatessen. Having opened the deli with his bar mitzvah money in 1960, Freddy Loeser has managed to hang on in a neighborhood that's lost much of its Jewish character. This is tough work, which is probably why Loeser himself is such a tough SOB. Wearing a hangdog expression on a face like Alan Alda's and a paper cap with his name written in pencil, Loeser set out to intimidate me from the moment I walked into his deli.

"How the fuck did you find me?" he asked, as though I'd just uncovered a secret lair. Loeser's was a relic so well preserved you could suffocate in atmosphere. There were faded family photos, old signs, clippings of political events, and handwritten notes from customers push-pinned to the wall. "I'm a natural, a switch hitter," Loeser told me, glaring into my eyes to make sure I heard every word. "I got the best pastrami in New York, the best brisket, the best soup, the best everything." He had the talk, the look, and the swagger of the consummate Deli Man—a creature disappearing with the deli itself, despite the self-assuredness of their own skills. And when he was done talking with me, he simply said, "Thanks for visiting," and turned his back. As much as it should have offended me, I was delighted. Because a substantial part of the fading delicatessen experience is getting treated like shit.

The Waiter: "You couldn't live with them, and you couldn't get a tongue sandwich without them. . . . They'd all been there ninety years, and none of those ninety years was any good." ("Oldest Living" by Alan Richman, *GQ,* October 2000.)

Richman's ode to this vanished specimen perfectly captured the love-hate relationship between the Jewish delicatessen waiter and his/her clients. It was a battle of sullen service vs. constant *kvetch-ing*, of walking misery vs. predetermined disappointment, but young Jewish men and women no longer view waiting deli tables as a lifetime occupation. "When I started [in the mid-1970s], 70 per cent of my staff were Jewish," said Ronnie Dragoon, the owner of Ben's. "I have customers complain and say, 'This is disgraceful, you only have Hispanics working here!' I say, 'Listen, if you have a family member that wants to come to work for me, I'll be more than happy to offer them a job. Just remember, they'll work nights, they'll work holidays. . . ' Then their tune changes. Who are you going to get to work here besides immigrants?"

Today, the delicatessen waiter is more likely to be female, gentile, and foreign-born. They may schlep a little less, and though the hostility of the old days is largely done for, the attitude and antics have gone nowhere. The deli waiter will tell *you* what to order and how to order it. "We usually volunteer what's best on the menu, we suggest what they should eat, what they should not eat, or if they're over-ordering and getting too much food," said Ida Berger, a former waitress at the 2nd Ave Deli. "Y'know, this is what you do in a deli, you don't do that in a diner or another type of restaurant. In a Jewish deli, it's more like a family." At Katz's, Carnegie, Stage, Ben's Best (a kosher deli in Queen's, unrelated to Ben's) and the rest, there's still plenty of attitude and *shtick* to go around.

Deli Eaters: By far the most important character in the Jewish delicatessen is the customer. In the world of New York Jewry, the delicatessen once represented the third pole of Jewish life outside the home. It was a role divided in importance with the synagogue and the *shvitz*. Delis weren't just restaurants to eat at, but places to exchange ideas and gossip, cut deals, network, and ruminate on the lessons of life. Commerce, social life, and politics all mixed and mingled at the cramped tables, where gangsters and street punks would break bread with bankers and lawyers. While the gentile power brokers had their country clubs and private dining rooms, the Jewish hustlers had their delis: the Stage was the haunt of show business, Lou G. Siegel's attracted the fast-talking garment dealers, and Berger's was the home of the diamond traders.

When election time comes around in New York, the delicatessen remains a powerful symbol. Ed Koch, the Bronx-born mayor of New York from 1978 to 1989, has his photograph hanging in practically every Jewish deli in New York City. Mr. Koch, like most savvy politicians, learned early on the political value of eating a pastrami sandwich. "It's a Jewish statement, and New York is an ethnic town," he told me, sitting in his Rockefeller Center office. Every time he took a bite out of a *knish* for the cameras, he sent a message to the area's Jewish constituents that Ed Koch was one of them. "Every politician does it," Koch said. (Though not always with conviction. Both Bobby Kennedy and George McGovern made the mistake of ordering a glass of milk at kosher delis and hot dog stands, a gaffe that some say cost McGovern New York's votes.)

The specter of gentile politicians eating *matzo* balls reveals the major appeal of Jewish delicatessens to gentiles. It is one of the few places where you can instantly immerse yourself in an organic Jewish experience. Unlike the simple initiation rituals of Islam, Christianity, or Buddhism, conversion to Judaism requires the study and dedication of LSAT-style entrance exams (a fact not lost on Jewish mothers). The very environment of a delicatessen somehow ensures that everyone inside will eat Jewish (lots and fast), get treated Jewish (with tough, sarcastic love), and talk Jewish (loudly). So long as they do not order mayonnaise on the sandwich or ask for white bread, no one will call them out on their lack of Hebraic heritage.

"A deli is guaranteed informality," explained William Helmreich, a professor of sociology at CUNY Graduate Center in New York and a lifelong deli fanatic. "Every nationality can go in, and during that time, the interactions they have are very, very rich." As we noshed away on pastrami and roast beef sandwiches at the back of the Kensington Kosher Delicatessen, in his hometown of Great Neck, Long Island, Helmreich outlined how the deli has evolved into a place to recharge on Jewish identity.

"Younger [Jews] who go into delis are practicing something us sociologists call 'symbolic ethnicity.' When the real trappings of ethnicity are gone—language, religion, practices—by the third or fourth generation people look for symbolic ways to identify, and food is the easiest. When two Jews go to a deli, they're ethnically bonding, expressing the common roots of our shared culture."

The same applied to other ethnicities. Italians venturing to Arthur Avenue for meatball sandwiches, Chinese Americans eating dim sum on Canal Street, or African Americans digging soul food in Harlem all served the same purposes. "In an era where everything changes fast, humans have a need to be rooted," Helmreich continued, "which is why you see Orthodox Judaism having such a resurgent appeal. But for one who doesn't want to be *frum* [orthodox], deli is the easy way. In the deli, you can walk in a goy and walk out a Jew . . . maybe a pound heavier."

With their numbers declining to dangerously low levels, Jewish delis now take on a different meaning for New York's Jews as symbolic representations of a fading past. "Why do we love these nostalgic places?" Helmreich asked me. Why is the sense of history, the unchanged decor, and the behavior of the waiters so important to the character of a Jewish deli? Helmreich saw that it was all about trying to stay true to who you were. When a person goes into a deli, he claimed, that individual is looking for authenticity. He is not just dreaming of the deli that he once went to when he was younger, but remembering what, and who, he once was. The young are validating the tradition of the Jewish delicatessen, even if they don't realize it.

Unfortunately, with each successive generation, as the number of delicatessens around New York has declined from thousands to mere dozens, the link between New York delis and New York Jews has grown perilously weak. The assimilation of New York's Jewish population is one of the crucial factors that brought the Jewish delicatessen to its current endangered state. Having come from the very farthest margins of European society, where persecution and exclusion was the norm, the Jewish desire to blend in and achieve acceptance in a Christian-dominated nation remains strong. Victims of anti-Semitism feel far less secure about their status and are more likely to do what it takes to gain acceptance. Intermarriage, which made up only 6 per cent of Jewish unions in 1950, is today present in approximately half of American Jewish households and much higher in younger marriages. As a consequence, children born in mixed marriages are less likely to be raised as either religious or ethnic Jews. Soon, the number of American Jews who will partic-ipate in a Jewish religious institution will be the minority, and the unaffiliated will become the majority.

Today's Jewish youth are far less likely to eat at a delicatessen than their parents, who, in turn, were less likely to eat at delis than their own parents. A large part of this is attributed to eating habits, but we must keep in mind that these are the same generations char-acterized by soaring rates of obesity. They're not forgoing deli for the salad bar, they're ditching it for burgers and BBQ. The delicatessen is so far removed from their own weakened cultural identity that it has no resonance for them.

"The Jewish deli will be a museum exhibit like at Ellis Island, with actors playing deli owners and everything." This was the pre-diction of Joshua Neuman, the editor of the irreverent Jewish youth culture magazine *HEEB*. "What is this culture?" Neuman asked me, when we spoke of deli, over tacos. "People hated the *shtetl*. The second they could get into that country club and file down their noses . . . forget it!" Today's Jews, Neuman believed, are looking to define their own experience in their own terms, not that of their grandparents. Neuman felt closer to a restaurant such as Mo Pitkin's House of Satisfaction (a "Judeo-Latin brasserie") than a traditional delicatessen. "Mo Pitkin's captures what's happening," Neuman said in late 2006. "It doesn't resist [the decline of deli]. Instead it poeticizes the crumbling of the culture in the food. In a way it feels more real to drink a Manischevetini [a vodka martini with a splash of Manischewitz kosher wine], than to eat a sandwich at Katz's. Katz's seems like something a German tourist does to see what Jews do, like he saw in a Woody Allen movie."

Trying to hang on to a fading culture was what Neuman called a "tremendous waste of resources." Nostalgic exercises, delicious or not, had no place in moving American Jewry forward. If the delicatessen had to die for that culture to be reborn, so be it. "I say nail in the coffin. Do it, let's get over it," Neuman remarked emphatically. "If we can live without animal sacrifice, we can live without the pastrami sandwich."

It was as stark an argument as I would face on the fate of the deli, but Neuman's opinion held a certain validity. Generations of American Jews had fought to shake off the rags of the *shtetl,* the victimization of the Holocaust, and the prejudices of white America. They had incorporated themselves into the highest levels of society, entertainment, business, and politics. Largely by assimilating so well, Jewish Americans had removed the barriers that had kept them on the margins of the world for over two thousand years. As Mayor Ed Koch told me when we sat in his office cluttered with photographs of him and various world leaders, "Our culture shouldn't be defined by something that we were fifty years ago. Jews are living in a golden era in the United States."

All true, but does it mean that the deli has to be abandoned for the sake of Jewish success in America?

I don't think so. In fact, I think the opposite.

New York City is the most dynamic metropolis on earth because there is no single dominant ethnic group. Each minority has given up certain elements of its native culture, while adopting aspects of others. The most visible manifestation of this is with food. New York is one of the greatest eating cities on earth in a way that is totally different from Paris or Tokyo. It is not the perfection of a single culinary style, but the coming together of innumerable cuisines.

New York is where they still sell *knishes* in pushcarts, and where *matzo* ball soup and pastrami are sold in every single diner, Jewish or otherwise. Only in New York would you have a Chinese restaurant such as Amazing 66, on Mott Street, create dishes such as pastrami fried rice, because the owner, Helen Ng, once ate at the 2nd Ave Deli and loved it. Only in this city would the celebrated French chef Joël Robuchon make his New York debut in the Four Seasons Hotel, and the first dish on the menu would be "Le Pastrami": a long platter of cold corned beef, poached for five hours with celery, carrot, bay leaf, rosemary, thyme, and spices, then interlaced with chive-kissed Alsatian potato salad, and shaved curls of foie gras.

If diversity is New York's strength, assimilation remains New York's culinary enemy. America's homogenization waits just off the turnpike. "What's replacing delis?" asked Ed Levine, head of the New York foodie Web site SeriousEats.com. "It's Benetton's and concepts. But deli is not a concept. It is real and it is honest, and people have a hunger for something real." Mo Pitkin's House of Satisfaction was an interesting concept, but it closed just two years after opening.

In the erosion of traditional cultures, the edible is often the last line of defense before total integration. New York's Jews' Yiddish language is largely forgotten. Many put Christmas trees in their houses, even though both parents are Jewish. A pastrami sandwich is often the only tangible connection assimilated Jews have to their heritage.

Which brings me back to Ruth Reichl. "It's sort of inevitable that our foodways move on," she said. "More than any other group Jews have assimilated. . . . To become Americans, people tried very hard to eat American food. It was the process of integration. In the 1960s, when you look at what kids brought to lunch, everyone brought peanut butter sandwiches. When you look at kids' lunches today, the Japanese kids are bringing rice balls wrapped in seaweed, the Korean kids are bringing *kimchi*, the Mexican kids are bringing *tamales*. There's a kind of pride in your own ethnic food, but I think Jews have been here too long to get that."

Did she feel it was too late for the Jewish delicatessen in New York?

"As long as there are two or three places making good pastrami I'll be happy," she told me with a comforting smile. "When they disappear, I'll be miserable."

YOUR
NUMBER
04
WHEN CALLED
IT'S YOUR TURN
FOR SERVICE
BY TICKET CO.
PRINTED IN U. S. A.

Pastraminomics: The Dollars and Senselessness of the New York Delicatessen Business

"Look at that!" Harry Rasp said, pointing with indignation as a waiter brought a tray of corned beef, tongue, and pastrami sandwiches to a table. "That's pure meat going out! What's the difference between a steak and steak sliced up on a sandwich?"

The same frustration that had brought Rasp into the deli business as an owner was now driving him out. In 1992, he was eating at a glatt kosher delicatessen with a friend. A big *fresser*, he and the friend had put away at least seventy dollars' worth of food during lunch, but on the way out the door Rasp spied a marinated pepper he couldn't resist. Not so fast, barked the counterman, buy a container or none at all. An argument ensued, and in a self-described "fit of craziness" Rasp decided then and there he was going to open his own deli (where he presumably could eat all the peppers he wanted). Essex On Coney was what Rasp ended up with, a glatt kosher deli on Brooklyn's Coney Island Avenue.

Rasp's dream had been to replicate the legendary Schmulka Bernstein's on Essex, a Lower East Side kosher deli/Chinese food restaurant that was the nirvana of his youth. "We waited two hours to get a table," Rasp recalled. "Bernstein's on Essex [a.k.a. Schmulka Bernstein's] was a schmoozefest from all five boroughs." Essex On Coney's menu was a near carbon copy of Bernstein's on Essex, with Sino-Yiddish dishes like Fon Won Gai. Rasp's meats were head and shoulders above other glatt kosher meats I'd sampled. His hot dogs, secretly made by an individual who worked for a large deli producer, were light pink and incredibly juicy, tasting of caramel without the repercussion of saltiness. Rasp pushed forward a few slices of what looked like corned beef.

"It's not corned beef," he said, arms crossed. "Try it and tell me what you think it is." I was astounded at the mellow sweetness that built as I chewed. There was a base of corned beef, but the candied flavor was altogether new and deliciously strange. "That's my honey beef," Rasp beamed from across the table. "No one else does that."

Rasp seemed to have everything: a solid track record, position in a heavily Jewish neighborhood, loyal orthodox clientele, and the food to back it all up. But Rasp couldn't wait to get out. In fact, he had just sold the business. "I wish I'd known fifteen years ago," Rasp said, his words laced with bitter regret. "If only I'd taken the money and bought property in New York."

As a business, the delicatessen trade was one of the toughest. For Rasp, owning a glatt kosher deli (the only option for an orthodox man) was even worse. At one point there had been over a hundred purveyors who sold glatt kosher meat to delis in New York, but now the number was down to just three. Retaining his glatt certification required Rasp to employ two full-time *mashgihim*, representatives of the chosen certification board (in this case Vaad Harabonim of Flatbush), who supervise glatt kosher restaurants. A *mashgiach*'s services started at fifteen dollars an hour, and in a glatt kosher deli one must always be present. Just for supervision alone, Rasp was putting out close to six grand a month, in addition to the thousands he paid to the certification boards for his license. With rent, labor, insurance, and equipment costs, Essex On Coney needed to sell a hell of a lot of sandwiches to stay afloat. Sadly, hawking pastrami didn't cut it.

Sandwiches, the most popular items on his menu, were actually the least profitable items for Rasp to sell. "If this place is packed on a Sunday night, and I sell six thousand dollars' worth of sandwiches I'm out of business. If we didn't have catering, we'd close. A sandwich is all meat. Chinese food is a little meat and a lot of vegetables. . . . I can't charge fifteen dollars for a sandwich, there's a resistance. People say, 'Hey, it's just a corned beef sandwich!' I can't cut costs either, because it's irresponsible and I'd end up with the worst quality meat. . . . These margins are why kosher delis are going out of business!" Rasp said, throwing his hands in the air, defeated.

I asked Rasp if he could go back, would he still have opened his deli?

"Hell no!" he said, without hesitation. "In ten or fifteen years there won't be anybody left."

For New York's delicatessens, rent and property values are what ultimately dictate life and death. Those who can pay survive; those who cannot will close. It separates New York delis into two categories: owners and renters.

Two of New York's most famous delicatessens are the Stage and Carnegie, set just one block apart on 7th Avenue, slightly north of Times Square. Both have been around since 1937. Both specialize in giant sandwiches that require a python-like dislocation of the jaw to ingest, as well as combinations named after celebrities. They are similar in size, roughly two thousand square feet apiece. A spirit of healthy competition exists between them. In 1988, the two delis went head to head in what the *New York Times* dubbed "The Pastrami Wars," and over the years both delis have tried to outdo each other by increasing the size of their sandwiches, like meaty towers of Babel. Today, the Stage's owner Steve Auerbach and the Carnegie's Sandy Levine maintain cordial, though hardly loving, relations. What really separates these two classic delis, and what will determine their fates more than opinions, food, or sales numbers, is property. The Stage rents 834 7th Avenue, whereas the Carnegie purchased 854 7th Avenue in 1991 (for $1.2 million).

"If you don't own the building, the landlord is your partner," said Sandy Levine. "That's what's causing a lot of the competition to go out of business. When their leases are up, the landlords are very, very demanding and you can't make deals. Landlords prefer leasing to Starbucks or to the bank because the risk is lower." Levine placed his annual insurance alone in the six-figure range, but at least he's secure in the knowledge that rising real estate values can only work to his deli's advantage.

Down at the Stage, owner Steve Auerbach laid out his dilemma in cold numbers: rent was roughly $500 a square foot per year, which came out to approximately $1.2 million for the deli, increasing on average 10 per cent a year. "What's happened in this area is that we're getting pushed out by the cheaper chain restaurants," Auerbach said. "We try and keep up by raising prices. We try to keep up by being innovative and bringing more people in, but with 135 seats, there's only so much innovation you can bring, and there's only so many people you can serve in the course of a day."

In the past, delis had the option of moving to a less expensive property when the rent increased, but in today's Manhattan, affordable areas of the city that can sustain a delicatessen are rare to nonexistent. For a midtown deli like the Stage, a similar location would cost the same amount or more. Factor into this the cost of rebuilding a deli's infrastructure (which Auerbach estimated at $1.5 million) and the loss of clientele, and the prospect of a move seems impossible. When I asked Freddy Klein (a veteran Manhattan restaurant broker who has been involved in the purchase, sale, and lease of most major Jewish delicatessens in New York, including both the Carnegie and the Stage) where in Manhattan a deli could find a reasonable lease that wouldn't drive them out of business, Klein didn't hesitate to answer: "There's nowhere to go." Period.

The primary reason that New York's Jewish delicatessens cannot afford New York rent is because of the foods they serve. As Harry Rasp said, if he sold sandwiches all night he'd go broke. How is that possible? The answer lies in the margins.

When you take the food cost of an item added together with the other costs needed to run a restaurant, and subtract that from the sale price, the resulting percentage is the profit margin. It is in these margins that delis live or die. To a deli owner, the most desirable items are those with high margins. Not only are they cheap for the owner, but they cost relatively little for the customer. The cost of an order of french fries to a deli is roughly 15 per cent of what it sells for (85 per cent profit). Fountain soda is 10 per cent (90 per cent profit), and a bowl of *matzo* ball soup is a healthy 23 per cent (77 per cent profit). "I love to sell soup and eggs," Carnegie's Sandy Levine said, as a table of four ordered bowls of *matzo* ball soup at $7.50 each. But customers line up outside the Carnegie and the

Stage for pastrami, not soup and eggs, and that's the problem. Why is that so?

Empire National is a small kosher meat and delicatessen purveyor in Williamsburg, Brooklyn. The company was founded in the early 1950s by Hugo Weinberg, a sausage maker from Germany who fled the Nazis. H. Weinberg and Sons supplied kosher deli meats to customers and two dozen–odd Jewish delicatessens spread around their small corner of the Bronx. After a fire in 1968, Empire National relocated its factory to Williamsburg, where it remains today.

Hugo's grandson Eddie Weinberg runs the company with his wife, Karen, from a cramped office with a hot dog–shaped mezuzah attached to the doorframe. Dressed in camouflage cargo pants, an army hat, and a black weightlifting sweatshirt, the solidly built Weinberg looks the part of a Marine drill sergeant. The company is regarded as one of the last boutique deli producers in New York, selling kosher corned beefs, briskets, salamis, hot dogs, and pickled tongues to such revered New York kosher delicatessens as Ben's Best in Queens and Liebman's in the Bronx. But it's the New York pastrami that Empire National is really famous for.

Pastrami is most commonly made from a cut of beef known as the navel. Kosher laws allow for the consumption of meat only from the front half of cattle, and the navel is found (should you go looking) directly behind the brisket, along the bottom of a steer's belly. Navels are tough and fatty, basically the bacon of beef, which is why pastrami requires such extreme treatment. A raw, trimmed, non-kosher navel ranges from twelve to fifteen pounds and costs roughly $1.75 per pound directly from the meatpacker. Kosher meat supposedly costs anywhere from 12 cents a pound to a dollar more, and glatt kosher would likely be another dollar on top of that.

Until recently, these cuts of meat were inexpensive. From 1960 to 1985, raw, non-kosher briskets sold between 30 cents a pound and 60 cents a pound. Navels cost even less. This meant that deli meats were cheap to buy and sell. But several factors have increased demand and prices for traditionally Jewish cuts of meat: the rising popularity of Texas-style BBQ brisket now has non-kosher briskets trading above the $1.50-per-pound range. Tongue prices, driven by exports to Asia, have shot up ten times since 1980. Domestically, new pressure is coming from the energy sector, where the rising cost of oil has created a boom market in corn ethanol, increasing the price of cattle feed.

To make pastrami, Empire National will take a navel and pump the meat with a pickling solution based mainly on garlic, salt, water, and nitrates. The navels marinate in large metal barrels for two days. Navels are then individually rubbed with pastrami spice, which consists of cracked black pepper, mustard seed, coriander seed, burnt sugar, and whatever secret ingredients Empire National uses. The traditional method of making pastramis, which is practiced by a select few New York purveyors, is dry curing. Rather than injecting the meat, a dry cure instead focuses on rubbing the raw navels with the spice coating, so the meat slowly absorbs the cure by osmosis and pickles over a period of one to two weeks. Dry-cured pastrami is naturally a darker red, is somewhat drier, and has a more complex flavor; however, it is less consistent and requires more care.

Once the black, caramel-like coating has marinated the meat, the pastramis are hung on racks and wheeled into one of three gas-fired ovens, each the size of a minivan. These smoke the meat for four to five hours at a low temperature (roughly 180°F). Though Empire National once used wood smoke, health regulations have eliminated wood from the process. The smoky flavor comes from the dripping fat sizzling on the gas element. To keep the meat moist, steam is pumped into the ovens during the smoking process. Each pastrami will lose anywhere from 10 to 15 per cent of its mass in the smokehouse. Once smoked, the pastramis are cooled, wrapped, and ready to ship.

"Twenty-five years ago I sold [pastrami] to a majority of kosher butchers and kosher delis," Eddie Weinberg said. "That's where our business was. The number of kosher delis has been dwindling and dwindling and dwindling. As somebody closes there's really nobody opening up [in their place]."

Weinberg recalled first noticing the decline in the mid-1980s. This was back when 65 per cent of his company's sales were to delicatessens. Since then, Weinberg estimated that forty or so of his kosher deli clients have closed down, representing a 90 per cent decline in the delis he services. Empire National's direct-to-deli sales currently hover around 15 per cent. When the 2nd Ave Deli closed in 2006, Empire National lost its largest customer, to the tune of 150 pastramis and 150 briskets a week. Weinberg has been forced to find new outlets for his products, including hot dog carts, nursing homes, and supermarkets. But the retail market is dominated by giants like Hebrew National.

The Hebrew National Kosher Sausage Factory Inc. opened in 1905 above a Lower East Side tenement. Twenty-three years later, it was purchased by "Issy" Pines (born Isadore Pinckowitz), who turned it into the most recognizable deli brand in America. Hundreds of kosher delis in New York once blazed neon Hebrew National signs. Issy's son Leonard Pines sold the business in 1968 to Riviana Foods of Texas for the tidy sum of $13 million (roughly $75 million today). Colgate-Palmolive purchased Riviana in 1976, but sales were so poor that Leonard's son Isidore "Skip" Pines brought the company back into family hands in 1980. Thirteen years later, Skip Pines sold off Hebrew National to the giant food conglomerate ConAgra for $100 million. Though many identify Hebrew National as the quintessential New York deli company, the meat has been processed at ConAgra's plant in Quincy, Michigan, since 2004 and the company is directed from ConAgra Foods' headquarters in Omaha, Nebraska.

ConAgra Foods is one of the largest processors of foods in the world, operating dozens of brands such as Chef Boyardee, Pam, Orville Redenbacher's, and even Gulden's Spicy Brown Mustard, in over a hundred countries. Profits in 2007 were over $2.6 billion from $10.5 billion in sales. As Hebrew National has grown with ConAgra, they have eliminated certain deli products and changed others because how Manhattan expects pastrami to taste is very different from how Montana expects it to. Eddie Weinberg feels that Hebrew National's meat has become somewhat "homogenized." "Hebrew National doesn't want to sell a few pastramis a week to small delicatessens," said a New York deli manager who uses their products, "they want to sell five thousand cases to a supermarket chain."

Empire National is one of the last family-run deli purveyors in New York, a fraction of the dozens that existed just a quarter of a century ago, and they face increased costs from corporate competition. Skilled meat trimmers and sausage makers have been lured away by salaries and benefits Weinberg cannot match. Empire National's forty-year-old plant is quaint and accounts for much of the food's taste, but it is inefficient compared to modern facilities. With regard to price, Weinberg cannot hope to compete with Hebrew National. "Here we are, like a little fly between mega giants," said Weinberg, pinching his thumb and forefinger within an inch of each other.

To survive in this hostile market, Empire National has focused on selling traditionally made products to delicatessens willing to pay a premium for a classic taste, though the kosher issue is a problem. The products that Empire National sells are kosher, not glatt kosher. Orthodox Jews will not eat Empire National pastrami. It might as well be lobster. Although gaining glatt certification could open up new markets to Empire National, the added cost of supervision would increase the price of Weinberg's meats beyond what his customers will pay. Empire National's business rests in the narrowest segment of the deli business, and one that tends to be disappearing the fastest.

"I don't want my kids to get into this business," Weinberg said, looking back at the photo of his son in full military uniform, "not unless they beg me. I told them, 'Don't figure on this, I don't have a good feeling about this.'"

A whole pastrami will yield between two and six sandwiches, depending on the size of the navel used. On average, your neighborhood New York deli serves an eight- to ten-ounce sandwich, though spots like Carnegie and the Stage will put a pound or more of meat in theirs. Waste is inevitable and as much as a fifth of a pastrami may end up in the trash. Yet, even with pastrami sandwiches at fifteen dollars and up, most New York delis are breaking even or losing money on their namesake item. Really good profit margins on a pastrami sandwich run from 10 to 15 per cent (that's an 85 to 90 per cent cost) though many in New York sell the item closer to the 5 per cent range. Other restaurants that serve slim-margin items make up for their losses in other ways. A place specializing in chicken wings can sell pitchers of draft beer at a tremendous markup. But alcohol is seldom sold at delis because Jews aren't big drinkers. Customers also have a perceived expectation that Jewish delis have always been, and will always be, cheap places to eat. Were delicatessen customers asked to pay the real cost of their sandwich, they'd surely revolt.

New York's Jewish delicatessens have found themselves sandwiched between skyrocketing rents, astronomical food costs, and a customer base unwilling to pay more. Many have taken refuge in the business of tourists, who will pay a premium for the chance to eat at a New York deli. But in Times Square, once the thriving heart of the deli trade, they're vastly outnumbered by glitzy theme restaurants.

"Look, [delis] were the original theme restaurants, okay?" said Stage's owner, Steve Auerbach. "You walked in and you could be sitting next to Milton Berle. That's a theme restaurant. The *shtick* was real, the gruff service was real. I just came back from a trip to Italy, and let me tell you, over there 'old' is old. Buildings are a thousand years old. Here in New York a building is a hundred years old and they tear it down. How many restaurants are seventy years old? You have twenty-year-old restaurants that are torn down and called 'institutions.' What are we? Or Carnegie? Or Katz's? We're national treasures. We should be saved! When . . . no . . . *if* we go, that's when people will realize it's the cashing in of an era, and by then it'll be too late."

Squirting a glob of the Stage's fiery pale mustard onto a plate, Auerbach rolled up a slice of pastrami, dredged the meat in the mustard, and popped it in his mouth. He chewed, paused for a few seconds, and finally pumped his fist in a sort of momentary victory. "Oh yeah," he exclaimed in triumphant satisfaction, "that's a good piece."

Death of a Deli: The 2nd Ave Deli

"A sandwich to a Jew is just as important as a country to a gentile. If the pastrami sandwich goes down the drain, there's no hope for this country at all." — Comedian Jackie Mason, on the closing of the 2nd Ave Deli

At the dark, cold end of New Year's Day 2006, Jack Lebewohl walked out the door of the 2nd Ave Deli, pulled down the gates, and turned the key. He stepped over the worn names on the deli's Walk of Stars, out from under the blue awning bearing his departed brother Abe's name, and walked away. There had been no prior announcement, no grand finale, no teary hugs from friends and customers. The 2nd Ave Deli's closing was so sudden and secretive that even the staff working that night had no idea what had transpired until they showed up to the shuttered delicatessen the next morning.

Word of the 2nd Ave Deli's closing spread quickly, first through panicked phone calls, then onto the pages of the *New York Times*. "My current rent is $24,000 a month for 2,800 square feet," Jack Lebewohl told the *Times*. "They want $33,000. I can't afford that." Most hoped that Lebewohl, a successful real estate lawyer with millions in personal property, could successfully reduce the 35 per cent increase. But things were more complicated than they appeared. Jack Lebewohl had actually negotiated the lease himself some fifteen years before, when his brother Abe still ran the 2nd Ave Deli. The landlord even claimed to have offered a $3,000 reduction to the deli. But Jack Lebewohl didn't mince words. "This is life," he told the paper. "Life goes on."

By the end of the week, workers were removing the deli's signature name from above the door. The two-foot-high Yiddish-inspired lettering of the 2nd Ave Deli lay dismantled on the sidewalk, like battlefield casualties in a Civil War photograph. Restaurant service companies carted tables, chairs, and appliances away. Slicing machines that had cut millions of sandwiches were packed up for sale. Tubs filled with chopped liver were dumped, cleaned, and stacked. Photographs of great entertainers and luminaries noshing on *knishes* went into boxes. The deli's big blue awning, emblazoned with the name of Abe Lebewohl, was soon sagging on the ground. In a matter of days the 2nd Ave Deli had gone from a bustling institution to a Manhattan memory.

Gone. Finished. Dead. *Toyt fahrtik gishtorbin.*

To the deli's regulars, it was the worst possible scenario. Fyvush Finkel, the Emmy award–winning actor from *Picket Fences* and *Boston Public*, had been a loyal customer since the deli opened, coming in for quick meals between shows at neighboring Yiddish theaters during the 1950s. Sometimes he'd walk around the deli, singing "Happy Birthday" to three tables in one night—in Yiddish of course. "When I passed by the deli and looked in and saw an empty shell . . . my heart fell," Finkel told me over frankfurters and Cel-Ray sodas at Katz's a year later. "It was very sad. Very sad. I felt terrible."

An editorial titled "Deli Down" in the *Forward* (New York's Jewish newspaper of record) on the closing of the 2nd Ave Deli had this to say:

> The closing of the Second Avenue Deli, the landmark Lower East Side kosher eatery, has all the classic elements of a modern-day Jewish cultural crisis: the struggle for historical memory. The quest for generational continuity. The never-ending battle for control of the land on which we stand. And, of course, the search for a truly great pastrami sandwich.

Abe Lebewohl was born in the territory of Galicia in 1931 on the shifting Polish/Ukrainian border. Captured by the Soviets, Abe's father was branded a capitalist and was exiled to perform hard labor in Siberia, while Abe and his mother were shipped to Kazakhstan. After the war, the family landed in an Italian UN refugee camp, where Abe's baby brother, Jack, was born. In 1950, the family made it to New York, and Abe took a job as a soda jerk in a Coney Island deli. After a stint at several other delis, Lebewohl scrambled together a few thousand dollars in 1954, bought a ten-seat lunch-eonette at the corner of East 10th Street, and opened up his 2nd Ave Deli.

Here was an area steeped in Jewish lore, surrounded by Yiddish theaters, synagogues, bathhouses, and other delis. But as the 2nd Ave Deli grew more and more popular, the theaters closed and the Yiddish actors who had built Abe's business were quickly forgotten. He created the deli's Walk of Stars in their honor, cementing their names in the sidewalk outside. Lebewohl also opened the

Molly Picon room, in a 1970s expansion of the restaurant dedicated to the Yiddish actress.

By the early 1990s, the 2nd Ave Deli was regarded as one of New York's top Jewish delis, if not its best. Unlike most other famous delis, it was kosher (though not glatt kosher). The food went beyond standard deli fare, offering a full menu of Ashkenazi dishes, including homemade *gefilte* fish, *flanken* with mushroom barley soup, chicken fricasee, and even *cholent*, the sabbath stew. Everywhere the deli's food went, Lebewohl seemed to appear, whether catering parties, Broadway openings, or *bar mitzvahs*. He could never refuse a hungry mouth. Any time the many homeless from the neighborhood came into the 2nd Ave Deli, Abe made sure they left full. Then he'd pack up the day's leftovers into the delivery truck and take it to shelters around town, his smiling face, bald scalp, and wild curls heralding a salty salvation for the most needy.

"He used to leave the truck unlocked so that this one homeless guy could get into the truck and go to sleep at night," recalled Abe's daughter Sharon. "One time he was in the truck sleeping. My father didn't realize it and at five o'clock in the morning he drove to the fish market. He didn't pay attention, he just threw the fish into the back of the truck and then took the truck to be washed. When the guys at the car wash took the hose to the back of the truck they suddenly heard a scream and realized that guy was in there. They were most shocked that my father wasn't surprised. He just casually said, 'Oh, I didn't realize he was in there today.'"

As Sharon and I chatted in a Union Square coffee shop one gray fall day in 2006, her words about her father revealed a deep love. In the weeks before, as I spoke to dozens of delicatessen owners and deli lovers around New York, the very mention of Abe Lebewohl's name brought those same words. He was a "*mensch*," a "legend," "the nicest guy you could ever meet," and "the last of the great Deli Men." But hearing Sharon Lebewohl talk about her father in a shaky voice, and seeing the tears well up in her eyes, I caught a glimpse of her painful burden. Abe Lebewohl was more than a legend to her, he was her father, and the 2nd Ave Deli had been all that she had left of him.

On March 4, 1996, Abe Lebewohl drove his delivery truck to the bank to deposit the previous night's receipts. Two men hijacked Abe in broad daylight and drove him around the corner to 4th Street, where a third was waiting. The men shot and killed Abe Lebewohl, took $10,000 he was carrying, and sped away, never to be found.

"My father was immortal in my mind," Sharon said. "It wasn't until I passed the deli, saw the news trucks and the gates down and saw people putting flowers and letters behind the gate," she recalled, a look of horror flashing across her face, "that I thought, 'Oh my God, it's true.'"

More than fifteen hundred people attended Abe Lebewohl's funeral at the Community Synagogue. Well-wishers spilled onto the streets and fire escapes of nearby buildings. Obituaries appeared in all the major papers. The prospect of the 2nd Ave Deli outliving its gregarious founder seemed impossible. Many assumed that it would close, yet days after Abe's *shiva* ended, the deli reopened. Abe's younger brother, Jack, put aside his law practice and manned the helm while Sharon helped out in the kitchen.

"There was something very comforting about it," Sharon recalled. "Customers would come with stories about him. It helped my healing. But it was very difficult. I can't tell you how many times I actually thought I saw my father in the deli. I'd see a man with a bald spot in the back where my father's was, and for one second I thought that if I hadn't looked in the coffin and saw my father I would have thought 'Oh my god he's here.' That part didn't get easier."

When I dined at the 2nd Ave Deli on a Friday night in 1999 (the only time I ever did), the place was perfect. Waitresses poured out fragrant metal bowls of chicken soup so densely packed with the fatty essence of the poultry that they glowed. *Knishes*, golden and crispy in their shell, revealed piping-hot potato mash with hints of pepper and a creamy texture. And of course the sandwiches were outstanding: pastrami hot, tender, and marbled, sliced thin so that chewing was almost unnecessary. With its wood trim, low ceiling, and hushed vibe, it felt more warm and welcoming than any other brighter, bustling deli. The servers were quick with the jokes and the walls oozed nostalgia. You instantly felt at home. This was a deli of the highest caliber, a fixture of the neighborhood, the city, and the greater Jewish world. Most every New Yorker I spoke with cited it as their favorite delicatessen.

With all this going for it, what on earth could have caused it to close?

"It took everyone by surprise," said Ida Berger, a waitress who had been working at the 2nd Ave Deli since 1993, and was now in her eighties. "No one knew a thing. It came Sunday night—[Jack] put a key in the door and walked away." Berger had been home that night recovering from hip surgery, when the other staff began calling her. "It was a blow to all of them." One day you're serving *kasha varnishkes*, and the next you are standing on the frozen corner, locked out of your workplace. Though many of the 2nd Ave Deli staff moved on to other delicatessens around the city, some were still adrift a year later.

I asked Mrs. Berger whether the reason for the closure surprised her, and she quickly shot into a tirade. "They wanted to increase [the rent] $9,000 a month!" she practically screamed into the phone. Customers were already complaining, and raising prices would have only pushed more away. Ida Berger had lived in the Lower East Side her whole life, had worked at a number of delis, and had seen many others shut their doors. Was there a future for delis in New York? "With delis? Forget it. It's a dying trade. Definitely not. They've all gone out. There's no way of reviving it."

But if that was the case, how did Abe Lebewohl keep the 2nd Ave Deli running when he was alive, facing similar challenges?

"Abe was a world-class nudge and he was the perfect Deli Man," recalled Steve Cohen, who managed the 2nd Ave Deli for twenty-two years until the day it closed. When we met, Cohen still sported a fading 2nd Ave Deli baseball cap. "Now it's a business, but to him it wasn't a business, it was a calling. It was run like mom and pop and now [the deli world] is corporate. When you're paying this kind of rent, you can't run it like a mom and pop. You gotta go on margins, you gotta think food costs . . . it's a whole different world out there."

Then why not change the deli? Modernize it to fit with the times, cater to the hip crowd moving into the East Village?

"You know, I like the past," said Cohen. "When people said to me, 'It's just like it was,' that was the greatest compliment ever." Cohen's philosophy was in line with what his customers cherished. After Abe's death, Sharon Lebewohl worked tirelessly on a series of low-fat items to add to the menu, in keeping with what other delicatessens were doing. The healthy menu failed dismally. Customers came to the 2nd Ave Deli as an escape from health regimes, not to find one. Abe had once famously boasted, "My food will kill you." His customers couldn't have been happier with those words.

What about Jack Lebewohl, I asked, how did his approach change from his brother's?

"He needed it like *luchenkup*, a hole in the head," Cohen said. "It wasn't his calling in life . . . at all. He was never enamored of the business."

The more deli owners and personalities I spoke with around New York, the more I heard skepticism about Jack Lebewohl and the death of the 2nd Ave Deli. Barry Friedman, owner of Friedman's in Chelsea and the Pastrami Queen on the Upper East Side, had offered to purchase the 2nd Ave Deli from Lebewohl months before. "I guess he'd rather close the doors," Friedman said. "The lease wasn't his problem. The landlord is a personal friend of my partner. It wasn't a surprise like all of a sudden the landlord was raising the rent. I think he just got tired of it, he didn't need it."

Despite dozens of messages left with his wife, assistant, and answering machine, Jack Lebewohl was not interested in telling me his side of the story after the deli had closed. However, my conversation with Sharon Lebewohl, Jack's niece and former co-owner, revealed similar sentiments. It had been close to a year since the deli closed, but her emotions were still raw. Sharon would purposefully walk two blocks out of her way to avoid even glancing at the corner where the 2nd Ave Deli had been. A Chase bank eventually occupied the space, but in late 2006, the deli's ghostly facade served as a sad reminder to all who passed by.

"I can't relive that feeling when I drove by right after [my father] died. I can't imagine nothing being there," Sharon said, staring into her coffee cup. "The deli was very cathartic for me. People ask me how often I go to the cemetery, and they're shocked to hear I don't. I was there for my father's funeral and unveiling and my mother's funeral and unveiling . . . that's it! I don't feel them there, but in the deli I feel them."

How did she deal with the closing? When did she know it was going to shut, and why didn't she tell anyone? And what about Jack? What went on between them in those tumultuous days? Was the 2nd Ave Deli's closing truly inevitable?

"I knew maybe a week before," she recalled, fighting back emotion, weighing each sentence with a long pause. "It was as much a shock to me as it was to the staff. I remember calling my kids and telling them, 'I just want you to know before the news hits' and them saying, angry, 'Why didn't you tell us earlier?' Because I didn't know earlier."

Over the course of the previous year, Jack had given no solid indication to Sharon that a decision needed to be made (they were co-owners of equal share, along with Sharon's sister Felicia, who wasn't involved at all). Occasionally Jack would wonder aloud whether they could sustain the business, but aside from a half-hearted proposal to drop the mail order service, its closure was never openly discussed.

On Christmas Eve, Jack told Sharon, "We have to close. We don't have a choice." Buying the building would have cost over $20 million and the banks strongly advised against it. Sharon contemplated whether she could operate the 2nd Ave Deli on her own. Her kids weren't involved in the business, and Sharon remembered that when her granddaughter was born, she had vainly hoped that maybe the deli could hold on long enough for her to grow up and take it over. She quickly came to her senses.

Over the course of the final week—that compressed space of *schmaltzy* nostalgia between Christmas and New Year's—the 2nd Ave Deli chugged along as normal. When it closed, none of the staff received so much as a phone call from Sharon and Jack, and it hurt many of them deeply. One of the deli's closest and most loyal staff members said that they would have expected it from Jack, but not from Sharon, Abe's beloved daughter. The least she could have done was make a few calls. Why didn't she?

"I was in such denial, in my wildest dreams I just didn't believe it was going to happen," she said. "I knew a lot of people were surprised about that from me. I think had I known months before, I would have put my foot down and said, 'They have to know now,' but I just had a week to kind of grasp it."

Jack Lebewohl certainly had the personal wealth and business experience to weather the financial storm and pony up for the rent increase . . . but for how long? Costs were not going to get any cheaper, the neighborhood was only getting more expensive, and a lease still meant he was beholden to the whims of the landlord. How soon until he had to charge $20 for a pastrami sandwich, or assume millions of dollars in personal debt just to float the deli?

Could he have sold the deli to someone else? Possibly, but what would it have become were it taken over by someone outside the family? What if it declined in quality, as many others had? Then people would have blamed Jack for selling out his brother's legacy. Jack was left with few good options. It all came down to this: were Abe Lebewohl still alive, approaching eighty, how much longer would he have lasted in the same circumstances? Steve Cohen remarked on that fantasy, "At some point, they just carry you out the door." Jack Lebewohl may have taken the decision to close the 2nd Ave Deli, but I would not blame him for doing so.

"If it wasn't for Jack," Sharon said with deep reverence, "we would have closed in 1996."

Part Two

USA: COAST TO COAST
WITH LATKES TO BOAST

A ccording to many New Yorkers, good Jewish deli simply doesn't exist outside New York City. Whenever they take a trip elsewhere, they inevitably whine about the pastrami and *kvetch* about the *knishes*. They'll harp away for hours about supposed violations of the sacred rules of New York deli—how the egg creams aren't made the same way or how the mustard is yellow, and not the proper spicy brown. And they will inevitably unleash pseudo-scientific tirades about the water—oh the precious water—without which no one can supposedly pickle a cucumber, let alone

When you encounter one of these grouchy New Yorkers, do as I do and act like they are bears. Nod politely and smile. Let them stomp and growl. Back away, keeping your hands visible at all times. Whatever you do, don't believe a word of it. Because while New York is the undisputed spiritual and historic center of the delicatessen world, only a fool believes that great Jewish deli is limited to its five boroughs.

Whenever Jewish communities have emerged in America, the Jewish delicatessen followed closely behind. And though the number of Jewish delis has diminished greatly around the country (as in New York), delis can still be found from the shores of the Pacific to the harbors of the Atlantic, just south of the Canadian border, north of the Rio Grande, and even in Hawaii. Without experiencing these far-flung delicatessens, the story of the Jewish deli's evolution in America would be grossly incomplete. And so, upon returning to Toronto from New York at the end of 2006, I started to plan a vast road trip across America's deli landscape.

Leaving at the end of January, and due back on April 1 for the first night of Passover, I would have two full months to drive around America's delicatessens, racking up an estimated ten thousand miles of highway time. I pulled out a map of the USA and started connecting the delis, until I formed a rough triangle from Toronto to Los Angeles to Miami and back home.

I knew it was never going to be a perfect trip. There were whole swaths of the country, like the Pacific Northwest and New England, that were too distant to explore. I wouldn't be able to visit places like the recently opened I Love New York Deli in Seattle, Kenny & Zuke's in Portland, and Sadie Katz in Burlington, Vermont. I really wanted to visit Shapiro's Delicatessen in Indianapolis, Jake's in Milwaukee, Zaftig's in Boston, Cleveland's Corky and Lenny's, and dozens more, but they were all out of the way. Toward the journey's end, as I realized I had under a week to make it from Miami to Toronto, I ended up skipping entire crucial areas of the East Coast. So my apologies go out to Attman's and

Miller's in Baltimore, 4th Street Deli, Koch's, and the Famous in Philadelphia, and the temple of New Jersey excess at Harold's, home of the largest sandwiches in America.

Even with all these omissions, I still managed to haul my ever-expanding ass across the entire continental United States, eating at up to four delicatessens every single day. At the end of it, I certainly felt that I'd gathered as complete a picture as humanly possible of the Jewish delicatessen business in America. If a solution to save the deli exists, it rests in the patchwork of states where over five million American Jews live.

Specials

Corned Beef on Rye
Fry (Small)
Pop (Small)

Mini 3 oz.
Corned Beef on Rye
Fry (Small)
Pop (Small)

YOUR
NUMBER
06
WHEN CALLED
IT'S YOUR TURN
FOR SERVICE

Detroit: Motown's Deli Blues
and Michigan's Suburban Jews

On the way to United Meat and Deli's inner-city factory, blocks of peeling postwar duplexes announced my arrival in America's starkest example of urban decline.

Sy Ginsberg was waiting for me in his office, a small room packed floor to ceiling with Detroit Tigers memorabilia, and greeted me warmly with a fat handshake and a big smile from below his cropped gray mustache. Born and raised in Detroit to a deli waitress mother and a father in the scrap business, Ginsberg began working in delis at fifteen, cleaning out the pickle barrels at

Lou's, in the Highland Park neighborhood. In 1968, he and a friend bought an existing deli called Hersh's, renaming it Mr. Deli. Up until that time there had been a dozen or so Jewish delis in Detroit proper, including Nate's, Brother's, Darby's, the Avalon, the Esquire (where Ginsberg's mother worked), and Alban's (which had closed just weeks before I arrived).

As early as the late 1950s, Jewish families began moving to the northwestern suburbs, first to Oak Park, then Southfield and West Bloomfield. Though the desire for bigger homes was a factor, so too was a growing fear that black communities were encroaching. The race riots that engulfed the city in July 1967 sealed Detroit's fate, and urban delis felt the shock as the remaining Jews fled the city en masse. "As the white flight/Jewish flight moved in a northwesterly direction," Ginsberg said, "obviously there was no business left for the delis. They either moved in that direction or closed up. Everybody fled Detroit. [Whole neighborhoods] picked up and left. Suddenly, my neighborhood went from being four square miles to forty square miles."

Seeing Detroit's Jewish community dying, Ginsberg wisely left Mr. Deli, later opening the Pickle Barrel in suburban Southfield, which he ran along with a partner, from 1975 to 1980, until he burned out. He then sold Chicago's Vienna Beef and Best Kosher deli meats around the Midwest. By 1982, Ginsberg was ready to strike out on his own and opened up United Meat and Deli in an old Detroit meatpacking plant. Perfecting his secret recipe over the course of eight months, Motown's corned beef maven was born.

Sy Ginsberg led me from his office through a curtain of heavy plastic into a brightly lit room. Nodding to the hard-hatted workers, each with a sizable knife in one hand and a sharp metal hook in the other, Sy took me to the edge of a tall plastic bin piled high with briskets. Cut from the breast of cattle and shaped like a flat teardrop, briskets are blanketed on the top by a layer of inch-thick fat called the deckle. When cured, cooked, and then steamed, all that fat makes for a moist, succulent sandwich.

Sy Ginsberg prides himself on the cure for his corned beef. After all, it is the core of his business. Catering to the Midwest market, which heavily favors corned beef over pastrami, he considers his product far superior to New York's, which he calls "flavorless." Traditionally, corned beef cures in barrels, much like pickles, over a period of time with a mixture of salt, garlic, sugar, and spices. As the briskets sit in the mixture, they soak up the brine and are ready to cook within a week or two. Several delicatessens still make their own product this way, though most buy a pre-pickled product like Sy Ginsberg's corned beef, which receives its cure via a flavor injector machine.

The Danish-built Fomaco M3 injector looks like an airport X-ray machine. Meat is fed into one end of the machine, until it reaches the center, where forty-eight needles rapidly plunge into the meat and inject the brisket with the desired amount of brine. Ginsberg's brine contains a small percentage of nitrates, which he uses to control bacteria, increase shelf life, and improve color. The M3 has the capability to inject up to 650 liters a minute, and when firing, the sound (*ch-PSST-ch-PSST-ch-PSST*) is nearly deafening.

"Everybody used to pickle their own corned beef," Ginsberg said, when I asked him why this wasn't more common, "but with barrels, curing corned beef through osmosis took weeks." By comparison, the meat we saw would be ready within twenty-four hours.

Most Jewish delicatessens buy uncooked corned beef from United Meat and Deli. Cooking on site allowed delis to customize their product, adding more spices to the water, boiling longer or shorter depending on the size and toughness of the corned beef. But fast-food outlets, supermarkets, and restaurant chains want something ready to serve the second it arrives. Ginsberg took me to the next room, where "idiot proofing" came into play . . . precooking. Hauling up the heavy lid on what resembled a giant metal coffin, Ginsberg took a big plastic paddle and stirred a few dozen corned beefs in individual plastic bags dancing atop what appeared to be boiling water. "Actually, the water isn't boiling, the bubbles are just aerating the corned beef, and making sure it cooks evenly and doesn't stick to the bag." Once the meat is cooled, a starting cut is made, so that when it arrives at the restaurant, people know which way to slice it.

We shed our coats and hairnets and went back to sit in Ginsberg's office. These days, United Meat and Deli is a medium-sized player in the non-kosher Midwestern delicatessen trade. The Detroit plant has 40 employees and ships 150,000 pounds of meat weekly, most of that being raw, cured corned beef—what Sy called his "bread and butter." Like Eddie Weinberg at Empire National in Brooklyn has found, the decline of Jewish delicatessens has affected just who Ginsberg's market is. "If I could quantify it," he estimated, "I'd say there are 60 per cent less delis [since the 1980s]. We're selling more and more product, but it's not necessarily going to the delis. In New York they're called diners, here we call them Coney Island restaurants, but they're just neighborhood restaurants. Even these chain conglomerates, these TGI Fridays, and Bennigan's, and Max and Erma's, they all have a corned beef sandwich on their menu."

These customers buy corned beef the same way McDonald's buys hamburgers—squarely focused on the bottom line. Most will buy extra-lean corned beef, or pastrami made not from the traditional navel, but from lean cuts generally used for roast beef. Some competitors will pump the meat full of excess chemicals, brine, and water, so it weighs more. Others use lesser quality beef, substituting steer meat or cow meat, resulting in a product that is dry and tough. Artificial flavors mask the difference.

"That's what we're up against on a daily basis," Ginsberg said. "We have customers who have some cognizance of quality and flavor, and they are willing to accept the fact that you build a business, and maintain a business, serving a quality and consistent product. But there are a lot of people that are only looking at one thing: 'How much does this cost per pound?'"

When a new delicatessen opens and contacts Sy Ginsberg for product, he will always offer to help the deli's owners start up. He'll demonstrate the way to cook a corned beef so that none of the flavor seeps out. He will don an apron, stand behind the counter, and show people how to properly trim the briskets. He will build sandwiches. He may even mop the floor. Sy Ginsberg does all this absolutely free of charge.

"When people come to me and say they want to get into the deli business, I always hesitate until I hear their background," Ginsberg remarked. "If they don't have a deli background, I shudder. In my opinion, the deli is the most difficult type of any food service establishment to run." He could just as easily ship the product with a book of instructions, but the man's passion for deli is limitless. Ginsberg has helped open delis around Michigan, Ohio, and even far-flung locales like Bozeman, Montana. In the long run, it makes for great business. One of Ginsberg's first consulting jobs was with Zingerman's in nearby Ann Arbor, where he taught Paul Saginaw and Ari Weinzweig everything he knew about deli. Today Zingerman's is one of the most successful delicatessens in the country, and they remain loyal customers of Ginsberg's corned beef.

Our bellies were emitting low murmurs, so we decided to head for lunch. Before we went, I asked Ginsberg if it would be possible to have a quick look at Lou's, the last original Jewish deli still in the city of Detroit. "Gosh, I haven't been there in years," he said, "but it's not too far out of the way. Follow my car and just make sure to stay real close. You don't want to get lost over there." We drove through a city that had been left to fend for itself. I had been to poor areas in other countries before, including slums in places like Rio de Janeiro, but the sheer scope of Detroit's blight—block after block of abandoned structures, gated liquor stores, and ramshackle Baptist churches—shocked me. Here I was, an afternoon's drive from Toronto, and it looked like a war zone.

"Wow," Ginsberg said, upon walking in the doors of Lou's deli, where he first worked half a century ago, "I don't even recognize the

place." The counter, kitchen, and cash now sat squarely behind a
wall of bulletproof Plexiglas, stretching all the way to the ceiling.
The customer placed an order through a microphone, then slid
their money under the glass. Food was served from a bulletproof
lazy Susan in the glass. Ginsberg beckoned me to come and look at
a lone photo adorning the wall. A faded Deli Man in Kodachrome
stared back at us. "This was the old man," he said wistfully. "That
was Lou." Lou Loewy's gray hair was parted neatly, his eyes hidden
behind thick Coke-bottle glasses. Lou had his hands squarely on his
hips, and the wry smile seemed to say, "*Nu*? Take the picture
already, I got a deli to run here."

I wondered what Lou would have said had he lived to see his
kitchen shielded like an Israeli embassy. Would he have been
pleased that his namesake was the last original Jewish deli standing in Detroit, one that still served classics like salami, pastrami,
matzo ball soup, and *knishes*, even though less than 1 per cent of the
city was still Jewish? Or would he toss in his grave at Felicia's
Chutzpah, a triple-decker sandwich of ham, pineapple, cream
cheese, lettuce, and tomato?

"They are capitalizing on the New Soul Food," Ginsberg
remarked after we sat down at the counter of the Bread Basket Deli
in nearby Livonia, a middle-class suburb ringed by auto parts factories. All around me guys in baseball caps, work boots, and union
jackets were hunched over big sandwiches. Everyone had a mustache. "I'd say that more corned beef is consumed by African
Americans in Detroit than Jews for sure. No question about it."
The Bread Basket was part of a small chain, owned by Alex
Winkler, Sy's former partner at the Pickle Barrel, and one of his
fastest-growing customers. In addition to the Livonia location,
there were three recently opened Bread Baskets in the inner city,
complete with the same bulletproof setup as Lou's.

"In the Jewish community people think delis are a Jewish thing,"
Ginsberg said, "but a lot of ethnic groups like deli, especially blacks.
Alex has tapped into a market that everyone else forgot about. I have

lost a lot of business in Jewish areas, but I gained it back and more so [in the inner city]." The key to this was what Ginsberg called the KISS principal, an acronym that stood for Keep It Simple Stupid. Rather than offer a full range of Jewish delicatessen items that required skilled labor, an informed clientele, and lots of kitchen space, pared-down delis like the Bread Basket or Lou's could operate in downtown Detroit by offering the basics: sandwiches and soups. No *flanken*, no *kasha varnishkes*, no *gefilte* fish. Simple, cheap, and not altogether stupid.

Our sandwiches emerged in front of us: two fat masterpieces of Sy Ginsberg's thinly sliced corned beef wedged between thick slices of double-baked rye. As my teeth sunk into the pillowy bread with its crisp crust, I quickly realized why Sy's corned beef was famous. Pink as a rare Sunday roast, it was so moist and tender that my jaw was actually surprised at the ease of chewing. The flavor was perfect, a balanced and somewhat sweet accent on the brisket, with just the faintest notes of mellow salt and garlic—the cure highlighted the meat like a fine fragrance on a beautiful woman.

The next morning I might as well have exited the freeway onto a different continent. The parking lot of the mall housing the Stage Deli in West Bloomfield was like a Lexus dealership. As I waited to be seated, a group of women in their sixties were departing from breakfast. They were clad along the lines of high school girls: skintight denim with colorful butt patches, fur-collared bomber jackets pressing forth silicone cleavage, Gucci sunglasses the size of ski goggles, and chinchilla boots with dangling pendants. They air-kissed goodbye, lest their taut, puffy lips explode upon contact. Overnight I had gone from one of the poorest neighborhoods in America to one of its wealthiest. This was how Detroit's other half *fressed*.

Since it opened in 1962, the Stage Deli (officially called Stage and Company) had always been grand. Its founders, an experienced army cook and Detroit counterman called Jack Goldberg, and his wife, Harriet, had the idea to open an upscale Jewish delicatessen. Jack's son Steve Goldberg now ran the Stage Deli. If the Bread Basket adhered to the KISS principle, then the Stage epitomized the grand suburban delis that emerged in America's postwar era. With its low ceiling, accented lighting, plush carpet, and deep vinyl booths, the Stage felt like the ultimate Jewish rec room.

A menu of five oversized pages offered up every imaginable treat. Sandwiches dominated, and between combinations the Stage Deli boasted some four dozen offerings named after Broadway shows or movies, most served on Jack Goldberg's famous double-baked rye, a Detroit specialty. The rye in New York generally comes pre-sliced, in small disks about half an inch thick. The best deli ryes have a crisp, amber-colored crust and soft center, though these are increasingly difficult to find, especially in New York, where rye has declined along with the deli. Back when he started, Jack Goldberg pioneered the process of double-baking his rye breads. In essence, the ryes at the Stage, and elsewhere in Detroit, are baked until almost ready, cooled, and then finished off again in a hot oven shortly before slicing. The warm loaf is cut into inch-thick slices on a diagonal. When you bite into a slice of double-baked rye, the difference in taste and texture is astounding. A thick, rustic crust greets your teeth, recalling the pleasurable chewiness of sourdough. The warm center of a double-baked rye has an airier density about it and doesn't break apart when stressed with a Bye-Bye-Birdie (house-roasted turkey breast, chopped liver, and Russian dressing). It makes New York's rye taste like pigeon food.

In addition to this, the Stage offered close to twenty appetizers ranging from the traditional (*kishka* and gravy) to the modern (spicy chicken quesadilla) to somewhere in between (french-fried chicken livers with sautéed onions and honey mustard dipping sauce). There were dozens of soups, salads, burgers, steaks, smoked fish plates, chicken dishes, and pastas, not to mention a separate breakfast menu. The huge takeout section was stocked with every imaginable item. But for the Stage to keep its regulars, Goldberg had to give them ever more. "In order to be successful in the marketplace, you have to offer a variety," Goldberg said. "The days of solid Jewish ownership of hole-in-the-wall delis is done. Look at any of the new delis created in the past decade or two and they're all big operations. That's what it takes in order to survive. [The Stage Deli] is an anachronism over here for forty-five years," Goldberg said. "In this country, [restaurants] either shutter or take the next step to move nationwide."

Across the country, delicatessens in strip malls and shopping centers emulated the Stage's example, offering bigger, glitzier versions of delis with menus as thick as phone books. Was this what it took for Jewish delicatessens to survive in suburban America? In the land where Hummers and Dodge Rams were proving the ruination of Motor City's automakers, was bigger definitely better? And where did it leave the few smaller, old-school places, like the nearby Star Delicatessen, whose European-born owner Sid Neuman operated from a small deli counter on a takeout-only basis? As I drove past the chain restaurants that would become an everyday sight over the following two months, I wondered whether there was a place in America's suburban sprawl for something that wasn't new or shiny or different.

"Look honey, I don't know who you are or what you're doing here, but if you want to talk I got no time to waste so you can come back in the kitchen because I'm freakin' *meshugah* this morning, you got it honey?"

Though close to eighty years old, Rose Guttman contained the energy of a woman half her age. In the blink of an eye, she could pull a scalding baking tray of heavy pound cake from the oven, open the walk-in fridge, stand on a crate and pull down another tray of cake, juggle the two in her strong arms, toss the hot one on the top rack, shut the steel door with her foot, slice the pan into perfectly even squares, wrap each one, scrape up the scraps and find a home for them in my mouth by waving a knife and slice of cake in my face, saying, "Here, eat! C'mon, honey, I don't have all day!"

Born in Romania, Rose Guttman was raised in her family's restaurant until the Nazis invaded. She ended up in Auschwitz, lost her entire family, but survived, and eventually settled in Detroit. Her husband, Irving Guttman, opened a delicatessen. Irving's Deli became the most successful deli chain in Detroit history. By the time the last one was sold in 1987, they had opened eleven outlets in total. "People lined up outdoors from eleven in the morning until nine at night," Rose said, grabbing a tub of corned beef scraps. "Everything was fresh in my store, nothing was canned. The other delis, they cheated. Well, you don't cheat the public, honey, you cheat yourself."

Rose was now a widow. At dawn each day (except Saturday), she could be found in the small kitchen at Tony's Ember's Deli and Restaurant, a roadside diner in the suburb of Orchard Lake that had previously been a Jewish deli and was now owned by Tony Perkovic, an immigrant from Montenegro. Tony brought Rose into his kitchen in September 2005 to revive the Jewish flavor, which had faded considerably.

"I just wanted to give the menu a boost. Meet customer demands for Jewish food . . . old-fashioned Jewish food," Tony said, in his thick accent. Rose had brought back *knishes*, noodle *kugel*, and other Yiddish dishes, which had increased business. She was a fair-haired firebrand octogenarian, with a voice that filled the room in no-nonsense turns of phrase. Tony was softer spoken, half her age, and towered a solid two feet above Rose's head. After years sitting at home lonely and miserable, Rose needed to cook.

"I'm not a talker! I don't care about what's happening in other people's lives and I'm not a luncher," she said, waving a knife for emphasis. "I don't need the money, honey, okay? This is something to keep myself going. It gives me a reason to get out of bed." She took softball-sized *matzo* balls from a pot and plunked them into a roasting pan, then skimmed the stock and poured it into a container.

Between asking the time and replying with a frantic "*Oy oy oy oy oy*" every few minutes, she set to task prepping corned beef hash. "If it kills me, I gotta make it!" she said, tossing the corned beef scraps in a blender with some onions. "I can't teach the others how to make it. They just can't do it, they screw it up, make it all into mush. The more you teach, the less they know."

Rose's way was the old way. Nothing came from a package, though it would have made life easier. It wasn't about money or the notoriety. Her name wasn't anywhere in the restaurant, and though she was proud of her legacy, that was never why she toiled away. She did it out of love. A love for the food, a love for her customers, and, I sensed, a love for Tony's family, immigrants from the same region as her birthplace. "Life is too short, honey, not to be nice. To be nice is easy, to be nasty is hard," Rose said, grabbing my arm.

"I work my frikkin' ass off here!" she said, cracking her thick calloused fingers and tossing on her coat. She ran around the kitchen, laying a big kiss on everyone's forehead, including mine. "Life is like a bowl of cherries, honey. You take the best and sometimes you get the pits!" Her tires squealed as she sped home to make dinner.

Tony began pulling out plates of Rose's food. First was a bowl of her *matzo* ball soup, the same one I had seen her making before. Little squares of translucent onion hung in the broth. Her *matzo* ball rose half out of the bowl, and when I carved off a chunk, I knew why Tony kept Rose around. Dense and packed with *schmaltzy* flavor, it somehow tasted light, with little pockets of soupy air throughout. I polished off the bowl.

Next came her corned beef *knish*, stuffed with the hash she'd made in the blender. Shaped like an egg and wrapped in a very flaky crust, it was baked to a George Hamiltonesque hue. I felt guilty for cutting into this beautiful thing, though callous greed was soon rewarded with little flecks of mashed potato and moist corned beef with just a hint of spice. I devoured the *knish*.

Finally, out came a pair of plump *blintzes*, one cheese and one strawberry. Both looked fantastic, each seared in butter until they were enveloped in bubbly crusts. First I tackled the cheese *blintz*, crammed with sweet, creamy farmer's cheese that was light and delectably warm. After two bites I moved over to its strawberry sister. As my fork pushed down, a surge of red filling burst out of the bulging *blintz*, and I greedily scraped it off the plate. I alternated between the two *blintzes*, finally combining both in my mouth for a Wimbledon-worthy strawberry and cream mélange. Sitting there, I thought of the first thing Rose told me when I walked into the kitchen that morning. "I got no recipes for you, okay? When I die a lot is going to the grave with me."

Rose was right. Her home cooking, like the Stage's institutional presence, was an anachronism in this land of franchises. It was food that couldn't be repackaged. To her, making those *blintzes* was keeping it simple, but her KISS method required a grandmother of six to work up to eight hours daily until her joints were stiff. This wasn't something that could be passed down easily. When she went, so would her food.

Driving to Ann Arbor, I thought about what I had seen over the previous few days. Here was the American socioeconomic-racial divide stark as ever. The only deli lovers left in the urban decay of Detroit were poor and black, eating their authentic Jewish sandwiches in fortresses. The Jewish delis in wealthy suburbs were under increasing pressure to branch out and modernize, to become nicer and prettier and offer more foods that had nothing to do with deli. To survive, they had to expand, which was inevitably risky and affected the quality of the food. Could these two models—the suburban and urban, with traditional food like Rose Guttman's and progressive thinking like Steve Goldberg's—work together and ultimately save Motown's delis?

Ari Weinzweig was reading his morning coffee when I walked up to the table. On a large paper filter were five different piles of ground Kona beans. Ari picked at each and sniffed, rubbing the grinds beneath his fingertips and rolling them in his palm. He tossed out various comments to one of his managers, banging away on a laptop keyboard so worn the letters had rubbed off. Finally, after twenty minutes of deliberation they agreed that this coffee would be best ground on setting No. 4.

Twenty minutes?

To decide how to grind one type of coffee, out of dozens?

What kind of place was this?

To refer to Zingerman's as a delicatessen is to refer to Times Square as an intersection. What began as a small deli is today nothing less than one of the most progressive and admired food businesses in the United States. The two minds behind this deli-based revolution are Ari Weinzweig and Paul Saginaw, college buddies who had worked together in local restaurants after graduating from the University of Michigan, here in Ann Arbor. Both Ari (from Chicago) and Paul (from Detroit) had grown up with a taste for deli. In 1982, they decided to open up their own, a venture that Ari's mother certainly didn't feel was the best application of his costly Russian History degree.

"What would your parents' reaction be if you told them you were opening a deli?" Ari said, shaking his head with the mischievous grin that perpetually adorned his bearded face. Tall and thin to the point of gangly, Ari looked younger than his fifty years. It was the dead of winter and he sported a healthy tan, black jeans, and black T-shirt with the sleeves rolled up. But there was something else to Ari, a kind of Zen that allowed him to walk around in shirtsleeves on a -10 degree day, when the plumper, younger staff were bundled in parkas. This guy was clearly happy in life, and happiness is a key component of the Zingerman's philosophy. It is right there in the company's mission statement:

We share the Zingerman's experience
selling food that makes you happy
giving service that makes you smile
in passionate pursuit of our mission
showing love and care in all our actions
to enrich as many lives as we possibly can

Certainly the boys at Katz's would cackle at such words, but Zingerman's lofty slogans and philosophies actually translate into something you can taste. As the deli's business grew from sandwiches to imported cheese, then olive oils, rare mustards, and gourmet chocolates, Zingerman's selection became legendary, on par with New York's Zabar's. Shelves are stacked with loose-leaf teas; in-house roasted coffees; and thousands of oils, sauces, spices, and spreads from every corner of the earth. Customers can freely taste anything in the store, from a slice of Sy Ginsberg's corned beef, to a $400 bottle of aged balsamic vinegar, for free, without any need to buy. Tattooed countermen and women with Ph.D.s lecture on the merits of aged Vermont cheddar or prosciutto di Parma. In-store classes on everything from polenta appreciation to the history of hot cocoa educate customers. Ari's newsletters and e-mails weave traditions and recipes into treatises on eating and ethics. Everything looks gorgeous and tastes incredible.

Avid believers in sustainability, Ari and Paul never wanted their business to be solely about the bottom line. "The classic model is 'strip mining,' where you run a business and take as much money out for yourself as possible," Ari said, noting that for the first few years of Zingerman's he only took about $200 a week to cover his living expenses. "A sustainable business leaves the community stronger than when it came in." Today there are eight operations encompassing the Zingerman's Community of Businesses (ZCoB), with more on the horizon. There is the Roastery, which roasts and sells coffee; the Creamery, which makes dairy products; a catering company; an events company; and a separate restaurant called Zingerman's Roadhouse, which serves high-end American comfort food. The largest operation is the Bakehouse, which specializes in traditionally made breads and pastries. Baked goods are sold in the deli, at supermarkets in the area, as well as through the Zingerman's online mail order business.

In addition to the food businesses, Ari and Paul set up Zing Train—a consulting outfit that allows outside clients to learn Zingerman's business model. Past clients include engineering firms, universities, grocery stores, as well as those wishing to start Zingerman's–style delis of their own (such as Katzinger's in Columbus, Ohio). Even traditional Jewish food institutions such as Russ and Daughters, the famous appetizing store on New York's Lower East Side, have applied the Zingerman's philosophy of management, training, merchandising, marketing, customer service, and staffing.

At Zingerman's everyone gets treated like shareholders, from managing partners to part-time fifteen-year-old busboys. Zingerman's practices open-book finance, keeping staff up to date on current numbers. "Our vision is that everyone who works for us leaves here with a better life," Ari said. To a hardened deli owner, it may sound like preachy hippie bullshit, but to the kid cutting corned beef at Zingerman's, it means that his job can lead to a real future. And while most every deli owner I spoke with complained about labor problems, in particular retaining skilled workers in a market dominated by low-wage immigrants, Ari had a surplus of talent. Everywhere I went, his staff were young, educated, motivated, and happy. He had master's students baking bread and Harvard graduates chopping scallions . . . not because they had to, but because they wanted to work at Zingerman's. The turnover rate was only 50 per cent, one-quarter the industry norm. "People do a better job when you're nice to them," Ari said, "big surprise there."

Still, there are many critics who claim that Zingerman's is hardly a Jewish deli; that their mountains of imported hams and truffle oils, training seminars and wedding cakes, have cut them off from their roots. To them I say: Taste! The Jewish food at Zingerman's is fantastic. As Sy Ginsberg sat down to join us for lunch, we received a plate of the greatest corned beef hash ever. Cubed potatoes, diced onions, and peppers were slowly sautéed together with chunks of Sy's juiciest corned beef trimmings, mixed with egg, and scrambled into a crisp omelet that was gooey in the middle.

Next came a grilled Reuben. Here was a perfect example of how the ZCoB benefited the whole business. The meat was trimmed in the deli, the coleslaw and Russian dressing were homemade, and the cheese was imported Emmentaler from the grassy pastures of the Swiss Alps. It all came together on the Bakehouse's own exquisitely complex dark Jewish rye. It was traditionally made with as much rye flour as possible (most rye you'll eat at delis is made up of regular white flour with a smidgeon of rye flour), then double baked. Touring the Bakehouse later that day, I saw and tasted similar Jewish breads, made with the finest organic ingredients, including whole eggs, homemade butter, and real honey . . . nothing powdered or frozen. There were great dark loaves of sour-smelling pumpernickel and a naturally leavened *challah* made without packaged yeast (the only one I've ever seen). Rose Guttman would have been proud.

But it was Zingerman's cheese *blintz* that really drove it home for me: a small square with a dark brown crust on the top. I could taste each ingredient: the velvet milk fat in the Creamery's own farm cheese, the floral sweetness of the chestnut honey, and the tropical complexity of real Mexican vanilla pods. In that first bite of *blintz*, I knew why the crowds were lined up outside on this frigid Sunday, waiting an hour to edge into the packed deli just to get a sandwich. I understood why people from all over the nation ordered Zingerman's breads, why they made pilgrimages to this college town in the middle of Michigan farmland for a corned beef on rye. Ari and Paul had successfully grown a small Jewish delicatessen into a business with over thirty million dollars in annual sales, and in the process managed not just to retain the food's Jewish tradition, but to deepen it.

Ari didn't think his and Paul's model was that difficult or radical, but Sy Ginsberg knew better. Few deli owners had the mixture of creativity, selflessness, and community spirit that Ari and Paul did. Fewer still found themselves in an environment as ideally suited as Ann Arbor: a rich college town with an endless supply of motivated, idealistic labor. It had the best of urban sophistication and suburban comforts, with a small-town insulation that worked to keep competition at bay. In the world beyond the town's borders, the deli business was more cutthroat, and many who had tried to emulate Zingerman's elsewhere succeeded only on a surface level.

"The Zingerman clones just don't match up," Sy Ginsberg said, wiping bits of *blintz* from his mustache. "It's like putting some extra chrome on a Chevy and calling it a Cadillac."

YOUR
NUMBER
07
WHEN CALLED
IT'S YOUR TURN
FOR SERVICE

Chicago: Can Deli Return to the Windy City?

A man walks into Manny's Coffee Shop & Deli, grabs a tray, and slowly starts down the cafeteria line. On the other side of the counter, a quartet of men in white button-up T-shirts and paper hats reaches underneath the protective glass to retrieve a rainbow of soul-warming dishes. It snowed two feet this week and the Bears got pummeled in the Super Bowl last night. He's earned this meal.

At the first counterman, he eyes browned strips of baked fish, golden salmon patties, crisp little fried smelts, and *knishes* big as grapefruits, but he's drawn to a softball-sized piece of homemade *gefilte* fish. The counterman hands it over, along with a bowl of *mishmosh*—chicken soup with the works, including a duo of dense *kreplach*, a handful of thin noodles, and two *matzo* balls.

Next, our man arrives at Gino. Manny's legendary counterman is furiously assembling overstuffed corned beef sandwiches. "Hey pal," Gino says in a flash, his wry smile emerging behind Einstein whiskers, eyes peering expectantly over spectacles that rest on the tip of his nose. Somewhere in the metronome tempo of two slicing machines peeling off strips of pink corned beef like soft cheese, our man in line falls into a trance, snapping awake only when Gino issues a quick "Hey pal? What can I getcha?"

The man orders a corned beef and Gino explodes into action. He slaps a big slice of rye onto the wood board, flips his fork in the air like a ninja, catches it, and stabs the growing pile of meat falling off the machine's blade. Gino drops the corned beef onto the bread, tosses another slice on top, and slices the sandwich in half. Then he grabs a plate and pickles, and in one swift move flips the plate into the air, catches it, slams the pickles down, drops on the sandwich, impales a crispy blond *latke*, and hands it over.

"Fast hands," our man in line says.

"Yeah," Gino quips, "and they're still attached too."

The man ignores the salad counter and waits while the cashier punches in his friend's order. Starving now, he takes a fork from the bin and tears off a fat hunk of *gefilte* fish. It's so good, almost creamy, that he barely chews, and is still savoring it, when he starts gasping audibly for air. His face turns red. The man is choking.

This is the point when my interview with Ken Raskin, Manny's owner, is interrupted, as he rushes over to save his customer's life. Raskin, a great bear of a man, wraps his arms around the choking man and lifts him off his feet, performing the Heimlich maneuver until the offending *gefilte* fish is dislodged. "Are you okay?" Raskin asks. The man wordlessly pats Raskin on the shoulder in brief thanks, then chews and successfully swallows the very piece of *gefilte* fish that nearly killed him. Without breaking stride, he joyfully saunters over to his table, where he rips into the rest of his meal with undaunted ferocity. No panic. No tears. No life flashing before his eyes. His only concern is to keep on eating.

"My arms are killing me," Ken Raskin said, returning to the table rubbing his forearms. I asked Raskin if the man's unruffled reaction was common. "Four years ago the roof caught on fire at lunchtime and people were fighting to get *in!*"

The Windy City has all the elements that should make for one of the world's best delicatessen towns. Its Jewish population clocks in at approximately 285,000, the fourth largest in the country (after Philadelphia), and is one of the few communities that is growing in size. Most of Chicago's Jews have Ashkenazi roots: Poles, Romanians, Russians, Hungarians . . . delicatessen stock.

Since the rise of the great stockyards in the 1880s, Chicago has long been America's meatiest city. Up until the 1950s and the advent of refrigerated trucks, if you ate beef in America, Chicago was its likely source. As a result, it was a hub of deli production. Vienna Beef, Best's Kosher and Sinai 48, Wilno Salami, Eisenberg, Oscherwitz Kosher, King Kold, Sara Lee, and Eli's Cheesecake are all Chicago Jewish food brands. Chicago's sausage makers still supply many delis west of the Mississippi.

The factors are all there for a Midwestern deli Mecca: lots of Jews, big carnivores, and a fair chunk of the deli industry. But why weren't Chicago's delis that well known? No one really discussed them. Were they still around? I had seen archival photos of delicatessens in the city from previous decades. Had they simply closed? Were the delis scattered among far-flung suburbs, like those I visited in Detroit? If so, why hadn't they come back to the city itself, which remained a thriving and wealthy metropolis?

"I don't think the mentality [in Chicago] was ever that delicatessens were the place to go, like in Cleveland or Detroit or New

York," Bob Schwartz said, recalling his own surprise when he moved to Chicago from Cleveland in the mid-1970s. "It's a hot dog town primarily." Schwartz, a short joyous man with a Danny DeVito rasp, was a senior vice president of Vienna Beef. He has published a book on Chicago's hot dog stands, and drives a red Audi with a license plate that says PSTRAMI. We had just finished a tour of Vienna's processing plant, a giant industrial facility that annually produces hundreds of millions of pounds of hot dogs and deli meats. Founded in 1894, Vienna Beef is one of the oldest Jewish deli purveyors in the country, predating Hebrew National by a decade, and is largely responsible for popularizing the hot dog in America.

Compared to United Meat and Deli, Vienna was playing in the national leagues. As I toured around with Schwartz, we passed racks of tens of thousands of hot dogs and walked along raised metal catwalks suspended above a dozen vats of bubbling corned beefs. Thousands of briskets and navels awaited entry into giant smokers, stacked onto the racks of metal trolleys suspended from a track in the ceiling. Schwartz said that Vienna sold half a million pounds of corned beef the month before St. Patrick's Day. With regard to hot dogs, they were making an average of 80,000 pounds a day, upping that to 120,000 pounds during baseball season. The plant runs twenty-four hours a day, seven days a week.

The majority of Vienna's products went to supermarkets, big box chains, and restaurant supply companies like Sysco. Schwartz estimated that sales to Jewish delis were less than half of what they had been in the 1970s, maybe 10 per cent of Vienna's total business, and a much greater decline from the first half of the twentieth century. The days of independent meat salesmen (whom Schwartz called "Wagon-jobbers"), *schmoozing* at their customer's neighborhood deli, were done. "That's why a company like ours has done very well, because we haven't relied on that one segment," Schwartz said. "A guy like Sy, for instance, that's his whole business. He'll get on an airplane and go to Bozeman, Montana. No one here will go to Montana just to visit one deli."

Consolidation had also cemented giants like Vienna, and the recent history of Chicago's deli purveyors reads like a meaty M&A report. David Berg and Company went bankrupt in the 1980s, and their Kosher Zion brand was absorbed into Vienna Beef. King Kold, Berg's glatt kosher dairy operation, was spun off independently and acquired the Ratner's brand name from the legendary Lower East Side dairy restaurant, which closed in 2002. Best's Kosher Sausage Company had merged with Sinai Kosher Sausage to form the Bessin Corporation, which then sold out to the Sara Lee Corporation. Sara Lee, which was established in 1935 by Chicago Jewish baker Charles Lubin, was acquired by the Consolidated Foods Corporation in 1956. Today Sara Lee is a publicly traded food empire with tens of billions in assets, including Shofar, Wilno, and Oscherwitz deli brands, LaVazza espresso in Italy, and Godrej insecticides in India.

All this consolidation had placed increased pressure on producers to leverage more profitability out of their products. Foods were being replaced with "foodstuffs"—engineered products with artificial flavorings, like Vienna's "Smoked Brisket," which was injected with liquid smoke. So long as the product could sell in Costco or Sam's Club, did it matter if it tasted *haymish*? These corporations had no loyalty to Jewish deli products. In January 2008, Sara Lee ceased all production of kosher meat products, ending the legacy of Best's Kosher, Sinai, Shofar, and Wilno in a penstroke. Best's Kosher alone had been around since 1886. Anyway, there were even fewer delis to sell to in Chicago, and they had been dying for some time.

"Benny Goodman first played clarinet in that old synagogue over there," Irving Cutler said, slowly driving his car around the West Side of Chicago's Lawndale and Douglas Park neighborhoods. "In this building, my sister sat and listened to Golda Meir, then a public librarian, give fiery speeches about the Zionist cause."

Retired as the chair of the geography department at Chicago State University, Irving Cutler has been spending much of his golden years as a historical tour guide of Jewish Chicago, and I asked him to show me the ghosts of Chicago's deli heyday. Up until the middle of the twentieth century, 125,000 Jews lived in Lawndale, but only traces of their community remain. Along Douglas Boulevard, a tree-lined street with a grassy median, Cutler pointed out the shells of once grand synagogues. Imposing stone structures rose from the sidewalks atop wide staircases, their turn-of-the-century grandeur unmolested by time. These were gorgeous buildings, some of the finest specimens of Diaspora architecture in America, now absorbed into the neighborhood's background. Most had boarded windows and barricaded doors. Many became Baptist churches, their Stars of David covered by bright signs enticing all to come and be saved.

As we turned onto Roosevelt Road, the area's main commercial street, Cutler began rattling off the delicatessens that had occupied various corners. The Blintzes Inn had become a day-care center. Silverstein's, once a banquet hall filled with seltzer bottles and *bar mitzvah* parties, was an empty lot. By the time of the 1968 inner-city riots, following the assassination of Dr. Martin Luther King, there were few Jews left in central Chicago, and even fewer deli-catessens. Those that hadn't decamped to the suburbs sold, went out of business, or burned up in the riots. Carl's, known for its corned beef and clubby atmosphere, was no more. Zweig's lasted until the mid-1960s. Gerwitz's, Sam & Hy's, and dozens of tiny corner delis . . . all were gone now.

In other areas of downtown Chicago, the story was the same. Cutler next took me to the historic Maxwell Street Market, once a dense collection of tenements and pushcarts just south of the city center that had been Chicago's equivalent of the Lower East Side. But Mama Batt's was gone, as was Leavitt's, and Gold's. The last holdout was Nate's Deli, formerly Lyons, which was owned by Nate Duncan, an African-American counterman who'd worked at

Lyons for many years. In *The Blues Brothers* film, Nate's exterior provided a stand-in for Aretha Franklin's soul food restaurant, but in 1994, the city tore down the Maxwell Street Market, including Nate's, to make room for condos and the growing University of Illinois at Chicago campus.

We drove on to northern enclaves like Humboldt Park, Roger's Park, and Albany Park, where Cutler explained how change came more gradually as Jewish families slowly moved out to the suburbs. Again, the delis were left to die: Moishe Pippic's, Itzkovitz, Joe Pierce, and Koppel's. Though Hasidic and elderly Jews remain embedded in West Rogers Park, there is nary a deli to be found for miles. Down in Chicago's South Side, Cutler remarked how Unique Deli and the legendary Braverman's are fading memories.

"The delicatessens that had relocated to the suburbs often didn't adjust well," Cutler said. "In the suburbs, they tried to open and failed. As you move away from the heart of the city, [the community] becomes more and more diluted." Where each Jewish neighborhood once boasted a dozen delis in its roster, now the whole of Chicago and its suburbs barely listed that many. It was fitting that the last stop Cutler made was in the suburb of Skokie. He pulled into the parking lot of the Barnum and Bagel Restaurant, a Skokie institution that had been teeming with business weeks before. Now it sat empty. White pieces of paper stating "CLOSED" were taped to the windows. Just a few blocks away, the only sign that Chaim's Kosher Bakery and Deli had closed the week before was its locked door. Chaim's stunned customers were now trickling across the street to Kaufman's Bagel & Deli where a sign beckoned "WINTER IS COLD. OUR HOT TREATS WILL WARM YOUR HEART." Inside, mother Judy Dworkin, daughter Bette, husband Arnold, a bevy of veteran countermen, and a big jolly baker named Herb Fingerhut were keeping Skokie's deli scene alive.

Physically divided in two, between a bakery and a takeout delicatessen, Kaufman's was not a restaurant, but a bustling Jewish food emporium. At Kaufman's I experienced my first great hope for

Chicago deli. Silver-haired matriarch Judy took me around the store, procuring various nibbles and tastes of anything she felt was worthy: cornmeal-rolled rye, dark Russian pumpernickel, sugar-speckled raspberry *rugelach*, sweet *gefilte* fish, coarsely chopped liver, dense noodle *kugel*, and a baked rice pudding. Bette, the gregarious daughter of already gregarious parents, was everything I expected in a Chicago woman: she greeted you with a huge smile, shot straight to the heart of the matter, and was one tough cookie maker when she needed to be. Only a handful of successful female delicatessen owners existed in the business, and as Bette (who was in her early forties) took over from her parents, the importance of the staff's respect was apparent. None showed that adulation more than her newly hired baker, Herb Fingerhut.

A seventh-generation baker, one look at Herb revealed that the occupation had crept into his genetic fiber. He had the solidly built frame of a man whose life had been surrounded by butterfat, which he said was a good thing, because you should never trust a skinny baker. Herb's face revealed the dimpled, cherubic smile of a grown-up kid who was having the time of his life. Bette hoped Herb's touch would inject something unique into Kaufman's, which continued to be successful, but nonetheless felt the constraints of the neighborhood and the slowing economy. Jewish Skokie had given way over the years to a more mixed community, and Kaufman's aging client base was dwindling, as the closing of the Barnum and Bagel and Chaim's illustrated. Traditional foods would remain the bedrock, but Herb could add touches of creativity that would bring new customers in the door. One of these was the daily special: his Reuben Strudel.

Herb stretched out four rectangles of pastry dough and spread roughly a pound of corned beef scraps on each of the pastry sheets. Next, he sprinkled sauerkraut, laid down thick slices of Swiss cheese, folded the pastry shut, scored the top, brushed it with butter, and placed it in the creaking oven. Twenty minutes later, Herb retrieved the tray. Though the golden dough was piping hot, he sliced one up, popping a scalding corner into his mouth. Slowly, a mischievous grin emerged. "It's very good," Herb beamed. Herb was being modest. The Reuben Strudel was freaking sensational, nothing short of a revelation in deli baking. Each bite was a mélange of decadent flavors; the buttery flaking of the dough meeting the gooey aroma of the melted Swiss, all brought together by the corned beef, steamed to a new life inside the pastry shell. I would never taste anything comparable to Herb's experiment that day at Kaufman's. If deli in Chicago was going to make its comeback, the Reuben Strudel was helping it off to a great start.

Unlike in most major American cities, people worked, lived, ate, and played in Chicago's downtown, though this wasn't always the case. For decades Chicago was known as a dangerous town, where gangs killed for nothing more than a pair of Air Jordans. Things began to turn around in the mid-1990s, with the revitalization work of Mayor Richard M. Daley, and Jewish delicatessens have slowly been returning downtown, looking to capture a slice of business from those moving into new condominiums, as well as those living in traditionally moneyed enclaves like the Gold Coast. In the winter of 2006, two very ambitious delis opened in downtown Chicago, stoking the hopes for a revival.

Eleven City Diner and Max and Benny's were both the product of suburban dreamers who'd set their sights on the big city. In the case of Eleven City Diner, its charismatic owner, Brad Rubin, had grown up in a big house with parents who constantly entertained. Rubin had worked in high-end restaurants around town, but after a decade in fine dining, Rubin (who was thirty-six at the time) wanted something else. Realizing the delis of his youth had disappeared, he developed the idea of an urban delicatessen/diner.

The Eleven City Diner opened on March 30, 2006, in the condo-crazy South Loop area, on Wabash at the corner of 11th Street. The space was lofty and bright, with white tiling along the walls,

Formica-topped tables, and an old wooden bar he salvaged from a strip club. By the register there was a mini candy store, and Rubin hung his bar mitzvah photographs on the way to the washroom. On weekends, his father worked the soda fountain, while his mother played hostess and *schmoozed* with customers.

The other deli, Max and Benny's, had been a going concern since 1985, when Lester Schlan opened it in ritzy suburban Northbrook, twenty-five miles north of the city. Max and Benny's excelled at everything a suburban delicatessen should. It was expansive (12,000 square feet) and comfortable. The menu at Max and Benny's offered everything from stacked corned beef sandwiches to breakfasts, salads, and an outstanding blueberry noodle *kugel*. They baked everything on site: bagels, breads, hot dogs wrapped in bagel dough, black and white cookies, and adorable bear-shaped Rice Krispy treats with mini Chicago Cubs hats. There was a huge takeout section packed with smoked fish, cold cuts, and breads. They catered *bar mitzvahs*, *shivas*, and *bris'*, and sold five hundred gallons of chicken soup each weekend and thirty metric tons of corned beef annually.

Schlan's son Max, then twenty-five, had recently graduated from Boston University's prestigious hotel/restaurant school, and Lester Schlan saw a double opportunity to give Max a chance at the head of his own shop, while establishing a foothold downtown. They would open a sophisticated delicatessen that could attract downtown Jewish residents, tourists, and office workers. Schlan secured a location at the base of the River East Center, a fifty-eight-story condominium and multiplex in the up and coming Streeterville neighborhood. The new Max and Benny's opened in February 2006 to much fanfare. Guests were greeted by lush draperies, expansive banquettes, high ceilings, etched glass walls, and flat-screen televisions galore, as well as a fully stocked bar.

Schlan was a proven entity in Chicago's deli landscape and served a product customers already loved. At Eleven City Diner, Rubin knew Chicago's downtown clientele but wasn't a Deli Man.

Both were risky ventures in newly gentrified, high-rent neighborhoods. So which of the two closed after only six months downtown?

"There's a reason there's not a deli in downtown," Schlan said, exactly a year and a day after his Streeterville location had opened. There was no single cause for his deli's failure, which lost an average of fifty thousand dollars a month. Large numbers of Jewish clients never materialized like they did in Northbrook. Locals rarely ate there at night or during the week. Though the decor was lavish, many felt it was ill-suited for a delicatessen. Staffing remained a constant problem. Tourists loved the place, and weekends were busy, especially at brunch, but Max and Benny's simply never sold enough food to make a profit. Smoked fish wilted in the display case like wallflowers at a school dance.

"Part of my success here is we know what people like," Schlan said, sitting amid the hustle of his original location. "My son didn't want to stay in the deli business. We thought we'd start with what we knew and we upscaled it a bit, but it just didn't take off. . . . It's possible that if we did an old-fashioned deli it might have worked." Schlan had no regrets, and business was doing better than ever in Northbrook. The only regret was Chicago's unrealized potential. "It's a shame in Chicago that I can count on my hand the number of delis," he said, "and less the number of good delis."

Over at Eleven City Diner, Brad Rubin was bouncing around like a pinball from table to table, back to the bar, over to the kitchen, into his office, around the deli counter, to the door, the cash, and over again, furiously pumping flesh, making jokes, teasing the staff in Spanish, fielding incessant calls, shooting the shit with suppliers, and handing kids candy. Eleven City Diner had survived its first year, a feat that was intrinsically tied to the kinetic energy of its *meshugah* owner.

Though he was nearly forty, Rubin looked far younger and gave off the image of an eccentric Internet wizard from 1992. He spoke quickly, punctuating words with his hands, and when I made a point he liked, he would grab my arm and say, "Yessssss! Exactly!"

I would be asking him about his meat supplier, and before he got halfway through the answer he was running to the counter to return with slices of maroon pastrami, heavily blackened, nicely marbled, and thickly cut. The man had no off-switch.

"It's not sexy to work seven days a week," Rubin said, the exhaustion showing in his eyes. "If I want to live in a restaurant, I want the place to be like a family to me. . . . I saw all the fancy restaurants trying to be the next big thing, but none of them had a forty- or fifty- or sixty-year longevity. I want to be around for a long time, to be part of this neighborhood." Upscale diners everywhere promised nostalgic food and atmosphere without grease-stained counters and dingy washrooms. What set Eleven City Diner apart was the Jewish delicatessen. The food certainly lived up to its billing. Eleven City's brisket, a hefty slab of sweetly braised meat atop stewed potatoes and carrots, peeled away at the touch of a fork. The chopped liver was superb.

I really enjoyed Eleven City Diner, so much so that I went back at night. There was Rubin, still kibitzing with everyone, from old Hebrew school friends to tables full of cops and booths packed with the city's top investment bankers. "With my education and experience I could work here four days a week," he said, completely drained. "I could sleep late. I could meet a nice Jewish girl, and make my mother happy. But instead I'm here all the time." I felt for him, but wasn't this what Rubin had signed up for? He wanted the life of the Deli Man, to be around for decades. Yet the more we spoke, the more I saw that Brad Rubin's ambitions went beyond that.

He talked about opening other locations within a year or two, possibly in a boutique hotel, maybe even Las Vegas. Then, in the spring of 2007, Rubin excitedly called to tell me that he was going to open up another Eleven City Diner on ritzy Michigan Avenue, the so-called Magnificent Mile, sometime in 2008 (though by the end of that year it had yet to open). It would have four hundred seats and a larger menu, more elaborate decor, and even pickled tongue. "But don't think we'll get modern on your ass!" he joked into the phone, assuring me that he still wanted to keep things authentic. In just over a year, Rubin had turned one restaurant into two and had plans to do more. So why was I worried?

Because, like most deli owners I met in Chicago, Rubin's hero was Richard Melman, the founder and chairman of Lettuce Entertain You, a corporation that owns over seventy restaurants across the United States with annual revenues estimated at over three hundred million dollars. Melman's career began behind the soda counter of his father's Chicago deli, Ricky's, where he cut strawberries with a spoon. When his father and uncle refused to sell him a piece of the business, Melman struck out on his own, opening R.J. Grunts in 1971, the restaurant that launched his empire. Though Lettuce Entertain You Enterprises has since opened everything from fine French dining establishments (Everest) to seafood restaurants (Joe's Stone Crab), Melman has yet to touch a deli.

"I have had an idea for what I think would be one of the great delis in the country," Melman said, talking to me from his Chicago home. "Every two or three years I get a group of Jewish guys who call me and say, 'When are you going to open that great deli?' and this is what I tell them: 'I don't know that I could make money in today's world running the type of delicatessen I'd like to run.' I always end it by telling them it would almost have to be like giving to Israel. It's just charity." Though Melman had the formula, experience, and money to save the deli, the risk wasn't yet worth taking.

Yet in Melman, both Rubin, Schlan, and other ambitious Chicago deli owners saw their dreams lived to their fullest, and they couldn't help but try to emulate his success. Many had tried over the years. Max and Benny's foray downtown demonstrated just how difficult that was. Eleven City Diner was a success, but one that seemed inseparable from its charismatic owner. What would happen when Rubin opened his second location, splitting his presence between two relatively new restaurants?

Chicago's deli revival was building up steam. Long-standing local delis such as Max's and Eppy's were adding more locations, and the popular Michigan deli Steve's had just opened in downtown Chicago. I openly confessed to Rubin that I feared he was spreading himself too thin. He worked ridiculous hours and in 2008 had to undergo three back surgeries from the damage he'd done to his spine at the restaurant. Eleven City Diner was a major part of that revival, but it needed to be nurtured and settle roots before branching out further. Aggressive expansion was tempting in the short run, but it increased the risk that Chicago's deli revival could fizzle. Rubin admitted he had those concerns too, but he was intent on sticking around as long as Manny's had. "I have one shot at making this succeed," he said, "and I don't want to fail."

Manny's was the biggest, best-known, and oldest deli in the city, and it was directly tied into Chicago's nascent Jewish deli revival. As owner Ken Raskin told the story, his grandfather Jack Raskin bought a cafeteria called Sonny's in 1945, and because it was cheaper to change two letters on the sign, he named it after his son Emanuel, ergo Manny's. From age thirteen on, Ken Raskin worked at Manny's every Saturday and summer with his dad. After the 1968 riots, Manny's closed at nights and on weekends, though the riot police took their lunch breaks at Manny's between cracking skulls at the Democratic National Convention. When Ken was just twenty-seven years old, his father suddenly died of a heart attack. It was a terrible shock. Ken's wife, Patti, had recently given birth to a second son, Danny, and the young family now lived in the suburb of Deerfield, thirty-five miles from the deli. Still, Ken Raskin never considered closing.

"I had been working here for half my life," Ken recalled. "I had a mortgage and two kids, but I also had a point to prove, because all the old-timers on the street were taking bets on how long I could last." Raskin worked tirelessly to maintain the original look, feel, and taste of Manny's. The potatoes were still peeled by hand and the *latkes* fried in cast-iron skillets. The antique water fountain, with a framed photo of Manny Raskin hanging above it, still anchored the deli.

In 2006, Ken's son Danny, then twenty-four, began working full time at Manny's, the fourth Raskin in an unbroken line of succession. Since coming on board he had pushed Ken for small modernizations. It was at Danny's insistence that Manny's took credit cards. He'd lobbied his dad hard to reopen Sundays and at nights for dinner and brought in free valet parking for customers, a move that drove up business during winter. The most important change had been to the food. Though Danny introduced chopped salads and a few "healthier" items, he'd also brought back traditional Jewish foods.

"I've noticed people my age started eating that food again, like noodle *kugel*," Danny said. "We were always afraid that when our older clientele died off, that food would too. The thing that makes you smile is that on Saturdays we're busier now than on any other day of the week. People my age come in with strollers and load up their trays with *matzo* ball soup and other Jewish foods. We are trying to modernize without changing the core of what we are. I don't want to stop those small things that make us Manny's, I just want to make it more efficient."

A new generation was on the cusp of rediscovering their past through the deli, and Manny's, the oldest and grandest of Chicago's delis, led the way. It wasn't the interior design that lured them; Manny's had no plasma televisions or plush banquettes. They came for what delis do best: *kugel*, *kishke*, *gefilte* fish, and fat sandwiches of tender, hot, pink corned beef. Danny Raskin's generation would save the Windy City's deli.

When Danny got up to help a young mother with a baby carry a tray to her table, Ken leaned in close: "He could have been an executive. It's a major regret of mine. But this has been a major part of the fun of working here. When I'm not here, Danny shines."

Danny returned and asked what we were talking about. Ken just smiled, put his arm around the boy's shoulder, and pulled him close.

The Yucchuputzville Diaries
Part 1: Goy West Young Man

(St. Louis–Kansas City–Denver–Boulder–Salt Lake City)

I left Chicago with just under two weeks to drive to California, well over half the width of the continental United States. To most deli lovers on the coasts, nothing exists in Middle America except cornfields, football, and ham on white. In 2006, barely 4,000 Jews lived in Utah, only 430 in Wyoming. But Missouri and Colorado both had substantial Jewish communities, and I knew that if there were Jews out there, then by god there

had to be some deli to feed them. Armed with a list of local contacts in each city, and the willingness to Google "Jewish Deli" and
a state's name in endless combinations, I was ready to seek deli in
some of the reddest states in the Union.

Protzel's Delicatessen, *Clayton, Missouri*

Above a single-story red brick storefront on a leafy side street, a
faded sign announced in hand-painted letters, "Bob and Evelyn
PROTZEL'S" with a nice blue Star of David to the right. Below, the
words FINE FOODS were sandwiched between CORNED BEEF and PAS-
TRAMI. It could have been the most perfect deli sign I'd ever seen. In
one glance you knew the proprietors, that they were Jewish, and that
you could find fine foods here, such as corned beef and pastrami.

Protzel's was a narrow takeout-only deli with a long counter
running down its length. Above the deli counter, the Protzel family
history was in full view. Photographs of Bob Protzel, the original
owner, elbowed up against *bar mitzvah* pictures of his grandchildren
Max and Erica, both of whom now worked behind the counter.
There were also humorous slogans written by Bob, a former free-
lance copywriter:

> ### CHOPPED LIVER
> #### $17,980.00 per Ton
> ##### May be Purchased in Smaller Quantities

Bob Protzel had grown up poor in St. Louis and managed to
open Protzel's Delicatessen in 1954 with his wife, Evelyn. During
that period there were over a dozen Jewish delis in greater St. Louis,
a city that held a significant Jewish presence because of its role
as a trade center on the Mississippi, including places like Louis',
Platt's, Sherman's, Fishman's, Solomon Deli, Eli's, and El and Lee,
which fed a largely urban community. But as downtown St. Louis
suffered white flight, and the Jews spread out amid the suburbs, all

the other delis closed. Though the Jews of greater St. Louis were now a smaller percentage of the overall population than they had once been, they remained a close-knit community, and on this Sunday the lunch lineup was snaking out the door. Most came for Protzel's specialty: corned beef derived from a secret recipe.

"My father knew nothing about the business," said his son, Alan Protzel. "Six months after he opened the store, a man came in called Braverman. He told my father, 'I'll give you the best recipe for corned beef under certain conditions.' My father wasn't allowed to sell the recipe and he had to pass it on to another young man if he ever sold the business. And that was that." The homemade corned beef also turned out to be the key to Protzel's survival. When supermarkets opened their deli sections in the 1960s, the other Jewish delis, who sold precooked corned beef that they purchased from Chicago, couldn't compete. But people were willing to pay a premium for Protzel's homemade product. Protzel's now sells over six hundred pounds of it a week, all barrel cured and cooked in the back of the cramped store. It is always served cold.

As I pigged out on slices of meats from a plastic plate— including the dynamite corned beef, moist even when cold, and a few slices of lovely tongue, which had a mild roast garlic aftertaste—I asked father and son about the importance of their family's legacy. "To tell you the truth," Alan said, "I would have closed the deli if Max didn't take it. Either that or sold it. And Max could care less about the legacy of the place. Look, nothing is forever, this place will either get sold or franchised."

I was shocked at how fatalistic it all seemed. Max, who was in his mid-twenties and recently married, didn't like the hours. "If I could do it without Sundays I'd be happier, but you just can't." Alan was even more direct. For decades he'd sacrificed advances in his career as an insurance executive in order to keep his late father's deli thriving. He made it clear that he was ready to cash out. "You put the right amount of money on the table for our corned beef recipe and I'll go out."

I couldn't believe it. He was talking about selling the very corned beef recipe that had taken the family out of poverty, paid Alan's way through college, and allowed Protzel's to outlast every other Jewish deli in St. Louis. The same secret corned beef recipe that was passed along on the explicit promise that it never be sold.

"Hey," said Alan Protzel, "that's my dad's promise, not mine."

New York Bakery and Delicatessen, *Kansas City, Missouri*

I didn't have high hopes for Kansas City. The city's Jewish population is fairly small, just shy of eight thousand, and it's a place made famous for the ultimate *treyf* cuisine, BBQ ribs. But when I saw the New York Bakery and Delicatessen, I immediately knew my preconceptions were way off. As I walked in the door, the sweet smell of baking *lebkuchen* cookies, danish, bagels, and breads assaulted me from all sides. There was an arranged chaos that only added to the feeling of a well-established institution: the sparse racks of *matzos*, portraits of previous owners, license plates that said BAGEL, BAGELS, and NYDELI, and old Star of David cookie cutters hanging on the walls.

The New York Bakery and Delicatessen happened to be one of the oldest delicatessens in the country, originally opened in 1905 by Esther and Isadore Becker, who'd come to Kansas City from Poland. When I arrived it was in the hands of Jim Holzmark, a sweet, laid-back gentleman with a crown of white hair around his bald skull and a lazy drawl. Holzmark, who'd grown up in the food business in Kansas City, had bought the delicatessen in 1981. With the other Kansas City delicatessens (Milwaukee Deli, Main St. Deli, and Schenkman's) having closed, Holzmark found himself at the helm of KC's only remaining Jewish deli and its oldest restaurant.

"We're a Jewish *delicatessen*, not a sandwich shop," Holzmark corrected me, when I referred to his establishment as a deli. "We're the real deal or as close as you're going to get in Kansas City." In the 1940s, the neighborhood had been the core of Kansas City's Jewish community, but time and economics had left it mostly in the hands of black families. When he first purchased the store, Holzmark estimated that up to 90 per cent of the delicatessen's clientele came from the Jewish community, and that a mere 5 per cent were black. Today, those numbers have almost completely reversed, with Jews accounting for a tiny 15 per cent of business and blacks for an overwhelming 60 per cent (the rest made up by whites). Holzmark couldn't have been happier with the arrangement.

"Blacks don't have problems with eating cholesterol," Holzmark said, as one of his regular clients ordered a towering Reuben sandwich at eleven in the morning. "If you've grown up eating barbecue, pastrami is a drop in the bucket. They'll come up to the counter and say 'Man, lay that fat on my corned beef sandwich!'"

This type of cross-cultural adulation, between African-American appetites and Jewish cooking, was one I saw many times—at Katz's in New York, Lou's in Detroit, or Manny's in Chicago—but the New York Bakery and Delicatessen had managed to take it one step further through its fantastic hickory-smoked brisket. Devised by the delicatessen's head cook, Sonny Taborn, this smoked brisket was the best combination of Jewish and black cuisines I'd yet seen. Sonny rubbed raw briskets with a mix of secret seasoning (the only hint I got was that it contained Lawry's salt), and then smoked them in a custom-built metal box with a puck of pure hickory for five to six hours.

"I jus' put a little touch to it," Sonny said, pulling aside a small vent pipe from the smoker to reveal a trickle of light smoke puffing up, "you know what I'm sayin'?"

It was mild, crumbly, and definitely smoky, a subdued and wonderful contrast to the powerful kick of a pastrami with far more wood flavor in each bite. Paired with a spicy brown mustard, it went down wonderfully.

"A true example of Black/Jewish fusion," I said to Holzmark.

"Mmmm hmmm," he hummed in approval, "KC cookin'."

In recent months, Holzmark was planning a return to the delicatessen's traditions. He proudly displayed a bag of chicken livers that he was getting ready to make into his first batch of chopped liver in a dozen years. But as we talked, Holzmark also confessed that he had put the delicatessen up for sale just a week before. His children, whom he had hoped to pass the business on to, wanted no part of the deli, and Holzmark was tired of working twelve-hour days, 365 days a year, when a timeshare in Mexico lay waiting.

"When you're in this type of business, you're in servitude," Holzmark said. "I'd hate to close her down, but as long as I get my money I'm happy." For the second day in a row, I'd been told by a Midwestern deli owner that it was time to flee the ship. History clearly showed that the survival chances of Protzel's or the New York Bakery and Delicatessen diminished once they left family hands. I promised to check back in a few months' time. As of early 2009, the deli hadn't sold. Despite a few offers, none had closed. "Cash talks, but bullshit walks," Holzmark said, optimistically adding, "I guess I'll stay here for a while." A glimmer of hope for Kansas City, however faint.

Mile High Rye, *Denver, Colorado*

Although I visited several of Denver's native delicatessens, including the stellar Zaidy's, the cozy Bagel, and the large, glatt-kosher East Side Kosher Deli, it was the so-called New York delis that really caught my eye in the Mile High City. For every five New Yorkers who leave for greener pastures, there will inevitably be one who decides that the new hometown needs a real New York deli, and he or she, a real New Yorker, is just the person to open it. This tradition dates back to the turn of the twentieth century, when Jewish immigrants would disembark in New York before setting off elsewhere in America. Many of them would open delicatessens named after New York, often as a telltale sign that they were offering authentic kosher food.

To many, a Jewish delicatessen and a New York delicatessen are one and the same. As one Texas deli owner told me, "We use New

York so we don't have to say Jewish. Though out here, New York means *Jew*." Across America there are dozens of delis with names like New York Deli, the New Yorker Deli, Manhattan Deli, Bronx Deli, etc. . . . Often, they are the first to enter a market where delicatessens never existed. The Eat This Deli was opened in 2005 in Rogers, Arkansas, by Dr. Ron Haberman, a cardiologist from Queens, and was located just miles from Wal-Mart's corporate headquarters. Unfortunately, Eat This Deli lasted only a year before closing. The *Arkansas Democrat Gazette* joyfully surmised that "it may have carried too much of a Yankee boast."

This is often the problem with exported New York delicatessens. They strive to be overly New York in every sense of the word, overwhelming locals with attitude. Each is decorated like a compressed version of Times Square. The owners of these delis are usually trying to impress one small subset of the local population—other native New Yorkers, who are ready within their first bite of a *knish* to accept the place as their deliverance or cast them down as charlatans. But for all their tacky bravado, these exports raise an interesting question. Does the salvation of the American Jewish delicatessen lie in maintaining a strong connection with its origins in New York or will a local approach ultimately win more hearts and mouths?

In Denver there were two delis competing for the title of most New York, with a third that leveraged its Brooklyn name to tremendous financial success. The New York Deli News had been around the longest, operating since 1989 in East Denver. Its owner, Al Belsky, came from Manhattan, where his parents owned the Fashion Luncheonette, a delicatessen in the garment district. When Belsky's parents retired, Al took over with his wife, Victoria, but soon moved to Denver, where they'd attended college, and opened New York Deli News, replicating the menu of the Fashion Luncheonette.

A sign outside the New York Deli News announced: "Leaving Denver, Entering New York." Their claim to fame was how much of their product arrived from New York. Meats and ryes came from outside Manhattan, the bagels from H & H, and the smoked fish from Brooklyn's Acme. Initially more than half Belsky's clients were Jewish ex-New Yorkers who craved a nostalgic nosh, though Catholic priests and Hall of Fame Denver Broncos quarterback John Elway also ranked as devotees. Clearly the New York attitude wasn't that hard-core, because they let Mr. Elway order his pastrami sandwich on white bread with mayonnaise, without so much as a sneeze.

When Belsky first opened, his partner at the time was Fred Anzman, an accountant from Long Island. Fred left the partnership after a few months, but reemerged on the Denver deli scene in 2002, when he opened Deli Tech with his wife, Barbara Simon. Whenever they went back to New York, Fred and Barbara invariably ate most of their meals at the Carnegie Delicatessen. One visit, Fred asked owner Sandy Levine whether he could open a Carnegie Delicatessen out in Colorado. Levine said franchises weren't an option, but he was happy to sell Fred and Barbara the Carnegie Delicatessen's product from his New Jersey commissary. Eventually they would import eight to ten thousand dollars a month of frozen Carnegie meats and cheesecakes, in addition to other New York deli staples. Fred and Barbara went ahead designing a delicatessen that would be more New York than the Yankees. Deli Tech (so named because it is located in the Denver Tech Center) was packed with enough New York kitsch to feel like a Broadway gift shop.

"You must be David!" Barbara screamed, pulling me into a big hug. Fred came over and gave my shoulder a squeeze with his huge hands. When they talked it was full of excitement, anticipation, and passionate interruptions of sentences. They waved their hands and forced food upon me. Like Deli Tech itself, Fred and Barbara were over the top in every way. Barbara had the funny habit of keeping her cell phone buried in her cleavage and fished it out repeatedly with her colorful nails. Fred looked like a biker, with a big shaved head and goatee. As big, loud, proud New York Jews, they felt it was part of their duty, as New Yorkers and deli lovers, to educate Denver's population in the rules of Jewish delicatessen consumption.

"When we opened I wanted to hire a guy with an NYPD hat and whistle," Barbara enthusiastically recalled. "When someone ordered corned beef with mayo, he'd blow the whistle and give them a ticket."

Bringing New York–style deli to a white bread city was always going to be a challenge. "People out here grew up on chains," Barbara said in disgust. Fred seized upon his wife's thought: "If we were to cater to people specifically from Denver you'd never have *this* stuff here." With that he brought over a pastrami sandwich stacked so high it toppled over, the glistening fat of Carnegie's signature meat steamed tender. As they went on about the superiority of Carnegie's products, I inquired whether they made anything in the delicatessen themselves. Barbara shot back in her seat. "Do we make our own stuff??? Suuuuure we do. It's the best anywhere."

She soon emerged from the kitchen with a wide bowl of blond *matzo* ball soup. The aroma was intense with lots of celery, and though the *matzo* ball was coarse, and oddly shaped, it was packed with the flavor of fresh chicken. Beside it floated a *kreplach* that was delicate as a Cantonese wonton, the paper-thin sheets of dough rolled neatly around soft minced beef. Next she plunked down the mother of all cabbage rolls, a huge steaming, juicy wrap of cabbage leaf packed with rice and ground beef, slathered in a sweet tomato jus. Their turkey, which came sliced from birds roasted on site, was so moist and tender the only word I could jot in my notebook was "perfection."

As good as Deli Tech's imported Carnegie products were, they tasted soulless when compared with the wonderful homemade dishes that Barbara and Fred were churning out. In their quest to be the most New York deli in Denver, they had unwittingly made some of the finest Jewish food in town. "I would love to duplicate this," Fred said, "I'd love to be able to franchise like Heidi's did, but I can't. If you're gonna put your heart and soul into a deli, how can you open up another restaurant?" He and Barbara were the soul of the place. Deli Tech's source for kibitz. Its *tam* (soul).

I didn't understand fully what Fred was talking about until I headed to the headquarters of Heidi's Brooklyn Deli. Started in 1994 by an Italian-American couple from Brooklyn and New Jersey as a bagel bakery, deli, and ice cream store in downtown Denver, by 2007 Heidi's had grown into a national chain of sandwich shops. There were more than thirty franchised stores, with locations all over Colorado and a dozen other states. Six times that many franchises were slated to open in the following years. Considering its franchising only began in 2005, Heidi's was spreading like wildfire.

Steve and Heidi Naples were constantly turning down people eager to pay $35,000 for franchise rights, plus $300,000 to $400,000 to build a store. Investors had to commit to opening three outlets, but successful stores could pull in upwards of $1.3 million annually. It was big business, a corporate American chain delicatessen, and people apparently wanted it bad. When Fred Anzman and Barbara Simon complained how people in Denver equated deli with a sandwich shop, this was what they were talking about. "A real Jewish deli cannot be duplicated," Steve Naples told me. "The reality is, if you don't systematize it, you're on edge all the time. You may make money, but your kids won't want it. For all the nostalgia of what we remember, the New York deli reality was fights, divorces, and eighty-hour weeks where people never saw their kids."

Naples took me into one of the newest Heidi's locations to show me what he meant by "systematizing." In the spotless kitchen, manuals outlined how to bake the large square loaves of airy bread, slice meat, and make sandwiches. Every single function was laid out, from how thick the tomatoes were to be sliced, to the best way to microwave the pastrami. Yes . . . microwave.

"Look," Steve said defensively at my look of revulsion upon hearing the *M* word, "we tried to steam it and grill it but we can't. The reality is that you have to sacrifice a bit of flavor when you take your product to the mass market." The further Heidi's spread across the country, the more mechanical it became. At Heidi's, the goal was for their Bronx Bomber sandwich (pastrami and egg salad on rye) to taste the same in Colorado Springs as it did in D.C. You couldn't teach each new franchisee how to properly steam navel pastrami. It took months, if not years, of experience. So you made the pastrami out of the top round cut, which is drier and has less flavor, but cutting it is like slicing cheese.

As I was driving northwest toward the hills of Boulder, it struck me that the answer to my question of local delis vs. New York–modeled delis wasn't so clear. Denver delis like the Bagel and Zaidy's were purely local, but their individual success hadn't spawned any surge in Denver's deli eating, and they didn't really have any distinctly Denver characteristics, no local equivalent of that hickory-smoked brisket. New York Deli News, Deli Tech, and even Heidi's were all connected to the New York deli experience in some way, but they were definitely Colorado operations, and in the case of Deli Tech, their locally made food was even better than what they brought in from 1,700 miles away on freezer trucks. My worry was that Heidi's microwaved pastrami would teach local mouths what a delicatessen should be, leaving little hope for a *haymish* Jewish deli to survive in the thin air.

Jimmy and Drew's 28th Street Deli, *Boulder, Colorado*

While in Denver, I'd heard rumors that a new deli had just opened in Boulder, and supposedly it was making everything from scratch. This place had the improbably long name of Jimmy and Drew's 28th Street Deli, which to me reeked of wannabe New Yorkism and, well, goyishness. My spirits picked up a bit as I read the notices for Torah study classes and other Jewish community flyers tacked up by the deli's door alongside fly fishing photos and ads for used Subarus. "Hey man, you must be David," Jarrett "Jimmy" Eggers said, coming toward me with latex gloves on. Tall, slender, and dressed in a fly fishing hat and fly fishing sweater, he hardly cut the traditional image of the Jewish deli owner (hint: fly fishing), but this was Boulder and I was hungry.

"C'mon back to the smokehouse," he said, "I've got some salmon that's just about ready to come out."

Salmon smoking in-house? Seriously?

Eggers pulled out gorgeous-looking salmon sides from the smoker. Each was colored a luscious mandarin orange and glistened with the fatty remnants of the sugar and salt cure that had permeated the fish over three days. "We try to smoke them fresh the night before, so people get the best lox at breakfast."

I was blown away. Though I'd seen delicatessens cure their own corned beef (which Jimmy and Drew's also did), and the rare one smoke its own pastrami (ditto here too), I'd never seen anyone smoke their own salmon. In fact, Jimmy and Drew's smoked *two* kinds of salmon . . . the cold smoked lox, and the hot smoked kippered salmon. Talking with Eggers, he rattled off the dishes they made from scratch in the store: *latkes*, chopped liver, noodle and onion *kugels*, several types of *knishes*, *gefilte* fish, herring in cream, stuffed cabbage polonaise (cooked slowly for twelve hours, like the braised corned beef), and of course *matzo* ball soup. Jimmy walked me over to the sandwich assembly area and ran a spreading knife through a metal vat.

"This is *schmaltz*," he said, letting me lick the knife. "We make this from the fat skimmed off the chicken soup, which is basically forty chickens boiled in a pot." Homemade *schmaltz*! I couldn't believe what I was tasting. Here I was in the mountains of Colorado, at a brand spanking new deli, and a tall blond fly fisherman was offering me a taste of the substance at the very core of Yiddish cooking. Imagine the creamiest, richest butter you've ever had imported from France, then multiply it by two and impart the mellow aftertaste of crackling chicken skin . . . that's what fresh *schmaltz* tastes like.

Eggers had grown up in Fort Collins, Colorado, but moved to suburban Chicago for high school, where he became best friends with Andrew "Drew" Marx. Every day after school the duo would end up back at the Marx house, where they'd raid the fridge filled with Drew's mother's Jewish cooking. Marx went on to graduate from the Culinary Institute of America and worked as a chef at high-end restaurants, but he and Eggers held on to a dream of opening a deli together. Finally, in May 2006, both living in Boulder, they opened their restaurant on 28th Street (hence the name). The meat was not processed, and most dishes were made from scratch. Cakes and pastries were even baked by Drew's mom, Sarah Marx, who had moved out to Colorado as well. Two blocks away from the nation's busiest Whole Foods store, an essentially sustainable, healthy, locally focused deli was being born. "Drew's philosophy has always been that if you do things simply with real fresh ingredients, the flavors are so much better," Eggers said.

Ahh the flavors. Even months later, as I'm sitting here, they stick out in my mind. There was the breakfast *knish*, a buttery little oval pastry packed with steaming corned beef hash, a thin layer of melted cheddar, and fluffy scrambled eggs. There were insanely large combination sandwiches: Jimmy's Favorite (which was a towering Reuben between two thin, crisp *latkes*), and Spudnik (hot corned beef and pastrami topped with coleslaw, melted Swiss, Russian dressing, and fresh-cut french fries). But it was a square of sweet noodle *kugel* that won my heart that afternoon. Dusted with cinnamon, it was as though the custardy starchiness of a rice pudding had been coaxed out of the noodles. "Oh my god," I said to Eggers, coming up for air before diving in for another forkful, "that is fucking brilliant!"

Since I'd left Chicago I'd had some good deli, but Jimmy and Drew's blew me away, largely because it was so unexpected. In that bite of *kugel*, I realized great Jewish delicatessens could happen anywhere. People, philosophy, and ingredients mattered so much more than place. Though Eggers figured they needed another year or two to feel completely stable, I knew they were going to succeed. And they were going to do it without selling out the food, trading on the image of other cities, or cutting corners by outsourcing products. Once upon a time all Jewish delicatessens had operated like this. I can say that I tasted more hope that night in Boulder than in any other delicatessen I had encountered on my journey so far.

Kosher on the Go, *Salt Lake City, Utah*

In the red states of North America, where the Jewish population of the state is lower than the number of Jews who pass through Zabar's weekly, the presence of Jewish food isn't a luxury, but a necessity. Spread between the Mormon capital, Salt Lake City, and the posh ski resort Park City, Utah's Jewish community numbers roughly four thousand souls. In this unlikely place sat Kosher on the Go, a tiny glatt kosher delicatessen run out of Israel and Miriam Lefler's living room.

An Israeli aircraft technician who moved to Utah in 1985 to calibrate U.S. Air Force fighter jets, the bearded, Hasidic Lefler still developed satellite communications for the CIA and FBI. He'd opened Kosher on the Go with his wife, Miriam (a diminutive Jew from the Philippines), in 2001, setting aside the front room of their small bungalow to prepare the only kosher meals in the state. With just two hundred Jewish families in Salt Lake City, most of whom were unaffiliated, 95 per cent of Kosher on the Go's business came from Jewish tourists or catering. In addition, Mormons will often order Jewish foods for the Jewish holy days. "They like Jewish food," Israel said of the Mormons. "Don't get me wrong, they'll still try to convert you, but once they realize not, you're okay."

The place certainly had a frontier feel to it. Most of the meat was pre-sliced, portioned, and frozen, as was the bread. Everything had to be imported from around the country, making it a costly and therefore very basic operation. Kosher on the Go's corned beef sandwich (at a quarter-pound) cost eleven dollars. Israel worked two jobs just to support his family and keep the place in business, but with far-flung delis like Kosher on the Go, the greater purpose was far grander than business. They were deli missionaries. "For us, it's not about the money," he said, twisting the ends of his beard between his thumb and forefinger. "It's a *mitzvah*. When someone comes to town, he doesn't have to eat sardines for the week."

I Left My Kishkes in San Francisco

Until very recently, San Francisco was a dying deli town. Only a handful of the several dozen delicatessens found in the city around the 1950s remain. The peak of the decline came in 2000, when the beloved Shenson's Deli closed after sixty-seven years in business, despite one of the last owners' attempts to give away the struggling deli in a poetry contest. It was a shame, because San Francisco is perfectly positioned to reinvent deli for today's palate. The city boasts one of the oldest and most established Jewish communities in the country. San Francisco has more in common with the tightly packed urban jungle of New York than it does with the sprawl of Sacramento.

Most importantly, San Francisco wholeheartedly stands in the vanguard of culinary America. The heart of the modern organic movement is still beating at Alice Waters's iconic restaurant Chez Panisse. With its armada of small boutiques, restaurants, and the spectacular Ferry Building Marketplace, San Francisco is a city that foodies dream about.

Until recently, the delicatessens in San Francisco seemed on the opposite side of the city's culinary evolution. Rather than pushing boundaries, they were letting traditions decline. Brother's Manhattan Deli, a once venerable institution, was now owned by Vietnamese immigrants, who added such items to the "kosher-style" menu as *pho* (soup) with BBQ pork. No one had anything good to say about the deli scene in the Bay Area for years, until a tenuous new generation of Jewish delicatessens began emerging, approaching deli with a locavore's take on the food. "Our growth came from our perspective that the reason deli did not taste so yummy anymore was that ingredients and their sourcing were ignored," Peter Levitt, the co-owner of Saul's Deli, in Berkeley, wrote me in an e-mail, explaining the sustainable philosophy that had brought Saul's back to life in 1999. "We have also been part of the local sourcing movement. Pastrami, rye, pickles, and bagels from NY are no longer cool or practical." Levitt, previously a cook at Chez Panisse, serves sandwiches with the Niman Ranch's naturally cured pastrami on old world rye from the famous Acme Bakery.

The Bay Area's gourmet deli renaissance even gave birth to high-end delicatessen meats. In 1997, foodie radio personalities Rachel and David Michael Cane were so dissatisfied with the state of overly processed pastrami that they launched their own brand. Conjured up through backyard experiments, David's Old World Brand Pastrami comes from USDA Choice 1st cut beef, contains no artificial coloring, is dry cured in barrels for two weeks, and is then smoked over real hickory.

"It's a different product," said David, as he fed slices of the rosy meat into a small steamer set up inside his recording studio. "It doesn't assault you, it has a much lighter feel." The subtle mélange of spicing—a heady mix of black pepper, caramelized sugar, and what tasted like salty sea breezes—demonstrated just a whiff of the Bay Area's gourmet deli potential: a product crafted by highly motivated, educated, and dedicated foodies, who strove to recapture the best of Jewish food traditions without compromise. They did this not through any new techniques imported from French chefs, but by eliminating industrial processes. "If deli customers only knew the ingredients they were eating in processed pastrami," Rachel said, "they'd be mortified." David and Rachel's had even made a limited batch of Wagyu pastrami, with briskets from the intensely marbled breed of cattle used to make Kobe beef. It sold for a whopping $47.98 a pound. Rachel described it as a meat so rich and fatty it was almost creamy and was best served in thin slices, because a full sandwich could stop the heart of a shark.

The delicatessen resurgence in San Francisco penetrated to the core of the city's Jewish community. In 2006, the SF-New York Deli, a glatt kosher delicatessen, entered the scene in downtown San Francisco. The brains behind the operation were four young men from Brooklyn and Miami, ranging from just nineteen to twenty-three years old, all fresh out of yeshiva. Two of them were ordained orthodox rabbis and one could even perform his own kosher certification in the store (which certainly cut down on costs). The same year saw the rise of the California Street Delicatessen, a bright nouveau-deli that opened in the San Francisco Jewish Community Center. It featured a menu created by notable chef Joyce Goldstein and had attractive servers and a minimalist look. The California Street Deli also shared a kitchen with a sushi restaurant, an attempt by owners to satisfy both the pastrami-craving bubbes in tracksuits and sashimi-loving granddaughters in yoga pants.

Still, San Francisco's delicatessen renaissance was far from solid. Even with its prime spot in a Jewish community center, the California Street Delicatessen closed in June 2007. The SF-New York Deli folded a year later. Though Saul's remains in business, it was apparent that the Bay Area's deli revival would take more than bold ideas. It needed Deli Men willing to stick it out.

"This is pathetic. How is it that the city with the best food in America, the city that can cook anything, can't have a decent sandwich?"

A decade ago, this was the central question that propelled Robby Morgenstein to forge a new deli beachhead in San Francisco. Like the great California icon at the time, Jeff "The Dude" Lebowski, the moment came when Morgenstein was in the midst of his bowling tournament. The Long Island–born Deadhead was looking for a mid-game nosh. Venturing down Filmore Street, he spied potential in a sign that boasted Coney Island Hot Dogs. When he beheld limp franks floating in greasy water, Morgenstein turned enraged to his friend and declared, "That's it, we're doing it!"

Morgenstein's family had a long history in Baltimore's kosher catering trade, but he was largely a novice. Days before Robby opened Miller's East Coast Delicatessen, his mother, Rae (who was seriously ill at the time), flew out to help. "She can barely walk, she's got pneumonia, and as soon as we open the restaurant she went back and got spinal surgery," he recalled. "And she sits here, you know—and this is the last viable thing she does as an adult— she sits here with me and we make everything. She can't walk, so she sits on a stool in the back, there's two amigos helping her get stuff, and she just tastes and seasons, tastes and seasons, until I get everything right."

Morgenstein endeavored to make as much from scratch as possible, and it showed. My San Francisco guide, music producer David Katznelson, devoured bite after bite of towering Reuben and Rachel sandwiches, plus a helping of sweet chopped chicken liver on a fat bed of sliced red onions. All of it was served in the atmosphere Morgenstein created, which can be described as Grateful Deli. An aura of hot meat hung in the air. He was proud his deli had some "*schmutz* on it." But elsewhere were touches that gave it a real West Coast feel: the wall of dog photographs from loyal customers, the Dead shows playing softly in the background, dreadlocked babies crawling around.

Morgenstein certainly looked the part of the West Coast slacker, but his visage (a sort of pudgy Tom Hanks), and paunch (his cholesterol was a whopping 638 . . . he called himself a "walking pastrami") hinted at a deli vet. The mix even filtered down to the customers, who included a few hippies, but also Herb Hirsch, an elderly Chicago retiree who came in daily to eat his franks, beans, *challah* toast, and potato salad. "It'd be a shame if there wasn't a place like this in town," Mr. Hirsch said with a broad smile.

"It's more important to me that Herb be happy than a bunch of frat boys getting drunk and coming in for Philly cheese steaks," Morgenstein told me. When he opened, the menu varied between traditional foods and "Californian-style" dishes, because that's what his co-investors thought would really sell. But the wraps and salads really pissed Morgenstein off. "Why let a hundred-something-year-old tradition in this country go away?" he asked. He'd recently revamped and expanded the menu, making it "uber-Jewy," by adding truly rare Jewish items like *kishke*, egg bean and barley, *kasha varnishkes*, tongue polonaise, cold borscht, *matzo brie*, smoked sturgeon, and pickled herring. "I can't say it's a business decision," Morgenstein said. "It's what I want to cook." He was bold, a bit brash, and ready to do anything to save deli in San Francisco. This made him an ideal Deli Man, though in this city, he was hardly a pioneer. It turned out that Robby Morgenstein wasn't the first deli lover who had tried to save the deli in San Francisco.

Over half a century ago, David Apfelbaum was looking to eat at a deli in the theater district with his wife, Nusia. First he went to Drapkin's, but it was dirty and smelled awful, so they tried a second delicatessen . . . this looked worse. By the end of the night, David

Apfelbaum had dragged Nusia to a dozen Jewish delicatessens around San Francisco. Finally he gave up, exhausted, but not before turning to his wife and stating his intention to open a deli. Apfelbaum secured a tiny storefront on Geary, in the heart of the theater district, and set about construction. Passersby tried to warn David off. "People said so many delis had closed before they opened," he said, "it was suicide."

Sound familiar?

David Apfelbaum wasn't easily deterred. Born in Lodz, Poland, he was the only family member to survive Auschwitz. David possessed the character traits typical of the survivor-generation immigrant—fearlessness, imagination, and an unshakable work ethic. Firmly grasping the potential of the American dream, he quickly succeeded in making David's Delicatessen a San Francisco institution. David's secret, like those reviving San Francisco's delicatessens today, was his focus on quality and freshness at a time when the competition was cutting costs and putting out an inferior product.

David's soon became home to San Francisco's theater crowd, journalists, sports figures, and intellectuals. David's quickly grew into a lavish cafeteria, with a large, U-shaped counter, and ornate banquet rooms. Apfelbaum began opening other locations, sixteen in all, and by 1965 David's dominated the city's deli scene. It was one of the most successful delicatessens in the country, known coast to coast.

Then it all fell apart.

"*A mentsh tracht und Gott lacht,*" Apfelbaum uttered to me in Yiddish, when recalling how the bank lost millions of dollars of his money at the peak of David's success. Man plans and God laughs. As reporters hounded Apfelbaum, he just smiled. "Any idiot can see daylight when compared to light," he told the cameras. "If I compare what happened today with what happened to my life between 1939 and 1945, it's nothing. No one will hang me, gas me, or torture me. I'll go home tonight, eat a good meal, sleep in a comfortable bed, and on Monday I'll figure it out."

Eventually, all the different David's Delis were sold and closed, until the original location on Geary was all that remained of this once proud deli empire. By the time I visited, the glory had clearly faded. The place was a drafty, rundown enterprise in a neighborhood that had lost its glamour decades back. The prices were exorbitant by any standards; a Reuben sandwich cost $18.95, soup cost $8, coleslaw $5. I ordered a plate of sauerbraten, a brisket in sweet gravy, and couldn't believe that it came with frozen vegetables straight from a bag. "Maybe we should go," my friend David Katznelson suggested. "This place is well past its prime." I considered leaving, but something compelled me to stay. My whole journey had been about preserving delicatessens, the older the better, and deep inside me burned a glimmer of hope for David's.

Then the *blintz* arrived that changed it all. It resembled a Parisian crepe: all flat, thin, and bubbled crisp along every inch of surface. It was smothered in a dark, sugary blueberry sauce and two generous dollops of sour cream. Breaking off bites with our forks, Katznelson and I inhaled our first mouthfuls in silence, gazing at each other in stunned wonder as we chewed on the crackling dough mixing with the sweet, creamy flavors. It was simply the best *blintz* I'd ever had.

Sitting back, scraping the plates for whatever was left, I took another look and started seeing David's Deli in a different light. There were the giant pastries lying in the display case—fat macaroons, massive *rugelach*, chocolate *babka* to die for, almond drops, mocha bee hives, rum balls, cherry strudel—in total some eighty-five varieties of baked goods. I ran my hands over the studs on the vinyl stools. I looked at the sandwich menu written out on a glazed wood panel in individual raised brass letters that hadn't changed in fifty-five years, and I saw a deli that was down, but not out.

With one hand on his cane and the other grasping the counter, David Apfelbaum shuffled over to us. The wild strands of white hair jutting out from the side of head gave him the appearance of Israel's first prime minister, David Ben Gurion. He spoke slowly, but his words were filled with razor-sharp wit. His most recent publication was a pamphlet titled *Some Hows and Whys of the Traditions and History of Jewish Cooking*, which he handed out to clients. Rather than the usual shtick-filled Yiddish clichés on deli foods, it was a philosophical and religious treatise on Jewish food. Here's just a sample:

> When my mother made spaghetti, it was smothered, bored to death, in the blandest sauce imaginable. This, the entire family understood, was spite work. The "inferiority" of such alien dishes became for her a self-fulfilling prophecy. The theory was this: One starts liking spaghetti and anything can happen. It's only a matter of time before you're on to chow mein or pizza. After all, a mother's job is to prevent her family's imperceptible drift into dissipation. . . . Spaghetti functioned to remind us just how good Pirogen could be.

On it went for nineteen pages, touching on everything from the origin of *knishes* to a Talmudic analysis of the biblical kosher laws. The menu, too, was packed with David's verse:

> Chicken Liver with Schmaltz: Eggs, onion, salt and pepper have been chopped in with the liver for as long as anyone can remember. The recipe is so unalterably classic, only a culinary Philistine would dare violate its venerable timelessness. The livers are chopped 1179 times. Some people consider this a rather arbitrary number. Who knows? It could be that David somehow believes this precise method adds something somehow. Then again it could just be his lucky number. In either case, he's the boss.

One thousand one hundred and seventy-nine? I turned to David and asked what the meaning of the joke was. The corners of his mouth creaked up a bit as he rolled up his sleeve to reveal the faded blue 1179 tattooed on his forearm. I felt a shiver. This man had taken the Nazis' branding and turned it into a joke on a deli menu. I thought I had a twisted sense of humor, but this would have made Lenny Bruce squirm.

Being at the deli was one of the few pleasures remaining in David's life. He loved seeing the sad, worn faces of people walking in the door transform as they tasted his food. But when I asked David about the future, he just turned his hands up in the air. "I would like to see it continue, but nobody will work as hard as I did," he said. "I lived it." His children had declined to enter the business and there was no clear successor. From what I'd heard around town, he was short tempered with staff, and his stubborn nature, which had increased with age, contributed to the further decline of his once great deli. The place existed only because he owned the building, and the property was worth a fortune.

Over the months that followed I heard that several prominent deli owners around the country were trying to buy David's. "David's is one of the great forgotten delis in America," said one. "It just needs love and care to make it great. To see it die off would be an absolute shame."

San Francisco's delicatessen scene had left me with a smidgeon of hope for America's. In a city that had forgotten deli, there was a real energy and excitement about the future that came from people like Robby Morgenstein, who were turning back the clock on the way food was made, returning Jewish deli to its flavorful roots. But I also felt a touch of remorse. David Apfelbaum had been filled with the same boundless optimism when he started David's two generations back. He'd revived deli in San Francisco, only to see it falter anew. Now he sat patiently in his broken palace, the last emperor of a deli dynasty that I hoped could somehow outlive its namesake.

Los Angeles: Hooray for Hollywood

Brace yourselves, New York, because what I am about to write is definitely going to piss a lot of you off, but it needs to be said: Los Angeles has become America's premier deli city.

Wait. . . Stop. . . Put the gun down. It's true.

Across the city's sprawling acres, there are more delicatessens of a higher quality, on average, than anywhere else in America. Every time I visited one deli, I heard about three more. Each one just kept tossing surprises my way. There were small old-school delis and large lavish chains, famous ones without famous customers, and little-known spots that were frequented by stars. There were even fast-food-type delis called pastrami dips (think a French dip with pastrami) like The Hat and Johnny's Pastrami. Despite their healthy image, far more Angelinos than native New Yorkers eat at Jewish delicatessens on a regular basis. Though the occasional tourist swings by, Jewish delicatessens in L.A. are thriving in the present, not trading on fabled pasts.

There has been no grand decline in the Los Angeles deli scene. Most are packed, sometimes around the clock, and not just with older Brooklynites like Larry King (who eats breakfast at Nate n' Al daily). The delis out there are bigger, are more comfortable, and ultimately serve better food than any other city in America, including the best pastrami sandwich on earth. Los Angeles is both the exception to the rule of deli's inevitable decline and the example for the rest of the nation of how deli can ultimately stay relevant. If we are to save the deli elsewhere, we can learn a lot from L.A.

When California was incorporated into the Union in 1850, there were just eight Jews in Los Angeles. Because of its distance from Europe, Los Angeles never experienced the massive influx of Ashkenazi immigrants that descended upon the East Coast in the late nineteenth century. The great sea change for L.A. came in 1913, when burgeoning film director Cecil B. DeMille teamed with partners Samuel Goldwyn (who would form MGM) and Jesse Lasky (who helped create Paramount) to make a movie, *The Squaw*, in a suburb called Hollywood, ushering in the golden era of filmmaking.

Many in the upper echelons of the early studio system were Jewish, forever implanting Hollywood with a disproportionate Semitic flavor that prevails to this day. As the film business grew into the postwar era, a migration west of Jewish entertainment talent swelled, lured by easy money, swimming pools, and golden-haired shiksas. And while delicatessens back east may have occasionally served the president of a Wall Street bank, out in L.A. the studio bosses and A-list movie stars ate at the deli almost daily.

The Universal studio commissary featured *matzo* ball soup, and the Academy Awards after-parties were catered by Nate n' Al.

Today, L.A.'s Jewish delicatessens are largely inseparable from the business of Hollywood, which is one of the key reasons the deli thrives in L.A. Art's, in Studio City, built its business delivering meals to the cast and crew of shows like *St. Elsewhere, Get Smart,* and *Gilligan's Island.* Owner Art Ginsburg credits 50 per cent of his business to the studios. He even caters the Miramax and Dreamworks private jets. When the writers' strike hit the industry at the end of 2007, L.A.'s Jewish delis really felt the pinch.

The link between delis and Hollywood goes deeper still. At Factor's Deli, on Pico Boulevard, owner Suzee Markowitz calls 1:00 p.m. "agent hour," when dozens of agents' black Mercedes line up at the valet and their owners head inside for an intense hour of horse-trading. Nate n' Al is the gathering spot for the upper echelons of Hollywood money and studio heads, who are rewarded with some of the finest chicken soup known to man—a wide bowl of silky broth dominated by a single, almost meaty, *matzo* ball— and corned beef, brisket, and short ribs made from certified Angus beef. Every year, billions of dollars of the world's entertainment is created, negotiated, and financed at delicatessens throughout Los Angeles. It's like the Cannes, Toronto, and Sundance film festivals all rolled into one.

"I've almost never had anyone object to a meeting in a deli," Sandy Climan told me, as we sat down to breakfast directly behind Larry King's entourage at Nate n' Al one morning. Climan is president of Entertainment Media Ventures, a media and investment company; was previously executive vice president of Universal Studios; and was a member of the senior management team at powerhouse agency CAA. Bronx-born and -raised, Climan explained to me the logic as to why delicatessens became Hollywood's watering holes.

"I see several reasons," he said, breaking up a chunk of smoked whitefish, which he placed on a bagel. "The creative industry is an ad hoc business. Projects are put together by people in small groups, and consequently everyone and their brother needs a conference room. The only one many people have is a deli table. In the entertainment industry, creativity is not necessarily enhanced by formality. [A deli emits] an accepted chaos in an industry where creativity comes out of organized chaos. Because genius isn't orderly. . . . The people sitting around here are trying to figure out whether the boy falls in love with the girl or not. Delis are about real life. Entertainment is about real life."

L.A.'s vast sprawl allows its delis the freedom to grow into hangouts suited for Hollywood's taste. Most delicatessens in L.A. own their properties. They have parking lots and valets, and have been built to feel like a cross between diners and country clubs. Few delis exist where tables are crammed together cheek by jowl. In L.A., the banquette is king. In L.A. you can find privacy in a deli. You can even find class.

At Greenblatt's on Sunset Boulevard, the dark wood panels and stained-glass windows lend the place the feeling of a refined steakhouse. The deli counter shares space with Greenblatt's high-end wine boutique, and if you want, owner Jeff Kavin will pair your brisket with a glass of Napa zinfandel or do a vertical tasting of *forshpeis* (appetizers) and sauvignon blancs. Many delis in L.A. offer full bar service, and, compared to other cities, the bottles actually get opened. In the rear of Factor's on Pico Boulevard, there is a gorgeous Mediterranean-style courtyard with big wooden tables, umbrellas, plants, and a fountain. There are no salamis hanging in windows at Los Angeles delicatessens, nor are there signs advertising Hebrew National or other products. "Our delis here are very laid back," one owner told me. "Hey, it's California."

In this setting, where bare bones casual meets West Coast comfort, the magic of Hollywood happens. If there is one subset of the entertainment community that benefits the most from the creative energy of Jewish delicatessens, it is comedy writers. I wanted to find out what it was that made delis such incubators of comedic creativity, but I needed a comedian, ideally a Jewish one, with some experience. I'd dropped names around town to various deli owners, but they freely admitted that asking celebrities to be interviewed would be impossible. Then, sitting in my car, I got a call on my phone.

"Hello, is this David?" said the raspy and highly familiar voice on the line. "This is Mel Brooks, where the heck did you get the *meshugah* idea for a deli book?"

Brooks had grown up as Melvin Kaminsky in Williamsburg, Brooklyn, during the 1930s, and his comedic career can be traced through delis. First, Brooks split his allegiances between two long-gone Williamsburg delis: Feingold's and Greenwald's. "Every Saturday night was deli night with my gang, starting at nine years old. My mother would set us free . . . the routine was deli first and then two movies. For fifteen cents I'd get a heavily laden pastrami sandwich, although if I had an extra nickel I'd order a corned beef sandwich, with potato salad. . . . Laden with deli mustard and a dill pickle, with a Dr. Brown's cream soda, it was incredible."

It was at those double features where Mel Brooks absorbed Hollywood's early comedians, rehashing the routines of Laurel and Hardy, the Three Stooges, and Charlie Chaplin in the deli with his friends. Later in life, when Brooks wrote for Sid Caesar's *This Show of Shows*, he and the other writers sustained themselves on food from the Stage or Carnegie delicatessens. "I got a little more sophisticated," Brooks recalled. "Sometimes I would have roast beef and Russian dressing from the Stage, and from the Carnegie (their pastrami was always so great), I'd have pastrami with coleslaw."

When Brooks finally moved to Los Angeles in 1972, he was based in 20th Century Fox and regularly ate at Factor's. He'd work the room, stealing an urn from the server's station, pouring coffee for all the customers. "I was cadging business. 'Don't forget to see *Young Frankenstein* opening next week!' I'd say. I must have cost them hundreds of dollars in free coffee over the years."

Brooks viewed delicatessens differently than other restaurants when it came to fostering creativity, especially in comedy. "There's nothing like a deli meeting," Brooks said. "Deli food keeps the brain cooking. It speaks to me of being nurtured and having some of that Brooklyn love. . . . Delis are magnets for Jews, and Jews, in order to survive emotionally, have developed tremendous humor. They don't have to be professionals. Every Jew is a good storyteller, and delis are bound in Jewish humor. Also, delis seem to be happy places. I've never seen anybody weeping at a table in a deli. I've seen them in cafés and smart restaurants dabbing their eyes, but I've never seen anyone crying in a deli. Never in a deli! No one ever has a bottle of Dom Perignon with their lover and says, 'This isn't working out.' Cel-Ray tonic doesn't cut it."

These days, Brooks is a regular at Junior's Deli, in West Hollywood, where he's a particular fan of owner Marvin Saul's *rugelach*, individual apple pies, roast turkey sandwiches, and chicken in the pot (it was Saul who put Brooks in touch with me). Junior's complimentary mini-*latkes*, which are small fried croquettes that come with each sandwich, are another story. "I don't know what they are," Brooks said, kibitzing, "but they're deep-fried and you got twenty minutes to live after you eat one. You might as well give it a name. You might as well call it Murray, because it'll be with you for days after you eat it. David, you must remember this: I as Jew do not chew!"

In many ways, L.A.'s deli culture thrived on the patronage of deli lovers like Mel Brooks and Larry King, who had grown up around kosher delis in New York, and reconnected to their roots via soup and a sandwich. In one of the largest, least traditional communities in the American Diaspora, where Jews actually compete among themselves for the lavishness of their Christmas decorations, the delicatessen for many *is* the full extent of their Jewish identity. "In many parts of L.A., the deli was established before the community center or *shul* [synagogue]," said Stephen Sass, the president of the Jewish Historical Society of Southern California. "For some, having a corned beef sandwich is their only link to the ancient temple in Jerusalem."

Even to Hollywood gentiles, the Jewish delicatessen offers a certain sanctuary. Take the case of Mr. T, the tough-talking, chain-clad 1980s icon from *The A Team*. When Mr. T first came to Los Angeles in 1981 to shoot *Rocky III*, the Chicago native knew nobody. But upon entering Junior's delicatessen, Marvin Saul took a shine to the young bruiser. "He didn't even know me when I first came in," Mr. T told me, in the midst of eating his way across L.A.'s delis. "Soon after, I called Marvin 'Dad' and 'Father' because he watched me grow." In a typical sitting at Junior's, Mr. T will put away three glasses of orange juice, a couple of eggs, potato salad, and a hot pastrami sandwich on four slices of whole wheat bread (I didn't dare suggest he try rye). Mr. T remains an adamant deli lover, and for those who say Jewish deli is unhealthy, Mr. T has a few choice words. "Anyone who says deli is bad for you: I pity the fool! That's a bunch of junk! A lot of people get caught up in health food, walk out, and get hit by a truck!"

Delis can provide an essential dose of reality for budding stars and fragile egos in L.A. This is precisely why young actors David Hirsh and Jonas Chernick formed a group called Pea Soup Wednesdays. Each and every Wednesday they meet for lunch in a Jewish deli. "In a city that exists in a state of fakery, where everyone wears their masks, I really look forward to it," said Chernick as we sat in a large booth at Canter's with Hirsh. Delis were an antidote to the soul-sucking Hollywood lifestyle. "I've got friends here who after two years will reference their psychics in passing," Chernick recalled. "There's a transformation that occurs if you're not grounded. This," Chernick said, holding up the fat chopped liver sandwich in his hands, "is the perfect antidote to Scientology."

Unfortunately for imperiled delis across America, there are very few applicable lessons that we can draw from the nexus of entertainment and deli. But don't despair. For all the glitz and tits of Hollywood, stars didn't make L.A.'s delis great . . . families did.

More than any other city I visited, the delicatessens in Los Angeles were overwhelmingly family-owned, mostly for two or three generations. That's an astounding fact. The Family Firm Institute, which conducts research on family businesses, notes that only 12 per cent of American family businesses make it to the third generation, and only 3 per cent to the fourth generation. While the children of delicatessen owners elsewhere were leaving delis to pursue less stressful careers, those in Los Angeles were maintaining the tradition.

"This generation, there's more at stake than just business partners," said Jon Startz, the owner of National Foodservice, a supplier to L.A.'s delis. "All of them take pride in it. They seem to really adhere to the ways of fathers and grandfathers, [but] in a way that's efficient to the twenty-first century."

Take the example of Brent's Delicatessen, one of Startz's largest customers, which has two locations in the San Fernando Valley. Brent's was purchased in 1967 by Ron Peskin, a counterman who had worked around the city. Rather than rely on the TV and film trade, he focused on the Valley's industrial areas and office parks. Brent's is now run by Ron Peskin's son Brent (the name's a convenient coincidence), his daughter Carrie, and his son-in-law Marc Hernandez. Brent's is the surprise heavyweight among deli aficionados in L.A. It lacks the star power of most other places, but the quality of Brent's food garners praise from even the most self-assured competitors.

At Brent's, as in many L.A. delis, you can get everything under the sun, from creamy whitefish salad and combination sandwiches to imported Polish ham or brisket tacos. My golden rule—the larger the menu, the worse the traditional deli food—broke at Brent's. Rather than eliminating classic Yiddish fare from its expanding menu, Brent's has elevated it to a level of quality that is often unsurpassed, especially their *kishke*. With regard to the decline of delicatessens, *kishke* (a.k.a. stuffed *derma* or *kishka*) is the canary in a deli menu's coalmine. A sausage-like dish of beef intestine stuffed with *schmaltz* and *matzo* meal, it was once a timeless classic on kosher delicatessen menus. But the difficulty of procuring the intestinal casing, and the labor involved in making the dish, has nearly rendered *kishke* extinct. Those few who carry it often use a processed product, which is made from an artificial casing and vegetable oil, arrives in a long orange tube and is sliced, heated in a microwave, and covered in gravy.

So when Marc Hernandez told me that Brent's made their own, I was taken aback. "You can't imagine what a bucket of cow intestines smells like," Hernandez told me, crinkling his nose as he handed me piping-hot, cigar-sized *kishke* on a small plate. It smelled positively amazing, a greasy tube of goodness that crackled when I sliced into it, revealing a warm, moist meal the color of amber lager. The finely ground beads of *matzo* meal soaked up the velvet *schmaltz* and left a smoky sweetness in my mouth. Imagine a sausage with the flavor of duck confit. Since Brent's had introduced the homemade *kishke,* it had been selling like crazy. Even better, the last time they removed an item from the menu it was fried shrimp, not pickled tongue. Family made this possible.

"There's not a lot of businesses today run by families," Hernandez said. "[Customers] don't like that. They want someone from the family here every day, or they're upset. Ron eats here every day. Brent eats here every day. I eat here every day, and my wife eats here every day. You have to control it. That's why I have three kids and I'm hoping to have a couple more. You cannot make deli a chain. It's just not possible." The only reason Brent's was able to open a second location in late 2006 was that a family member would always be present. Hernandez, who worked in hotels for years before returning to Brent's, saw how employees looked out solely for their own interests. By contrast, a family business is communal, with each family member holding shares.

The same went for other delis in L.A.: Junior's owner Marvin Saul's sons, David and Jonathan, basically ran the restaurant now. Nate n' Al was in its third generation, with brothers David and Mark Mendelson (grandsons of Al). Greenblatt's was operated by

Jeff Kavin, the third generation of his family in the business. Art Ginsburg's son and daughter were aboard at Art's. The Markowitz sisters were continuing their late parents' tradition at Factor's. Even the most corporate of L.A.'s delis, Jerry's Famous Deli, was run by Guy Starkman, the son of late founder Ike Starkman.

Many of the best delis that I'd visited across America— Michigan's Stage Door, Bronx's Liebman's, Brooklyn's Mill Basin, Chicago's Manny's—had been passed from generation to generation. When you have children, parents, and grandparents all putting in their two cents, the compromises that emerge ultimately leave stronger delis in their wake. On the other hand, delicatessens that were sold outside the family were always discussed in tones of sadness. "Oh them," someone in the business would say. "Yeah, it's a shame. It used to be such a great place, but it's changed hands so many times." When I saw David Apfelbaum, alone in David's Deli, this became crystal clear. Sure there were exceptions, but most Jewish delis with a family legacy thrived better than those without.

"There's something unique about L.A. delis," David Mendelson told me, as I sat in Nate n' Al chatting with him and his brother, Mark. "Deli owners here aren't only multi-generational, we're also all *friends*! We all help each other. We call each other all the time." When Nate n' Al installed a new computer system a few years back, the Mendelsons personally went around to all the other delis in town, helping set theirs set up. In other cities, Jewish deli owners seemed to silently pray for the demise of their competitors, regarding any overtures of camaraderie with outright suspicion.

"We need each other, we know that, and if we support each other we'll grow," said David Mendelson. "On the other hand, if you stop talking [to other delis] you'll lose your customer base and your control over suppliers. It's the fear of losing something you have, or something you want, that generates negative relationships. We'll always take a call from someone else at a different deli." David's brother, Mark, who was by far the trimmest and most soft-spoken deli owner I'd ever met, saw the success of any individual delicatessen as beneficial to all Jewish delis. Family kept them united, family kept them pure, and family ultimately surpassed New York on deli's signature sandwich.

"The hot pastrami sandwich served at Langer's Delicatessen in downtown Los Angeles is the finest hot pastrami sandwich in the world," wrote Nora Ephron, in *The New Yorker*. "It's a symphony orchestra, different instruments brought together to play one perfect chord. . . . [It] is, in short, a work of art."

Langer's can be found nearby downtown L.A., kitty-corner to the infamous MacArthur Park. The long, low deli stands as an anomaly to a bustling street scene grinding to a rhythm of Mexican pop songs. The color scheme inside Langer's is all shades of orange, brown, reds, and yellows, like a 1970s shag rug, and at the rear hang a trio of large oil paintings depicting countermen slicing pastrami.

Waiting for me at a booth sat Norm Langer and his father, Al. The day before, Norm and I had spoken and he'd insisted that his father, who was ninety-four and in poor health, was not up for an interview. Still, when I arrived, a frail and diminutive Al Langer was sitting with his oxygen tank alongside his sixty-plus-year-old son, who now towered over him. Even at this age, Al bristled with enthusiasm, his big aquamarine eyes twinkling as he told tales of his youth. Though his white hair was fine and his voice quivered somewhat, his thin hands grasped Norm's strongly.

Al Langer was born in Newark, New Jersey, in 1913, and entered the deli business at the tender age of eleven, to earn money to have his *bar mitzvah*. After stints as a waiter in the Catskills and Miami, his parents moved to Los Angeles. Al quickly got a job at a deli, then went on to open various delis without success; first in Palm Springs, then in a bowling alley, where he met his late wife, Jean, a waitress who'd once slapped him with a whitefish. Al finally established Langer's Delicatessen in 1947, and it remains in business today.

Langer's originally catered to the Jewish retirees who frequented MacArthur Park and to the business crowd from downtown. But by the late 1980s an economic downturn and the rise of crack cocaine turned the area into a borderline ghetto. Prostitution went on right outside the door, and clients were afraid to visit after dark. At first Al and Norm cut their hours and staff, then they put locks on the bathrooms. Finally, they considered shutting down the deli. It was only the construction of the Metro Red Line subway in 1993, which stopped directly in front of the deli, that saved Langer's. "The Tuesday after it opened," Norm Langer recalled, "we had five hundred people outside on a waiting list trying to get in." Newspapers dubbed it the "Pastrami express."

Langer's has always used pastramis from RC Provisions, one of the larger deli purveyors in Southern California. The seasoning RC uses is no different for Langer's, but the secret unfolds in several phases. First, Langer's orders a two- to two-and-a-half-pound piece of pastrami, smoked tender. The pastramis are smaller than most other delis', leaner, and custom cut for the delicatessen. "I want a certain thing," Al told me forcefully, "and I don't care how much it costs. I'm a stickler."

After two and a half to four hours of steaming, the pastramis will ideally reach an internal temperature of 209° F. Only then are they are ready for the cutting board and the skilled hands of Langer's cutters. Norm, who exuded the swaggering confidence of a member of the Rat Pack, stepped behind the counter. "Look, anybody can take a knife and cut thick or thin," he said, standing over the deli's cutting board. "In hand-cutting you have to work with the meat. You need to read the navel and meet the grain. Every pastrami has a piece of short rib on the side. You can't chew it, it has the consistency of a diaphragm. But if you have a knife and a fork, you can cut it out." Norm plunged a carving fork into a steaming pastrami and popped on a pair of reading glasses.

"Can I? You think?" he said, daring me to challenge him. He slowly sculpted perfect slices off the pastrami, working his blade thoughtfully, while talking with bravado. "You want to send me back to the East Coast?" he taunted. "To New York, where they can teach me how to cut?" With a few turns of the knife and a flick of the wrist, Langer flipped the pastrami over on its back. "If you put it on a machine, they're not going to cut out *this*," he said, as he excised the aforementioned diaphragm. He tossed it to the side of the cutting board, a slimy, yellow membrane that would surely have ruined a sandwich. "If you put it on the machine, *that* is going to go in it," he said, stabbing his fork into the wood resolutely. "That's the difference."

And yet, as he gloated, one of the countermen began cutting a pastrami on a slicing machine. I looked at Norm quizzically. We sat back down and Norm explained. "I'll tell you who the best cutters I ever had were: Art Bebovitz, Leo Ginzburg, Al Factor, Gene Goldstein, and Joe Harmenstein. These men were the hall of fame in this city. During the 1950s, 1960s, and 1970s, I had six or seven countermen that were all A's. They were the cat's meow, they couldn't possibly cut better." His father nodded in agreement, muttering their names in appreciation.

"Today I got one A, a B, a C+," Norm said, "and two I haven't yet decided on." Some people could hand-cut and some couldn't, and those who couldn't were better off using a machine. Over the years, supermarkets and discount delicatessens had left Langer's with a shallow roster. Rather than try to keep them all, Norm and Al selected a few A's and hoped that they could pass along their skills. Even still, no matter how well a counterman or manager was trained, they'd never be family. "It's a feel," Norm said, patting his belly with a smile. "When you have your name on a sign, the customer can easily relate to that. It's real. But the second you pay a manager a percentage it becomes corporate. . . . It's gotta be you!" Langer's was Langer's because a Langer was at the helm. Norm was training his daughter Trisha in the business. His wife, Jeanette, worked the cash register. Their family name *was* the business.

When Langer's Delicatessen celebrated its sixtieth anniversary in June 2007, the intersection of 7th and Alvarado was renamed Langer's Square. With his legacy ensured, Al Langer slipped into death just two weeks later. Though his passing was marked by warm obituaries from across the nation, the greatest tribute to Al Langer's life was his incomparable hot pastrami sandwich.

The Langer's pastrami sandwich is a sculpture of delicatessen that encapsulates perfection at every turn. The bread it rests between is the finest west of Detroit: two thick slices of caraway seed–infused, double-baked rye, still warm on the fingertips from the heat of the oven and cut fresh for each individual sandwich. Steamed until the pastrami is ready to disintegrate, the expertly carved sheets lie in a flat pile between the slices of bread. Most delis stack the meat in their sandwiches high in the middle, to give the illusion of size, but the Langer's pastrami, still a respectable seven ounces, is consistent throughout, and every bite delivers equal amounts of meat. The pastrami itself boasts an almost surreal appearance; the color is too ruby, the slices too perfect to seem like something you can actually eat. Before the first bite, the tangy aroma of warm yeast, Romanian spices, and vaporized *schmaltz* teases the nostrils and entices the taste buds. It almost feels shameful to alter such perfection, but Al Langer's handiwork is art that's best consumed, not admired.

How do you describe the taste of a perfect pastrami sandwich? No matter what I write, it won't be satisfactory. The specific flavor profile—at once peppery, smelling of the sea, and hinting of butterscotch—would sound contradictory and confusing. Any cute turn of phrase or illustrative metaphor—how the peppercorns and salt and sugars dazzled my taste buds like a Chinese New Year's fireworks show going off in my mouth—would never measure up to the real thing. It is simply legendary, beyond any descriptive qualities I possess. As I tore through America's finest sandwich that day in March, Al and Norm stood over me smiling.

L.A.'s family deli legacy had fortified the city's ranks, but there was one small problem. The working environments of most family-run delicatessens are less apt to be *Brady Bunch* scenarios than they are to be a kosher-style version of *King Lear*. When family politics mix with matters of commerce, often the resulting animosity can be disastrous. I saw this first-hand when I went to Canter's, on Fairfax Avenue.

In 1929, brothers Ben and Jerry Canter, who had owned a delicatessen in Jersey City, New Jersey, moved into the Boyle Heights neighborhood and opened up the Canter Brothers Delicatessen. Canter's became so successful that during the Depression banks approached the deli for loans, and over the years it grew into L.A.'s largest delicatessen. Gary Canter, the grandson of founder Ben Canter, greeted me with a box of incredible *rugelach*, a platter of meats, and a heaping serving of aggravation. Since the death of his grandparents in the late 1970s, the deli's ownership had been spread over various branches of children, siblings, uncles, aunts, and cousins. No fewer than nine different members of the Canter family held a stake in the deli and their authority was ambiguous. As one waitress put it to me, "It's like nine chiefs and no Indians."

Gary, whose responsibilities were mostly dealing with staff, was fed up. A fast-talking man, he could easily pass for a member of the Soprano crew with his perfectly coiffed hair and fancy tracksuits. Shuttling me through a rapid-fire tour of the giant delicatessen, he fired off salvos about the waste, mismanagement, and lost opportunities that had come from a business with too many hands in the jar of macaroons. Canter's did an astonishing $8 to $10 million in annual sales, but Gary felt it could be as high as $18 million if his relatives agreed to modernize certain aspects of the business.

Everything worked on a haphazard basis, Canter said, pointing out the squeaking antique toasters at the rear of the deli. His brother Marc preferred to repair everything himself. Gary led me upstairs into a massive room jammed with junk, spare parts, and old equipment. "You see? You see?" Gary said, kicking antique vacuums out of his path. "Do you know what this junkhouse once was? Huh? It was a ballroom. Yeah. Lucille Ball and Bing Crosby used to come up here for banquets after the Oscars. This was a beautiful place where the history of Hollywood's golden age unfolded, and now look at it," he said, staring around in disgust. "Here, the wrong way is the right way."

Staff acknowledged the confusion, but said it wasn't as bad as Gary felt. The place just ran on instinct. People loved coming into Canter's and watching the hubbub in action. It was an environment that brimmed with possibility and chaos, which is what drew people like Jimi Hendrix and the Beatles here in the 1960s. On a given night at Canter's, you can find film students studying, NBC executives hashing out sitcom episodes, famed producer Michael Mann working feverishly on a script, and a waiter who is also an aspiring dancer practicing his pirouettes by the cash register. One of L.A.'s up and coming bands will be tuning up in the Kibitz Room, an adjoining bar and club that is the dark, boozy footnote to the bright hubbub of Canter's. Frank Zappa used to play there, and Lenny Bruce would occasionally perform impromptu gigs, though more often he'd score heroin in the bathroom. The Red Hot Chili Peppers jammed there, and the Wallflowers crafted their sound on the Kibitz stage, but the most famous group to emerge out of the Kibitz Room was Guns N' Roses, whose picture still hangs behind the bar.

Canter's at night was like New York's Katz's meets Alice in Wonderland. The trippy decor, including plastic owls spinning on the roof exhausts, added to the funhouse charm. I can't say whether the food suffered because of what Gary said. Some dishes were better than others, and the baked goods were among the best anywhere, especially the chocolate *rugelach*. Yet there was something deeply unsettling about the ten-dollar bill Gary Canter slipped a waiter to make sure no one touched my briefcase while we walked around. In any other delicatessen, the owner's word should have sufficed.

Gary wanted some form of escape and he'd found it in Las Vegas. In 2004, he had opened a Canter's branch in the Treasure Island casino. "Vegas is my dream," he said, cherries spinning in his eyes. "In Vegas they have fine-tuning. They have rules. They have a system." On some days, the Las Vegas location pulled in more money than the Fairfax delicatessen. Soon, Gary hoped to open another outlet in Mandalay Bay with even bigger payoffs. "I just can't use my time to play with my fucking family. Why break my back? If this works out with Mandalay Bay, they'll be giving me fifty thousand dollars a month! Who could refuse that check coming to their house?"

Gary Canter wasn't the only one thinking Las Vegas. All over America I'd met deli owners with designs for the desert. As David Mendelson told me, "I sure as hell don't plan to be busing tables, cleaning washrooms, and changing light bulbs forever."

Las Vegas: Luck Be a Brisket Tonight

The concept of Las Vegas as a deli Mecca isn't too far a stretch of the imagination. After all, it was delicatessen-loving, New York Jewish gangsters like Bugsy Siegel who transformed the city from a Mormon frontier outpost into an oasis of green felt, free booze, and busty broads. Caesars Palace was started by Jewish "businessmen" Jay Sarno, Nate Jacobson, Moe Dalitz, and Morris Kleinman. Sam Tucker opened the Desert Inn, while Hyman Abrams, Carl Cohen, and Jack Entratter ran the Sands.

A few individual delicatessens did exist in Vegas's swinging heyday. In the delicatessen at the Flamingo, Catskills comedians

Myron Cohen and Freddie Roman would share late-night pastrami and corned beef sandwiches with crooner Tom Jones. Foxy's Delicatessen, started by Abe Fox in 1966, was close to the intersection of Las Vegas Boulevard and Sahara, and Jackie's Deli was a favorite hangout for sports bookies. The last of Vegas's old-school delis was Max C's, owned by the larger than life Max Corsun, who used his deli in downtown Las Vegas as a pulpit to reward friends and attack his political enemies. Max C's closed shortly after Corsun died in 2002.

These delicatessens were part of old Las Vegas, which has mostly disappeared. Its hotels, like the Sands, were theatrically demolished with dynamite and fireworks. The new Las Vegas, a gargantuan playground that magically sells the city as a sort of Disneyland with whores, is where out-of-town delicatessens want to make their mark. While old Vegas was the sinister kingdom of the underworld, new Vegas came to life under the guise of corporate America. And although a taste of old Vegas lives along the dollar blackjack tables of Fremont Street and the champagne rooms of obscure strip clubs, it is the family-friendly Vegas that calls the shots. Even though the recent advertising slogan "What happens in Vegas, stays in Vegas" is uttered by shmucks everywhere, a large part of Vegas's infrastructure caters to the American family.

With regard to food, the days of casinos offering all-you-can-eat shrimp buffets may not be over, but it has been superseded by an even greater indulgence. Casinos have brought in the world's celebrity chefs, built giant palaces of gaudy gastronomy, staffed the kitchen, and mailed checks. All the chef has to do is create or approve a few new dishes, appear on the rare occasion (flown in on a private jet and put up in a luxury suite), grace the hundred-foot television screens around town, and smile. With an army of restaurant consultants and designers at their disposal, the developers of Las Vegas casinos have managed to conquer the last stranglehold of independent eating in America, turning the upper end of the food chain into another packaged concept.

Now it was the turn of the Jewish delicatessens. With names like Canter's, Carnegie, and Stage already established in Las Vegas, others were vying for a slice of the action, enticed by the casinos. Again, it made sense for both parties. Delicatessens, by nature family-run businesses, had reached the max in profits they could squeeze from a single location. No matter how many bowls of *matzo* ball soup Nate n' Al sold in a week, there'd be a limit. But in Vegas, with forty million tourists flying in annually, costs paid by the casino, and a systematized management and production system, they could rake it in. Across the nation, deli owners spoke about Vegas with the same unbridled excitement their forefathers in the *shtetl* spoke of America. One thing was for sure; these wouldn't be *haymish*, family-operated delicatessens. They'd be franchised and licensed versions of the original, with an eye on maximum profits for all involved.

"Equity partners are looking for concepts," the food purveyor Jon Startz said back in Los Angeles. "They're not looking for a great restaurant. They are looking for something there can be a thousand of." If it could work in Vegas, I was told, why not elsewhere? Las Vegas was the front line for Jewish delis that could spread to malls nationwide. It was deli ready to take a slice of America's fast-food pie. Many deli owners saw it as their future, but what kind of future did Las Vegas really promise?

Before hitting the Strip, I wanted to see what action there was away from Las Vegas Boulevard. With an exploding Jewish population, Las Vegas certainly had enough numbers to support a local deli or two, and I needed a baseline comparison to judge the casino delis against. In Henderson, the city on the far end of the Las Vegas airport, Weiss Bakery and Deli opened in March 2006.

Originally from New Jersey, Michael Weiss had been working in the restaurant business since he was a kid and had lived in Las Vegas for over half his life. Seeing the absence of true Jewish delicatessens in the area, he set about rehabilitating a deli called Samuele's with his Turkish-born wife, Aysegul, with the sort of mom-and-pop attitude that now seems foreign to the Vegas formula. A tall energetic man with a positive grin glued onto his face, Weiss reveled in every challenge the deli business threw at him. As he made a brisket sandwich on the eggy *challah* bread he'd baked himself that morning, he told me, "Here, the challenge was perfecting what I had. So I took the recipes that were here already and tinkered with them. I used a lot of my grandmother's recipes, and I went back to making everything I could from scratch."

Weiss pickled his own corned beef and tongues, cured and smoked his own pastrami, and baked his own bread and pastry. Nothing went to waste. The fat skimmed from his soup was rendered into *schmaltz*, which made its way into the *matzo* balls, the finely diced chopped liver, and his *kasha varnishkes*. In my previous experiences, I'd never really discovered the appeal of this starchy side dish of bowtie pasta and buckwheat. I often found them dry and bland. Weiss showed me otherwise.

"The trick with *kasha* is that you sauté the onions in butter, *schmaltz*, and olive oil until they are caramelized. Then, you toss the *kasha* groats in a hot pan, without the onions. After a few minutes the kernels will separate, and then you add it all together." The bowties with fat kernels of *kasha* were covered in a rich, chocolate-colored homemade beef gravy. Flavored by the sweet, fat-drenched onions, the individual kashas burst in my mouth like moist beans.

Weiss Bakery and Deli reminded me of Jimmy and Drew's 28th Street Deli in Boulder, Colorado, where a pride in ownership of the food had turned out so much promise in such a short period of time. It was an attitude of deli owners that had long faded from the landscape, but Weiss knew that if his name was on the door, he had to answer directly to customers. "If it says Weiss, it *has* to be nice," Weiss said half-jokingly, before reflecting on the delis inside casinos, where I was heading that night. "Those guys are doing it to get a paycheck. I'm doing it because I love cooking."

8:00 P.M.: Greenberg's Deli, *New York, New York Casino and Hotel*

Once again, my deli odyssey kicked off in the Big Apple, or in this case, a soundstage replica of New York. The sprawling complex boasted a mini-Brooklyn Bridge, mini-Empire State Building, and in an ode to modern-day Manhattan, a small Starbucks. Down in the pint-sized Lower East Side/Little Italy/East Village, where café patios pushed onto the "worn brick street," was Greenberg's Deli. Gigantic couples sat in matching NASCAR T-shirts, their ample flesh stuffed like *kishke* into advertisement-laden casing. At the best of times, Las Vegas attracted the very kind of big eaters often seen at New York's midtown delis with whole sandwiches visible in their throats like a snake's dinner. But I'd lucked out. My visit coincided with Vegas's NASCAR race. The largesse was abnormally high, even for a city that sold deep-fried Oreos at ninety-nine cents per bag.

Greenberg's Deli was not affiliated with any deli past or present. In the plate-glass window, a giant neon bagel shone blue and red with the words Greenberg's Delicatessen flanked by two stars of David. The floor had the requisite checker tiling, and raised shelves were stocked with neatly arranged jars of Manischewitz *gefilte* fish and boxed *matzos*. I looked at the short menu hanging above the counter and asked the woman working the register what was homemade. "Ummm, like, I'm sure something?"

Scanning the board, I picked out the few items that would actually appear in a Jewish deli. Mesquite Grilled Chicken toasted sandwich? Not likely. Homemade chicken *matzo* ball soup? Sure. Smoked Ham and Colby Jack Cheese toasted sandwich? I hoped not. Greenberg's Reuben? Okay. But aside from an egg cream, bagel, lox and cream cheese, and a black and white cookie, it seemed like standard sandwich shop fare. I opted for the *matzo* ball soup, figuring it was the toughest to screw up. I got two midsized, pale *matzo* balls in a little paper bowl filled with dark, onion-colored soup.

I unwrapped my plastic spoon and dug in, slicing a *matzo* ball that had the firm consistency of a baked apple. Searching for a taste, I soon realized that I'd found none. The soup tasted not of chicken, but of water, bouillon, and celery. Nothing resembling a chicken had ever come close to it. I tossed the soup in the trash, walked over to the nearest blackjack table, and lost five consecutive hands.

9:00 P.M.: Stage Deli, *Caesars Palace Forum Shops, Caesars Palace* Over the years, New York's Stage Deli had opened franchises and licensed outlets in Cleveland, Atlanta, Boston, Atlantic City, and Los Angeles. All except Las Vegas and Atlantic City (in the Taj Mahal casino) had closed when I arrived in Vegas. In New York, Stage's owner Steve Auerbach told me that the out-of-town branches were extremely troublesome, because you couldn't control the quality. At one point, there was a Stage Deli in Bally's, the Flamingo, and two in the MGM Grand.

When I visited, there was just one Stage Express kiosk in the MGM Grand, and a full-service restaurant at Caesars Palace. The Broadway-style marquee of the Stage Deli of New York rested between two giant columns amid the Forum Shops, a luxury mall catering to the gaudy tastes of high rollers. The Stage Deli represented its famous namesake on 7th Avenue quite well, despite the fact that it was twice the size of the original. The long deli counter had the right look—topped with brushed steel and etched glass panels, but there was no steam wafting in the air, no clatter, and no deli smell. It felt a bit too sterile to come close to the Stage's beloved tumult. The half a corned beef sandwich and bowl of cabbage soup I ordered came to only $9.99, a fraction of what I'd have paid at the original. The Stage in New York had to pay over a million bucks in rent each year, while this was a building where people traveled great distances just to surrender their money.

When it arrived, the cabbage soup was packed so densely with cabbage that I could hardly find any bits of meat or even tomatoes. It had sufficient tang, but little else, like glue stock doused with some pepper. My half sandwich arrived, and I pushed the soup aside. It was on caraway-seeded rye, which, while lacking any crunch to the crust, didn't taste awful. It was easily half to two-thirds smaller than the gargantuan monstrosities they served on 7th Ave. Unfortunately, the corned beef was too lean and tasted like it had withered in the freezer. Unsurprisingly, the Stage Deli closed just over a year later.

1 1:00 P.M.: The Carnegie Deli, *Mirage Hotel and Casino*

Here, once again, the Stage shared the same block with its rival the Carnegie. Carnegie's Las Vegas operation opened in 2005, just beyond the Mirage's shrine to Siegfried and Roy. It was the first expansion for the delicatessen since its unsuccessful franchises in the 1980s and 1990s, when the Carnegie, like the Stage, had opened seven new locations around the country, licensing the name to local owners. The franchises almost always opened with great fanfare and closed shortly after in quiet disgrace. The problem, according to Carnegie's current owner, Sandy Levine, was that Carnegie's old owner, Milton Parker (Levine's father-in-law), had no control over their far-flung outposts. Local owners who were trying to recuperate investments cut costs by using inferior products from other suppliers. No two Carnegie delis would be serving the same pastrami. It was an unsustainable situation.

But Vegas was a different story, and part of the Carnegie's new strategy. "I will open other delis," Levine told me in New York, "but only in tourist areas, never competing with local delis." Selling to locals required a level of service and pricing that was difficult to

replicate. You could charge tourists more, make more, and put yourself in a high-rent area that catered to those willing to eat massive
sandwiches for the photo-op alone. Levine insisted that if a deli had
the Carnegie name on the sign, it had to be owned and operated by
him. Among other conditions were the following: the deli had to
have table service; it could not be a kiosk or a self-service counter; and
it had to exclusively use Carnegie products, from the meat to the
mustard. The Carnegie's commissary in New Jersey produced all the
cheesecakes, breads, and pastrami that supplied the Manhattan
delicatessen, Las Vegas, and wholesale customers like Deli Tech in
Denver. Carnegie had recently begun producing vacuum-packed,
pre-sliced pastrami for Costco outlets around the United States. Just
pop into boiling water and voilà . . . hot pastrami.

The Carnegie Delicatessen inside the Mirage occupied a sort of
open triangle in the middle of the casino floor. It was surrounded
by hundreds of bleeping slots and a gigantic sport betting area. At
the entrance was a low wall with the logo of the Carnegie
Delicatessen—a big red heart with an arrow through it. Along the
back, salamis hung along a deli counter. The servers, all dressed in
bowties, shirtsleeves, and black aprons, were friendly and served
with just the right touch of attitude. Even late in the evening, the
place was pretty much packed. Best of all, it smelled like a deli,
which is no small feat in a building where the air is continuously
pumped with oxygen to keep gamblers awake.

Next to me, a large geeky couple in matching Halo T-shirts
were struggling to finish a Woody Allen pastrami/corned beef
sandwich. It had toppled over in a meaty avalanche, and though the
wife appeared to be falling into a diabetic coma, the pair kept shov-
eling forkfuls of salty meat into their mouths. I ordered a *latke* and
a small plate of pastrami, which the waitress was kind enough to
give me for no extra charge. The meat was excellent, and though
it was closer to warm than hot, the Carnegie's trademark spicing
shone through. There was an initial sweetness, followed by a building peppery barrage, carried along the way with an overtone of

liquefied salt and the cool hints of coriander lurking devilishly in the background.

The *latke* came out soon after the pastrami, the oil from the fryer still bubbling on the brown ridges of its wavy surface. I tore a scraggly chunk off the end, dipped it in applesauce, and danced the scalding treat around my tongue. It was excellent: airy inside, really crisp on the outside, and blessed with just enough sizzling fat to make it decadent, but not greasy. I polished off the *latke* and meat just in time to hear the couple pay and the husband say, "I wanna get drunk like a Klingon." I hit the nearest blackjack table and in half an hour won back my previous losses, plus the combined total of my deli grazing. Satisfied, I walked across the street to Treasure Island to hit up Canter's, but it had closed at midnight, as had Zoozacrackers, the delicatessen/coffee shop in the Wynn hotel. I couldn't believe they all shuttered so early, considering that Canter's in L.A. was open twenty-four hours. By the time I got back to my hotel, my head was pounding from the drinks, lights, and noise. I walked up to an empty blackjack table, put down my remaining cash, and doubled it in four hands.

10:30 A.M.: Canter's Delicatessen, *Treasure Island Hotel and Casino*

Given what Gary Canter had said in Los Angeles, my hopes for Canter's were high. Designed like the set of a futuristic spaceship, complete with swiveling captain's armchairs, I can only describe the architecture as late George Lucas. There was no deli counter or slicing machine visible. The menu consisted mainly of sandwiches. Only a few of the baked goods from Canter's incredible bakery rested in a small case. Each was individually wrapped, and didn't really look like any I'd eaten in L.A. Because the deli meats weren't going to be ready for another few hours I opted for a bagel and cream cheese. What I got was a plastic plate, a plastic knife, two little packages of Philadelphia cream cheese, and a plain bagel.

There was no tomato or onion or cucumber, and apparently they were out of lox. I looked down at this sad bagel, which I wasn't even sure came from Canter's (it tasted like a supermarket bagel), and sighed. I could have had this exact meal on an airplane.

If the Vegas model is to be the next frontier of delicatessens, as those like Gary Canter and others predicted, we have a disappointing future. Though deli owners saw easy fortunes to be made, none acknowledged the sacrifice required to do so. No matter how good the plan was, or the infinite piles of money they put into it, a delicatessen branch in a Las Vegas casino would never equal the original. The best of the lot was Carnegie, and even that was a shadow of the 7th Avenue location.

There would always be something lacking because casino owners wanted predictability above all else. Deli owners wanted the money, but they didn't want to live in Las Vegas. The customers would always be new, changing, and transient. The Las Vegas Strip wasn't a community. For that, residents went to Weiss Bakery and Deli, for food that was head and shoulders above the corporate delicatessens in the casinos. If I had to choose the future of the Jewish delicatessen based on what I saw in Vegas, I would bet on the home cooking of Michael Weiss any day. As for the corporate franchises and licensed operations, I just hope that what happened in Vegas remains in Vegas.

The Yucchuputzville Diaries Part 2:
Schmaltz by Southwest

(Scottsdale—Austin—Houston—New Orleans—Atlanta—Washington)

From Las Vegas I had just over two weeks to drive to Florida, do my research, and hightail it back to Toronto for the first night of Passover. Once again I was leaving the urban, historically Jewish coasts and venturing into the goyish heartland: the southwestern desert, the Gulf Coast, the Deep South, and even the nation's capital. By now my skepticism, though apparent, had eased somewhat. I wasn't sure which delis

I'd find here, or what they'd be like, but I knew that no look at America's delicatessen landscape would be complete without a journey through its warm underbelly.

Goldman's Deli, *Scottsdale, Arizona*

It was pushing eighty-five degrees outside Goldman's Deli, and noon was still an hour away. Inside, a crowd largely made up of retirees in their mid-sixties slurped up hot borscht. The tanned flesh of their faces crinkled in anger as they watched Fox News, loudly commentating on the grave injustices of the day.

"God damn Mexicans," one man told his golf buddy, to scenes of immigrants being chased through the desert, "they get what they deserve."

At the counter, Sam Goldman, a squat young man in a baseball hat, chatted with a customer about their hometown team, the Chicago Cubs. This migratory population was the core of Goldman's business; a full two-thirds lived in Scottsdale only during the winter. The Jewish population of cities like Scottsdale has been growing steadily over the past fifty years, fueled by the Sun Belt's retirement developments, which cater to northern baby boomers and their parents.

Rozalia Goldman didn't particularly care about the deli market when she and her husband, Gregory, moved down from Chicago around 2000. Both Roza and Greg had worked together as colleagues at Kaufman's in Skokie, and after Roza's first husband passed away, she eventually fell for Greg, the Mexican cook. When I visited, Roza and Greg were vacationing in Mexico, so Anat, Roza's daughter, took me back into the kitchen, where the cooking staff, made up entirely of Spanish-speaking Mexicans, brushed butter on the tops of flaky, delicious potato and mushroom *knishes* about to enter the oven. In every single delicatessen I had visited thus far in America, those doing the cooking were almost exclusively immigrants. In New York, deli workers were a mixture of Dominicans, Puerto Ricans, Arabs, and Chinese. In Florida, they hired Cubans, Haitians, and Central Americans. But overall, Mexicans were the predominant nationality.

Mexican workers are picking the cucumbers in Mexico that are then shipped to Los Angeles, where they are pickled by Mexicans, shipped to a deli by a Mexican driver, unloaded by a Mexican stock boy, then paired with a sandwich full of pastrami that was smoked by Mexican workers in New York, from cattle that were slaughtered by Mexicans in Iowa, on bread that was kneaded and baked by Mexican bakers in Detroit. Even the soda was stirred, canned, packed, and shipped by Mexicans. Sure, the deli will boast "Cooking just like bubbe used to make," but in reality, it is Jose's hands that make the difference between a well-rounded *matzo* ball and one that falls apart.

According to the National Restaurant Association, one in five people involved in food service in the United States is Hispanic. Restaurants employ more foreign-born people than any other U.S. industry, but some Jewish customers have a grand expectation that nothing but Jewish hands will touch their food. Some even talk with open disgust about the cleanliness of Mexican workers. The perception of many deli owners toward their own immigrant staff is outright racist.

Watching the golfers in Goldman's watching a Mexican invasion on Fox news, chowing down on crisp sweet cherry *blintzes* prepared by the deli's Mexican cooks, it all struck me as incredibly hypocritical. Gregory, who owned Goldman's, was a product of Mexican migration. As Anat Goldman said, "He's more Jewish than all of us, especially in the kitchen." Mexican and Latin American workers had silently become the new Jewish mothers. Delicatessen fans nationwide owe them an overdue *gracias*.

Katz's Deli, *Austin, Texas*

Sure, it was the state that brought George W. Bush to power, but Texas was also home to 130,000 Jews, mostly centered in Houston and Dallas. Texan Jews included oilmen, like Max Jaffe and Kinky Friedman, the cigar-chomping, Stetson-wearing author/politician/musician who fronted the band Kinky Friedman and the Texas Jewboys. Friedman was fond of the expression "May all your wishes be little *gefilte* fishes," and when we spoke briefly on the phone, he personally recommended Katz's Deli in Austin.

Located just off the main streets of downtown Austin, Katz's remained open twenty-four hours a day. The night I arrived was the start of the massive South by Southwest music festival, and I shared a table with a nice couple from Seattle who helped me devour two of Katz's contributions to Texan/deli fusion: a platter of deep-fried, cornmeal-battered half-sour kosher dill pickles (with tangy ranch dressing), and a trio of kosher-style tacos filled with cubes of grilled salami, chunks of *latkes*, hot salsa, and fluffy scrambled eggs. It was a fine prelude to my meeting with Marc Katz the next day.

To own and operate a Jewish deli deep in the heart of Texas requires a personality of enormous proportions, one that can appropriate the state's famous swagger as its own. Marc Katz had this in spades. Upon my first bone-crushing handshake with the bald giant I was assailed by his sinister cackle. A native of Queens, N.Y., Katz was a descendant of kosher butchers. From his teenage years on, he worked in restaurants and delis around New York, including Meyer's, the Turnpike Deli, and Charney's. In 1977, he moved down to Austin for love and opened up Katz's, an unabashedly boisterous New York deli (not at all related to the landmark on New York's Lower East Side).

"We're selling an experience," he told me as we sat over lunch. "A little bit of abruptness and you get it the way they do in New York City." Texans, who were accustomed to a sort of y'all come back now civility, knew New Yorkers from the movies. They came in expecting to be insulted, and Katz played to that. "The main thing about Katz's is that it's a fun experience," Katz told me. On cue, a customer leaned over and told Katz how much he loved

Jewish food. In fact, the man said, he had a Jewish friend in Detroit. "Oh yeah?" Katz shot back, quick as Clint Eastwood on the draw. "Let me find someone that gives a shit . . . . *boo ha ha ha!*"

Jewish clientele had always represented a small part of Katz's overall business, around 10 per cent. "We promote ourselves as a New York deli, not a Jewish deli," Katz said rather seriously. "A Jewish restaurant only appeals to Jews." Liberal as Austin was, overt anti-Semitism still existed there, and Katz had been called a "Jew bastard" by rednecks more times than he cared to remember. Rather than throw his considerable weight around, though, Katz simply tried to win them over with kindness.

"I love this restaurant so much. When I tell some guy, 'I'm glad you're here!' that son of a bitch knows I mean it!"

With that, he handed me his signature beverage, the Cheesecake Shake: a milkshake with a slice of Carnegie cheesecake tossed into the blender. Katz billed it as a "heart attack in a glass." It took all of my lung capacity to coax a drop out of the straw, and as I sat there struggling to breathe, Katz shouted at my waiter.

"Make sure this son of a bitch pays!"

Kenny and Ziggy's, *Houston, Texas*

"Hey David, I'm Ziggy. So . . . *nu?* What's the *emmis?* You want a nosh or a *shtickl* of something? Maybe some *gehakte* liver, or a *bissel* of *matzo* ball? *Oy veysmear*, my phone is ringing, hold on a minute, *bubuleh*."

At the start of my journey, sitting with Sy Ginsberg in Detroit, the first person he recommended I meet was Ziggy Gruber. "You won't believe this guy," Sy told me. "Ziggy's like an old-fashioned Deli Man from the 1950s in the body of a young guy. You'll just love him." Ziggy was the first to admit that he was a rare breed— part of a new generation of old-fashioned Deli Men. I could easily have been talking to an eighty-year-old veteran of the New York deli scene in an established Manhattan delicatessen. Instead, I was staring at someone in his early forties, whose deli stood in a Houston strip mall.

Ziggy had literally grown up in the New York deli world. His uncle and great-uncle owned Berger's in the diamond district, and the Woodrow Deli in Long Island. His grandfather owned the famous Rialto Delicatessen on Broadway, where young Ziggy was put to work at the tender age of eight, stuffing cabbage and making *knishes* on top of a crate. He was every bit the seasoned Deli Man, except he watched Bugs Bunny on his coffee breaks. Eventually, Ziggy's father and uncle initiated him into their own deli, Crest Hill Kosher, north of the city in Rockland County.

Ziggy Gruber walked and talked with the confidence of his predecessors. He seemed to know everyone in the American deli business, their stories, problems, and family secrets. In my travels I'd met many second- and third-generation deli owners, but never anyone like Ziggy. He was more of a New York deli owner than most of the deli owners I'd met in New York, wielding Yiddish as though he had just stepped off a ship from Poland. Deli was Ziggy's life, and he knew from an early age that if he didn't try to save it, it would surely die.

After the death of his beloved grandfather, Ziggy enrolled in culinary school in London. He worked at the famous Waterside Inn and did a stint in the kitchen with a young Gordon Ramsay. ("He wasn't such a tough guy then," Ziggy said, laughing. "I've seen him cry.") When he returned to New York with his chef whites, his father hoped that Ziggy, then eighteen, would stay in fine dining. But all that changed when Ziggy and his dad attended the annual dinner of the Delicatessen Dealers' Association of Greater New York. The association of Jewish deli owners had at one time boasted several hundred members. Its main purpose was to establish a collective presence for negotiating with unions and suppliers, but there was also a strong social element to the association, based on gambling and eating. But with delis closing down so frequently, the organization dwindled to just a few dozen members, disbanding in the late 1980s.

"I'll never forget. I looked around the room, it was all sixty- and seventy-year-old people, and it was sad to look. I said to myself: 'Who is going to perpetuate our food if I don't do it?' That was my calling. The next day I went back to my dad and my uncle and I said, 'I've had enough of this fancy-shmancy business, I'm going back into the delicatessen business.'"

Ziggy quickly got to work, soon tripling sales, but when Rockland County's demographics started shifting away from Jews, the family sold the deli. Ziggy headed to Los Angeles (where his brother was living) and opened up Ziggy G's Delicatessen on Sunset Boulevard, but after just three successful years he was forced to close because of a rent dispute with the landlord. He returned to New York in 2000 and began looking around for a deli to buy with Freddy Klein, the restaurant broker known for buying, selling, and leasing New York's delis. Klein had heard that a friend's son was looking to open up a Jewish delicatessen in Houston. Ziggy flew down and met with Kenny Friedman, who showed him a tightly knit Jewish community that was the largest in Texas and the Gulf Coast. The delicatessens that had once existed in the city were long gone, and the last one, Guggenheim, closed shortly before Ziggy arrived. "I took a look around and realized it wasn't such a cow town," Ziggy joked.

These days, Ziggy presided over the deli alone, having bought out Kenny's share. In Ziggy's mind, there were two types of people: restaurant people and deli people. You could take a deli waiter and successfully put him in any five-star restaurant, but placing a restaurant waiter in a deli would be a disaster. The philosophy echoed famed New York writer Damon Runyon's quote, displayed in Ziggy's deli: "There are two types of people in this world, those who love Delis and those you shouldn't associate with."

Ziggy wanted to make a further distinction, between full-blown Jewish delicatessen mavens, like himself, and people who happened to serve pastrami and corned beef sandwiches. To Ziggy, deli was a complete immersion in Yiddish culture and cuisine. Sure, lots of delis had corned beef, but his was pickled in barrels on site. He served rarely seen dishes like stuffed breast of veal, and *gribenes*, which are fried bits of crackling chicken skin, paired with chopped liver. He sold lox by either the Nova or belly cut, and hand-sliced the fish lengthwise over the whole side of salmon—so thin that you could actually see through it. His was a deli of the finest caliber, from the *flanken* short ribs boiling in the pots, to the Hebrew National salamis drying above the counter.

Ziggy's giant cabbage roll, the very kind he'd been making since he was in grade school, was so surprisingly light and fluffy that I assumed the meat inside had to have been veal. Nope, just beef stewed perfectly over the course of five hours, until every fiber melted into a stock that tasted like a French ragout. Every dish had a lightness to it, from the fluffy *kasha varnishkes* and egg-mushroom-barley sides, to the massive vegetable *latkes*, made from carrots, zucchini, and garlic and then served with a stewed apricot glaze. The giant noodle *kugel* had the airy consistency of a soufflé.

Kenny and Ziggy's was undoubtedly one of the best delis in the country. In Ziggy, I saw a traditionalist succeeding in the modern market. Sure, he did what was necessary to stay current, like adding large salads to his menu, but he did so without sacrificing the core of his cuisine. "The key with my deli," he said, "and I think this is a *shanda* [shame], is that there aren't too many places or people who take the pride that I do in this. Yes, some small places do here and there, but if you went to a deli back in the early twentieth century, I'd guarantee you that each was better than the last, and better than most you find today. Why? Because they were family places, they had lots of competition, and they made everything from scratch."

Here in suburban Houston, Ziggy was cooking the way his grandfather had taught him. It was the same care and deliberate attention that Rose Guttman put into her *matzo* balls in Michigan. If a new mold of Deli Men were going to save the deli from extinction, Ziggy Gruber would make an ideal leader.

Kosher Cajun New York Deli and Grocery, *New Orleans, Louisiana*

TOUGH TIMES Don't Last
TOUGH PEOPLE DO!!

These defiant words, written in colorful chalk and presented in an elaborate, gold-embossed frame, spoke to the pain of Hurricane Katrina's destruction and the strength of renewal. Driving into New Orleans, I saw abandoned neighborhoods rotting on either side of the highway. New Orleans had survived Katrina, but only in shattered fragments.

"We kinda saw the storm brewing before *Shabbos*," Joel Brown said, retelling his story as we sat in his recently renovated glatt kosher delicatessen and grocery store. Brown was a short man, with dark, full cheeks, and a soft demeanor. No one in the family watched television or turned on a radio that day, but Brown knew things were bad when he was walking to synagogue. People were frantically packing cars and boarding up windows. "As soon as *Shabbat* was over, we turned on the TV and saw it coming," he recalled. "Sunday morning we boarded up the store and the house."

For twelve hours, the Brown family, including Joel's wife, Natalie, and their three young daughters, crawled on choked freeways toward Memphis. The sky turned pitch black. Somewhere along the road, their dog had a heart attack and died. For two days they lived in a motel, glued to the television, and when the levees broke on August 29, Joel turned to Natalie and said, "Oh my god, the city is destroyed." He prayed everyone had made it out alive, and then he thought about his deli.

New Orleans had never been a large deli town, despite its love of fatty foods and big sandwiches. As Southern Jewish food historian Marcie Cohen Ferris wrote in her book *Matzo Ball Gumbo,* the city's German Jewish community was obsessed with integration into the halls of elite society and eschewed kosher eating. But by the turn of the twentieth century, a small Jewish area had taken shape around Dryades Street, populated by increasing numbers of Eastern European immigrants. Small delis opened to serve them, like the Southern Matzos Bakery, and then later Pressner's, the Kansas Deli and Bakery, and Ralph Rosenblatt's.

The city's last kosher deli, Ralph's, closed in the 1970s, and for three decades New Orleans' Jewish families had to drive to Alabama just to buy kosher food. Joel Brown and his wife were both natives of New Orleans. Though the community was small, roughly ten thousand before Katrina, Brown characterized it as one of the closest he'd ever seen in America. "I'll tell ya,' we're stronger Jews for it. I look at my customers from Gulf Coast communities, who have to drive two hours here and two hours back just to shop for kosher food, and I see strength."

Sensing an opportunity in this, Joel had opened the Kosher Cajun New York Deli and Grocery in 1987. Jewish clients came for kosher groceries, while deli sandwiches attracted gentiles. Brown began catering all over the Deep South and was even hired by supermarkets to consult on their kosher purchases. Then Katrina drowned it all.

"Ten days after the storm, we got six guys from the community together and drove back down," Brown said, in a syrupy voice thick with Delta drawl. "When we came into the city there were helicopters flying over, flashing searchlights, and Humvees prowling the streets with armed troops pointing guns out the windows. It looked like a war zone. Around our neighborhood, trees were uprooted and tossed through houses like toothpicks. We were speechless."

Metairie, eight miles west of downtown New Orleans, had escaped the worst of the flooding, though two feet of water had nevertheless inundated the deli. When Brown pried open the doors, he was quickly overpowered by the smell of rancid *gefilte* fish floating for a week in 100°F heat. Before he could make it out the back door, Brown threw up in the middle of his deli. Kosher Cajun sustained over $300,000 in damage (covered by insurance) and had to be completely rebuilt. Over three months, Brown commuted twenty times between Memphis and New Orleans during construction. He often questioned reopening.

"I had a building that was standing, but no one was around. I could lose more money reopening than just shutting. I mean there was no electricity, no water, no anything. If the building had blown down, the insurance company would have written me a big fat check and that would have been that." But Brown felt he was needed in New Orleans and Kosher Cajun reopened on November 17, 2005, less than three months after Hurricane Katrina. His initial clients for the first few months were FEMA workers, construction crews, and contractors from out of town. Though more than 30 per cent of the Jewish community never returned to the city, Kosher Cajun gained new customers from locals and foreign relief groups. A year and a half later, Joel Brown's eyes still welled up with tears when he discussed the ordeal.

"Hey," he said, snapping out of it, "let me get you a sandwich." Brown came back a few minutes later with the J&N special: hot corned beef and pastrami on dark rye with mustard, horseradish, and coleslaw. The bread was hot, studded with caraway seeds, and had a dark crust that boasted a crispness I hadn't tasted since L.A. Up to that point I could honestly say that every glatt kosher deli sandwich I'd eaten was a disappointment, a symptom of the industrial processing that suppliers used to cut down on high costs. In contrast, the J&N was simply wonderful. First the wallop of steaming pastrami on the roof of my mouth mixed with the cool tang of coleslaw. Then the spicy mustard and horseradish kicked in with the pastrami's pepper, building to an incendiary crescendo. In a time when delis the world over were dying from man-made troubles—real estate, profit margins, and assimilation—Brown's delicatessen had risen from one of the worst natural disasters in American history. That sandwich was a minor miracle.

The New York Corned Beef Society of Atlanta, *Atlanta, Georgia*

Deli in the Deep South. Sure, Jewish families have lived in south-ern states for as long as Jews have been in America, but the prospect of pastrami and gravy-covered biscuits in the Bible Belt just seemed wrong. To misquote Lenny Bruce, if the north is Jewish, the south is goyish. But deli wasn't foreign to the south. Charleston, South Carolina, once had a thriving deli scene in its "Little Jerusalem" neighborhood. Gottlieb's was once a legendary spot in Savannah, Georgia. Memphis had Rosen's, Goldstein's, Segal's, and Miner's. In Atlanta, dozens of delicatessens used to occupy Jewish neighborhoods, including Siegel's, Gold's, Merlin's, Mazian's, Nathan's, and the Economy Deli. Jackson, Mississippi, once hosted places such as the Olde Tyme Deli.

In their early years, Jewish delicatessens walked a precarious middle ground between heavily restrictive white society and segregated black communities. In many cases, neighborhood delicatessens were among the South's first integrated restaurants. There were exceptions. Leb's Pig Alley, a Jewish delicatessen in Atlanta owned by Charles Lebedin (a.k.a. Charlie Leb), firmly refused to integrate in the early 1960s. After tossing a black cus-tomer onto the street in 1963, Leb's became the focus of sit-ins and clashes between demonstrators and the police, who stood shoulder to shoulder with Ku Klux Klansmen in hooded robes. Under tremendous pressure from the Jewish community, includ-ing Jews who participated in sit-ins, Lebedin grudgingly relented and served blacks, but Leb's Pig Alley went under shortly after the passage of the Civil Rights Act in 1964, one deli that many were undoubtedly content not to save.

One by one, the South's Jewish delicatessens disappeared. Today there are very few Jewish delis operating in Southern states. This is not because the Jewish population has declined in the South. In fact, the population in places like Atlanta and Charlotte is growing steadily, thanks to retiring Northern baby boomers. But for deli lovers who make this migration, the disappointment awaiting them between slices of lifeless rye provokes much kvetching. One man decided to do something about it.

One Sunday each month, crowds of people jostle for tables at Twain's, a bar outside Atlanta. They come not for the house-brewed ales or chicken wings, but for a brief membership in the New York Corned Beef Society of Atlanta (NYCBSA). They'll pay a few dollars for initiation and in return receive a steaming, hand-sliced hot corned beef or pastrami sandwich, plus coleslaw, potato salad, and a pickle. Walking through the crowd will be Howard Wurtzel, a retired Freudian psychoanalyst and artist originally from Williamsburg, Brooklyn, whose obsession with Jewish deli created this phenomenon.

Drafted into the army in the late 1960s, Wurtzel was shipped down to Fort Bliss, in El Paso, Texas, where he and other Jewish doctors rhapsodized about Katz's deli. On a whim, Wurtzel bought some briskets from a local supermarket, cured his own corned beef, and threw a party on the base. Four decades later, both of Wurtzel's children moved down to Atlanta to operate Twain's, and Wurtzel followed suit with his wife, Ettie. He soon began exploring Atlanta's deli scene, much to his disappointment. His solution was to throw a corned beef party. In October 2005, he printed up a few flyers, stating that the New York Corned Beef Society of Atlanta would gather at Twain's the following Sunday. Wurtzel and his family cured, cooked, and sliced the meat for thirty-five or so ex-northerners. Next month the crowd was slightly larger, including a reporter for the *Atlanta Journal Constitution*, who wrote a story for the paper's front page. Close to three hundred people showed up the following month. Around town Wurtzel is known as the "Corned Beef King." He considers this the biggest accomplishment of his life.

Pickled Politics, *Washington, D.C.*

Though home to a good number of Jews, many of whom occupy positions high and humble, it must be stated that the nation's capital is probably the WASPiest place in America. This is a city where bowties are actually cool and creamed corn regularly appears on menus during Republican administrations. "Washington is a place where Jews were outsiders even when they were extremely powerful," remarked Franklin Foer, editor of *The New Republic*. "The culture of the city is one of a club-oriented atmosphere, which almost by definition shuts Jews out."

Jews may hold some influence on Capitol Hill or even in the west wing of the White House, but their acceptance by mainstream America has always been a delicate matter. D.C. represents the average American, and Jewish culture hasn't quite won his heart. Though delis existed over the years around D.C. (Frisco's, Baltimore Deli, Terlitsky's, Posin's, Hoffberg's), they were never really adopted as something sufficiently "American." Despite classic delis like Attman's, Weiss's, and Lenny's just an hour away in Baltimore, D.C.'s attempts to mix political power with pickled peppers had fallen flat.

There was one grand exception though, and its name was Duke Zeibert's.

From the Truman administration until the early years of Bill Clinton's reign, Duke Zeibert's ruled Washington power dining. Less a deli and more of a "Judeo-American Restaurant," Duke Zeibert's was *the* place for big names to be seen in D.C. At its zenith, it was the D.C. equivalent of Le Cirque, with the dapper Zeibert greeting guests, complimenting powerful women, and reinforcing D.C.'s social hierarchy.

Positioned just five blocks from the White House, Duke Zeibert's quickly became the toast of Washington soon after opening in 1950. Real estate honchos, baseball players, lawmakers, politicians, and gamblers made themselves at home, dining on such classic Jewish dishes as chicken in the pot and chopped liver. Duke Zeibert's was a place of white-gloved service and starched linens, where champagne was served alongside broiled tongue, and the menu contained not just corned beef, coleslaw, pickles, and *flanken*, but clams casino, steaks, and spring lamb chops. It was Jewish enough to bring chutz-pah to the city, but had enough WASP standards on the menu to satisfy regular customers like President Harry Truman.

"The first time I came in, I thought it was a Jewish wedding," recalled Mel Krupin, who managed Duke Zeibert's as its powerful maître d' from 1968 until 1980. "It was all mink stoles and suits." As head of the house, Krupin quickly learned the importance of Zeibert's ranking when it came to assigning tables. The most coveted were those closest to the windows by the front. These would be reserved for luminaries like Howard Cosell, Muhammed Ali, Milton Berle, J. Edgar Hoover, and Robert Kennedy. In the center of the room would sit less important regulars, like Jimmy Hoffa or junior congressmen. A second section, found behind a wooden trellis, was reserved for nobodies and those whose power had been stripped. They called it Siberia, because it was akin to being thrown into the social gulag. Krupin remembered bejew-eled women wrapping their arms around the divider in protest, saying "I don't eat in *that* room!"

In 1980, the building was sold to developers, and Duke Zeibert retired to Arizona. Mel Krupin received Duke's blessing to carry on the torch in his absence, opening Mel Krupin's just blocks away. But Duke was restless, and within four years, he returned to D.C. to reopen his namesake restaurant, forty feet away from Krupin's. The press dubbed it a "Matzo Ball War," and for a brief period the streets ran red with borscht until Krupin went out of business. "I worked for the man like he was my father," Krupin said, still bitter. "I really don't want to talk about Duke. It has no meaning to me." Perhaps fittingly Duke's didn't last much longer.

Dreams of marrying delis and political elites still seduce the occasional ego in D.C. In 2002, an Orthodox Jewish Republican lobbyist named Jack Abramoff opened Stack's Delicatessen, the only glatt kosher deli in D.C. Abramoff expected Stack's to attract Jewish power brokers, kosher lawmakers, Israel lobbyists, politi-cians, and representatives from Jewish organizations. When the

Jewish press found that a five-hundred-dollar-a-plate fundraiser at Stack's broke campaign finance laws, the "Picklegate" scandal emerged. Months later, charges were being brought against Abramoff for a number of political kickback schemes. Stack's closed shortly thereafter, and Jack Abramoff ended up in jail for fraud, conspiracy, and tax evasion.

Florida: Where Deli Goes to Die

"**D**id you hear about Rose?"

"No."

"Cancer."

"What about Pearl?"

"Kidneys."

"How long?"

"Who knows. . ."

"*Oy.*"

"Such a pain in my *tuchus* I got."

"You should get that checked out, it could be Crohn's."

"God forbid."

"I'm going to see how much longer we have to wait."

"Tell them we're wasting away to nothing out here!"

I'm waiting outside 3G's Deli in Delray Beach, Florida, for a big loudspeaker to call my name. The youngest person out here, besides myself, is in her late sixties. Most are in their eighties. It's late March. It's sunny. It's warm. No one has anywhere else to go, so they sit and wait for deli and *kvetch*. To some this would be living hell, but to elderly Jews in Florida it's a heaven just miserable enough to know they are still alive.

"DAVID SOX!"

I stand and walk toward the door. Dozens stare with contempt. Inside wait freshly baked loaves of crusty rye, moist roast turkey breast carved right off the bone, and bowls of chicken soup packed with life-giving *schmaltz*. When their turn comes, a smile will broaden on the creased faces waiting outside, and their rumbling bellies will emit a soothing gurgle of content. For a brief moment they'll be happy. Then, the *kvetching* will begin anew.

Florida is deli's last stop in America. It is the place where Jewish delicatessen owners and eaters head into the mustard-colored sunset. There are innumerable little delis spread around the strip malls of Ft. Lauderdale, Boynton Beach, Delray Beach, Sarasota, Hollywood, West Palm Beach, Boca Raton, and Aventura. These communities, many of which didn't exist just twenty-five years ago, represent the third largest population of Jews in the United States, numbering roughly 850,000.

Deli in Florida is plentiful, omnipresent, and largely inexpensive. There are deli carving stations in the dining halls of retirement villages. In Pompano Park, a racetrack in Broward County, you can eat at the recently opened Myron's. Even Florida's Subway chain advertises a hot pastrami sub with one full pound of meat. But like that Subway sandwich, quantity seems to trump quality in Florida's delis. Aside from my brief meal at 3G's, which was the last deli I visited on the way out of Florida, very little stood out as exceptional. There were some good deli meals, but nothing remarkable.

This wasn't how I remembered Florida, though I had been to Miami only once before, with my family, when I was six. Each morning I'd wake up, run into my parents' room with my little brother Daniel, and jump up and down on their bed shouting, "Rascal House! Rascal House!" I recall long lines under a canopy outside and my mother trying to explain what a rascal was (which went something to the tune of "You and Daniel are rascals"). But mostly I remember the danish, because at Rascal House they brought out baskets of hot, sticky danish with every breakfast, and hot, steaming rolls with every lunch. I can't recall what I ate besides those danish, but even now, over twenty years later, I can still picture my greedy little fingers, sticky with melted sugar, grabbing another.

When I heard the news late in 2006 that the Rascal House was going to be torn down and replaced by a condominium, I was crushed. The culprit behind it was none other than Jerry's Famous Deli, a Los Angeles–based chain of delicatessens much reviled by deli owners. How could the most successful deli in one of America's most populous Jewish communities possibly meet the wrecking ball? What factors had brought Florida's delicatessens to the point where their greatest temples were being destroyed?

The Jews who populate Southern Florida are old. In Broward and Palm Beach counties, those over sixty-five years of age account for roughly half the Jewish population—more than twice the national average, though it is a relatively recent development. Jews were actually forbidden to buy property in Miami Beach up until 1936, when real estate signs for new houses boasted "Always a view, never a Jew." Soon after the war, Miami Beach became a Jewish vacation destination and the area's Jewish population rapidly swelled, overwhelming any attempts to restrict it. There were kosher hotels like the Saxony and delis galore, such as the Southbeach, the Uptown, Villa, the Gourmet Shop, Junior's (of Brooklyn cheesecake fame), Wolfie's, and Wolfie Cohen's Rascal House.

The large migration of retirees to Florida didn't begin until the 1960s. As the GI generation began retiring, many simply moved down to Florida full time. Grand Jewish hotels made way for more profitable condominiums. High-rise, low-cost aquamarine apartment buildings dominated the skyline as pensioners came to live out their golden years. According to Ira Sheskin, a demographer at the University of Miami, in 1982 62 per cent of Miami Beach's population was Jewish. But that soon changed. Drug violence invaded Miami in the form of *Scarface*-style "cocaine cowboys." Most of the retirees living in Miami Beach survived on fixed incomes, and their frugal lifestyle negatively affected economic growth in the area, which felt like a cross between Rio's mean streets, and a *shtetl* by the sea. Delis began closing down, as fearful residents moved to communities farther north in Broward and Palm Beach counties. Many of these were gated suburbs, which offered a protective way of life. The lawns were larger, the houses more spacious, and security monitored the premises day and night. To skeptics who lived outside the gates, these new suburbs were "Fancyville Ghettos."

Toward the end of the 1980s, many of Miami Beach's ocean-front properties were reoccupied by a burgeoning gay community. South Beach became the retreat of Madonna and Versace, and the city spawned countless low-fat, low-carb diet fads. Real estate began soaring in value, and the remaining elderly Jewish residents who hadn't fled from the crime now fled the rising rents. Between 1994 and 2004 alone, Jewish households in Miami Beach dropped by over 50 per cent. Today, there are fewer than seventeen thousand Jewish residents of Miami Beach, a tremendous decline in just two decades. Synagogues have closed down or sit empty. In less than a generation, an entire community was built up and taken apart. But hey, that's Florida, where little is made to last.

"Miami Beach was Jewish back then. Period!" said Arnie London, the former owner of Arnie and Richie's, the last original deli in Miami Beach until it was sold to the Roasters' n Toasters chain in 2008. When I spoke with London a year before the sale, his local clientele were quickly disappearing. As we talked, a friend walked in and told London that yet another patron had passed away the night before. A tall, lean man, with a cropped gray mustache and perpetual look of scorn, London just sighed loudly and shook his head. "These are the old-time regulars, the first generation who came in," he said, staring deep into my eyes. "I can name them all. These were sweet people, real people, down-to-earth normal people. It's the end of an era."

The point, London made sure to note, was that his older customers weren't being replaced by deli eaters. While Florida's Jewish population overall is actually growing, the demographic shift is occurring away from retirees, toward younger families and the orthodox. On the surface this is positive. Delis need new clients. But younger Jewish families are less inclined to eat deli, and businesses that rely on a steady stream of golden oldies are in the unenviable position of watching their customer base literally die off.

So much of Florida's deli business is seasonal. At some Floridian delicatessens, seasonal clients (who stay from Thanksgiving until Passover) add an additional 30 per cent or more to sales. This creates intense periods of business, where the place might be packed from breakfast until dinner, but it also ensures up to eight months when things are dead quiet. Older clients tend to be demanding customers. Often the price required to keep them loyal is enough to make a deli owner lose whatever hair he has left.

"Old Jewish people? Do you want to know what they're like?" London asked, raising a crooked eyebrow, leaning in close and lowering his voice. "They know what they want and they want what's good, but they don't want to pay the true price for it because they remember what it once was."

Bob Weinstein, the handsome owner of the Bagel Cove, in Aventura, put it differently. As he stared out at a sea of silver heads, all of whom were loudly slurping soup, he said to me, *sotto voce*, "This is not a yuppie community. These people aren't working in a stock market making $25 million a year. *This* is their job." Every complaint was just another day at the office. The more they made, the more productive they were. "They want raisin muffins without raisins and apple danish without apples! Forget it."

A large number of delicatessen owners and workers in Florida are also in various stages of their golden years. Most came to retire and soon found themselves working harder than ever. Bob Weinstein owned twenty-one bakeries and four restaurants back in New York, before retiring to Aventura, but soon grew bored. "I was going out of my mind," he said during Bagel Cove's packed lunch hour. "How much golf can you play? How much bullshit can you talk? That's the plight of 99 per cent of people here who have retired. They're here because they have no choice." Old Deli Men migrate around Florida like flamingos. In many cases, they cut meat right until their very last breath. One owner told me a story about a seventy-five-year-old counterman who went home the week before to take a nap between shifts and never woke up.

None of this leads to a warm feeling within Florida's Jewish delicatessens. With owners and customers who are cantankerous and counting down the days, the atmosphere is decidedly grouchy. Florida's deli owners greeted me with a sense of suspicion that I never encountered elsewhere, and they extended the same ill feelings to their competitors. Floridian Jewish deli owners didn't know about other delis, didn't like talking about other delis, and certainly didn't associate with other deli owners. If Los Angeles taught me that the overall health of a deli community could benefit from friendly relations between Jewish delicatessens, Florida demonstrated that it can ruin a town for deli.

Florida also tends to be dominated by bagel-delis. These are combined bagel bakeries, appetizing stores, dairy restaurants, and delicatessens. The decline of the deli has been shadowed by the meteoric rise of the bagel. Once the specialty of Jewish bakeries, bagel orders in America grew 92 per cent between 1993 and 1998. I've encountered bagel-delis elsewhere in the country, but never to the extent that I witnessed in Florida, where their presence was near total. I found them all largely disappointing. With so much effort put into baking bagels, deli meats and kitchen dishes suffered.

One of the few stand-alone delis I encountered in Florida was the Pomperdale Deli in Ft. Lauderdale. Its owner, Larry Vogel, another ex-Brooklynite, was in his late seventies, well-sunned, bald, with a set of pearly dentures. People were always pleading with Vogel to broaden Pomperdale's menu away from deli, but he firmly refused. "This is what I do," Vogel said, pointing to the towering pastrami-corned beef combo sitting before me on the counter, a flash of spicy brown mustard seeping out over the meat. "I have men here who know how to slice and build a sandwich." It was a fine sandwich, among the best in Florida, but even Vogel knew that a great sandwich wasn't enough to survive in this climate. "I always worry about what's going to happen to this place," he told me. "There's so many other corporate restaurants here. All they have to do is just huff and puff and blow delis down." I knew exactly what he was talking about.

Since opening in 1954, Wolfie Cohen's Rascal House had been a sensation. The deli followed on the success of Cohen's eponymous Wolfie's, which had debuted in the heart of Miami Beach seven years earlier, at the peak of South Beach's postwar Jewish boom. Wolfie's set the standard for deli in Florida, and when Cohen expanded his burgeoning empire, he set up shop in the then under-developed suburb of Sunny Isles. (Over the years Wolfie's prospered under different owners, eventually in three separate locations, but the last one closed in 2001.)

The infrastructure of Wolfie Cohen's Rascal House was purpose built for crowd control. To shade those waiting for up to an hour, a canopy snaked along the side of the expansive delicatessen. Once in the doors, you entered a type of human sorting apparatus: several rows of rails separated parties with large signs clearly marking where "Singles," "Parties of 2," "Parties of 3 or 4," and "Parties of 5 or more" waited for seats.

Rascal House went on to become the most famous deli south of New York. There were three full-sized rooms, a huge oval counter, and a separate takeout section. In all, it could seat 425, making it one of the world's largest delis. No visit to Florida was ever complete without a trip to the Rascal House. During peak tourist season, crowds would line up from breakfast until four in the morning.

Even though I hadn't been in over twenty years, the first thing that struck me when I walked into the Rascal House in 2007 was how easy it was to do so. It was Sunday at 11.30 a.m. in March, as prime time as it got for deli anywhere, let alone Miami Beach. There should have been dozens of people waiting, but we waltzed right into a large circular booth of rose-colored Naugahyde. I had gone with my cousin Eric Katz, who was in town for business. Within minutes of sitting, our waitress deposited a small plate of buttery mini-danish on the table.

"Do they just give you these?" asked Eric, as if he'd just won the lottery. Sticky, messy, and sinfully sweet, the little butter-soaked temptations were every bit as good as I'd remembered. Small, warm *rugelach* were flaky and filled with dense, sugary veins of chocolate. Beside them lay two-bite cheese danish, with dough the consistency of a Parisian croissant, containing oozy cheese that tasted of sweet ricotta. Buried beneath was a single apricot roll, which Eric dispatched in one greedy chomp. The waitress returned a minute later with a quartet of fist-sized cinnamon buns studded with raisins and covered in frantic Jackson Pollock brushstrokes of melted icing sugar.

This scene was played out under the watchful eyes of Wolfie Cohen's Rascal, which resembled a sinister version of Casper the

Ghost: a white, soft-edged little man with a pointed tail and giant head, topped by a white sailor's cap with a big red R on it. Behind his back, the Rascal held a trident, but above his head burned a glowing halo. No character represented the complex relationship between a deli and its customers more. Here was a place where one indulged in the holiest of sins, a sort of blessed gluttony that was reviled by cardiologists but approved by psychologists; where guilt in the mind met pleasure in the belly; where one's stomach could take a holiday in the midst of vacation.

This was the Rascal House I remembered and would soon mourn. It was destined for the junkyard sometime a year later, in 2008, when The Epicure, a mixed-use condominium complex, was set to rise on its footprint. The Epicure would be a fourteen-story behemoth of glass and steel, with swimming pools, a luxury gymnasium, and spa facilities. According to the developers, Jerry's Famous Deli Inc., the whole project would be designed for discerning culinary customers, with top-grade kitchens in each unit and delivery from the Epicure gourmet market on the ground floor of the building. The original Epicure Market, in South Beach, grew from a small Jewish grocery into a place where celebrities now shop for extravagant foods and wines. There were no plans to preserve any part of the Rascal House in the new development. It had a standing date with the wrecking ball. "Rascal House has been here since 1954, and it's an institution," Jerry's Famous Deli Inc. vice president Jason Starkman told the *South Florida Business Journal*. "But we're basically replacing one institution with another."

Basically??? Here you had a revered Jewish deli institution torn down by a corporate Jewish deli in the service of a luxury Jewish grocery. It was all just too disgustingly ironic—cultural cannibalism at its most repugnant.

Whether The Epicure condominium complex will ever be revered as an institution on par with the Rascal House is doubtful. If it's ever built, The Epicure will be seen as a late entry to Miami's millennial condo bubble, announced right as the subprime melt-down hit. Though the condo was indefinitely shelved, Rascal House was still torn down in April 2008 and replaced with an Epicure market. Rascal's death will be seen as another bold move by Jerry's Famous Deli Inc., the nation's most controversial deli.

Jerry's started in 1978, when Isaac "Ike" Starkman, a retired Israeli air force lieutenant, and his then partner (named Jerry), opened a delicatessen in Encino, California. Starkman soon took full control and transformed Jerry's into a general restaurant, expanding the menu tremendously with dishes that had no relation to Jewish delicatessen. In interviews over the years, Starkman stated his belief that while traditional deli foods have a nostalgic value, he feels no loyalty to them. By the late 1980s, the success of Jerry's as a twenty-four-hour restaurant allowed Starkman to open three other outlets in greater Los Angeles, plus a cigar lounge adjoining the Beverly Hills location.

Then in 1995, Starkman did what no other deli had ever done. In a highly risky move, he took Jerry's Famous Deli Inc. public, listing the stock on the NASDAQ exchange, under the symbol DELI. The IPO quickly raised $9.2 million, which allowed the company to finance further expansion. In 1996, Jerry's opened a Pasadena branch and purchased Solley's, a well-known deli in the San Fernando Valley, as well as another deli, which was closed and reopened under the Jerry's name. Further stock sales generated $11 million, which financed the purchase of Wolfie Cohen's Rascal House and its property in 1996 (for close to $5 million). Cohen had died ten years previously, and his family ended their involve-ment in the business. Epicure was purchased in 1998 for over $9 million in cash and stock, though members of the Thal family were retained to manage the business. In 1998, Starkman opened a second Rascal House in Boca Raton, Florida, and in 2001, Jerry's Famous Deli opened a location in South Beach.

But the stock of Jerry's Famous Inc. never really performed. Fewer than 150 investors purchased shares, mostly the Starkman family (Ike and sons Jason and Guy . . . also vice presidents) and several institutional investors. Though revenues grew from over $40 million in 1996 to over $70 million in 1999, with income nearly tripling, the stock price declined amid great market volatility, fluctuating from $6.66 to $1.88 per share in one quarter alone. By the end of 2001, Jerry's Famous Inc. (DELI) had lost 80 per cent of its value. NASDAQ delisted the company and the Starkmans took Jerry's Famous Deli Inc. private in a share buyback that cost $3,815,000. But what may have seemed like a misadventure in the stock market turned out to be crucial to Jerry's success.

"What Starkman did was brilliant," said an L.A. deli owner. "He brought the company public, used the cash to finance a huge expansion, then bought it back cheap. It wasn't great for investors, but for him it couldn't have worked out better."

When I visited the gorgeous art deco South Beach location of Jerry's Famous Deli, which was filled with young, mostly gay, tourists eating breakfast, it was a disappointment. The vast menu, with everything from Cajun pitas to lobster tails, lost much in the mix. The *blintzes* my waiter brought, which were two small, luke-warm blond squares, arrived long after I'd ordered, during which time a fistfight broke out in the kitchen. The cheese was grainy and lacked any trace of creamy sweetness. They were served with cold strawberry jam. Along with a glass of freshly squeezed orange juice, the total came to just under twenty dollars! At the hostess's desk near the entrance, Jerry's had placed the very same quote I'd seen at Kenny & Ziggy's: "As I see it, there are two kinds of people in this world: people who love delis, and people you shouldn't associate with." Jerry's may have started out as a Jewish delicatessen, but I didn't feel any love there.

Corporate delis run on a different foundation than other delicatessens. Theirs is the rationale of spreadsheets and consultants over tradition and instinct, and for many, it is the future of the deli business. Florida is a place where chains of corporate restaurants thrive and their effect is obvious to anyone who drives through the state.

Exit off the freeway and pull into any town or small city. You'll soon be assaulted by the bright signs of the same food service outlets found off highways everywhere; Applebee's, Friendly's, TGI Friday's, Cracker Barrel, Cheesecake Factory, Ruby Tuesdays, etc. . . . But go a little farther, as I always do, past the Wal-Mart and the Home Depot, and drive into the historic center of town. There, you'll likely find archeological traces of what was once the American Main Street: empty gas stations, graffiti-covered town halls, and the dusty facade of a forgotten family diner. No one walks the streets here. The people are all back where the lights are brighter, drawn like moths, while Main Street quietly perishes. In this way, the death of America's Jewish delicatessens isn't unique. The problems that affect Jewish institutions continue to be harbingers of what will eventually happen to everyone else. When it comes to where Americans eat, corporations have leveraged your appetite into stock options.

The most successful corporate deli in Florida, and likely in the United States, is TooJay's Original Gourmet Deli. It began, as almost all chains do, as a single operation in 1981 by Jay Brown and Mark Jay Katzenberg (two Jays), who were looking to start a lower-priced Jewish deli in Palm Beach. These days, TooJay's (which no longer involves Brown or Katzenberg) has twenty-five locations, has more than seventeen hundred employees, opens an average of two new stores each year, and generates substantial profits in multiples of millions. The TooJay's menu, while hardly bare bones, remains mostly true to classic Jewish dishes, featuring smoked sable, *knishes*, brisket platters, and all the usual soups and sandwiches. They cater *bar mitzvahs*, *shivas*, and *bris'*; arrange full dinners for the high holy days; and remain involved in local Jewish communities.

At the head is Bill Korenbaum, the CEO and president, a friendly, straightforward middle-aged man from Long Island. The objective of a corporate chain, Korenbaum explained, is to control every aspect of the business in an efficient and predictable way.

Most of the food served at TooJay's is made in a large central commissary, where it is frozen, shipped to various outlets, and then prepared for service. Rarely does the word "cooking" enter into it. Instead, food is "reheated," baked goods are "finished off," and meals are "assembled." Nothing is left to chance. "How many different ways are there to make a *blintz* or a stuffed cabbage?" Korenbaum asked me, pointing to TooJay's *blintz* and stuffed cabbage, which would presumably look the same in the other twenty-four outlets. "There's a hundred different [potential interpretations] for every type of Jewish dish. For us, we'd like to outsource as many products as possible if the quality is there."

Every decision, event, and transaction is computerized, sent to the head office, and reduced to statistical format, down to how many hours each store's lights were on. Store managers cannot even select dinner specials without corporate approval. In corporate (deli) culture, the decisions that are the most important are made in boardrooms by CAS and MBAS. Nowhere does the knowledge of the DM, the Deli Man, come into play. His is a world of feeling and texture, but the Deli Man's is experience that can't be analyzed and multiplied, and corporate delicatessens must multiply in order to survive.

"Individual, family-owned delis today are dead. They're dead," Korenbaum said. "Are they opening new ones? I don't see it much. There's such a barrier to entry because the costs are so high. This is an industry with the highest failure rate of any in the United States." Still, family-owned delis, like the small Best Deli one plaza over, remained a threat. "Every restaurant is competition," Korenbaum said. "I don't care what it is, it's going to affect your business. . . . If a mom and pop opened up next to us, they'd do more damage than another chain . . . more so than the Cheesecake Factory, because a deli is doing exactly what we do."

When it came down to taste, a family-run deli was likely going to give TooJay's a run for their money. This isn't to say that I disliked the food at TooJay's. The bread was warm and crusty, and the meats were well steamed and sliced (they hired experienced countermen for stores in Jewish areas). But something was definitely missing in each bite. They all fell a little flat, as if the desire to appeal to what Korenbaum referred to as a "mainstream" customer base had dumbed down the flavor, as had all the freezing, outsourcing, and processing. At a family-owned deli I could look behind the counter or in the kitchen and see the person who had made my meal from scratch. Here I couldn't, and that made all the difference.

Corporate chains generally lean toward less remarkable food, but this needn't be the case. One of the best delis I visited in Florida was Ben's Kosher Deli in Boca Raton, an outlet of the Long Island chain. Ben's owner, Ronnie Dragoon, is regarded as one of the most respected Deli Men in New York. Ben's corned beef and tongues are pickled in barrels in each location's kitchen. They serve rarely seen dishes like tongue polonaise, a hot casserole of sliced, fatty tongue, covered in a gooey sweet raisin sauce, and crisp, bubbly, fried *kreplach* packed with chopped seasoned beef and smothered in thick chunks of candied onion. Since opening in 2004, the Boca Raton location represents one of the most successful outlets in the whole Ben's chain.

"We're selling more *kishke* out of this store than all the other stores combined," says Boca's manager, Michael Ross, a young, slim, experienced Deli Man with a dry wit. "I don't want to cut this stuff out, and neither do the customers. When we put wraps on the menu we nearly had a revolt. One man came up to me, shook his finger, and said, 'It's a *shanda* that you sell wraps in a kosher deli.'" Ben's succeeds with a kind of compassionate corporatism. Dragoon and Ross are both men who learned the business from behind the deli counter. Their fingers bear the scars of knife blades. Yes, they're in the deli business to make money, and they know expansion is an element of that, but they are also in it because they truly love deli . . . something I suspect the Starkmans do not.

Of all the deli owners I contacted for this book, Isaac (who passed away in summer, 2008) and Jason Starkman were the only ones who ignored my requests for an interview. But the visits I made to Rascal House during my brief time in Miami gave me a glimpse into what the corporate philosophy of Jerry's Famous Deli Inc. could do.

I went back to the Rascal House with my friend Jeffrey Kofman my last day in Miami, nearly a year before it was torn down. It was the middle of the week, and the small crowd that had been present the Sunday before was gone. We took a big booth underneath a Rascal statue and waited for a waitress. After ten minutes, I walked to the counter to get some service. As I came up, a young man with a pierced lip was screaming at one of the old waitresses. She was asking Adam (so said his name tag) for juice. She had a tray full of food; he was behind the counter with the juice dispenser. He must have been no older than twenty-five, and she no younger than seventy, but he just barked at her to "Fuck off!" When she backed away indignant, he smiled at me.

"If it wasn't for me, this place would be falling apart," he said, folding his arms.

"How come?" I asked.

"I'm an all-star here," he boasted. "I worked at Jerry's before and I'm one of their personal favorites. They brought me over here to sort shit out, to get these old bags moving a little."

Another waitress walked up, and Adam snapped, "What the fuck do you want?"

Though tempted to grab a hard salami and beat him over the head, I didn't want to leave without one last taste of Rascal House. The waitress finally came to our table with a basket of hot *challah* rolls. Each roll was a small, perfect, golden loaf that exhaled a mini steam bath when you broke the crust. The food was another story. First came the bowl of chicken soup, a light broth with thick egg noodles and a small, single *matzo* ball. Jeffrey took a bite and put his spoon down, pushing the bowl toward me.

"What, no good?" I asked.

He shook his head. It was weak. Real weak. Watery broth had soaked into the *matzo* ball, rendering it a sponge of nothingness. A trio of meats arrived on a plate in front of us with a stack of rye. I laid the pastrami on a piece of dry rye and took a bite. It was cold in some places and warm in others. On my third bite I caught a tough fiber and had to chew like a hyena. The brisket was drier than the Sahara. The salami we ordered was actually bologna. Five minutes after the bill arrived, the waitress brought us the *latke* we'd ordered. It tasted like it was made of wood chips. I actually spat it out. Even though my breakfast there just days before was great, this was an atrocity. But hey, if the place was being torn down, what incentive was there to put any effort in? None.

The deli's manager, Nate, came over as I was taking photographs. I asked if I could talk to some of the staff. He went away to call his bosses at Jerry's. I walked over to the nearest table where an older couple from Baltimore was just about to tear into a sandwich. I told them about the book, my trip, and how Rascal House would be closing. When I said that, their tanned faces dropped to the floor. They hadn't known it was terminal and I'd just sucked away the joy of their visit. I felt awful.

"Where will we go?" the wife asked her husband, genuinely worried.

"I guess a hot dog stand or something."

Just then the manager returned. I wasn't allowed to take any pictures or talk to any of the staff without the permission of Jerry's Famous Deli Inc. "Sorry," he said, "it's corporate. You can't do nothing without corporate. You gotta do what corporate says. They decide."

Part Three

TRAVELS IN THE DELI DIASPORA

A few years back, when I was living in Buenos Aires, Argentina, a city with plentiful beef and Latin America's largest Jewish population, I felt sure there had to be some pickled brisket kicking about. Friends led me to Big Mamma, Argentina's take on a New York Jewish deli. I ordered the Big Fresser's Hot Pastrami on Rye, and what I got was some pre-sliced, microwaved semi-corned beef on spongy bread, drowning in sour mustard. I bit in, tasted the tangy, rather tough meat (which had no spicing to speak of), chewed on the "rye," and was nevertheless transported back to a place I loved. By the standards of American deli it was atrocious, but the sheer chutzpah of eating that sandwich in Buenos Aires was the most affirming moment of my deli-obsessed life.

When you remove a deli lover from his native land, his obsession for pickled meats intensifies. I have known people who have bribed border guards in Bangladesh to enter the country with a suitcase full of Montreal smoked meat. People have spent considerable sums exporting the Jewish deli concept abroad. Hong Kong, a city with a sizable foreign-born Jewish population (commerce + dim sum = Jews), has several delis. The city's Jewish community center has a kosher restaurant, there's a small deli called Archie B's, and there's also the Main Street Deli in the luxury Langham Hotel, which features something called the "Rudest Wall of Chocolate Cake." There have even been Jewish restaurants in Havana, Cuba, where Jewish restaurants such as Moishe Pippic's, Cafeteria Boris, Cooperativa, Waxman, and Sandberg served the burgeoning community there until Castro forced them all out of business.

One place that's never taken to Jewish delicatessen is Israel, even though it boasts more Ashkenazi Jews than anywhere else. You could not find a pastrami sandwich in Jerusalem if you had the Mossad looking for you. Yes, *matzo* ball soup and other Ashkenazi dishes exist in the Holy Land, but they're pretty much cooked exclusively by grandmothers in private homes. The Israeli culinary landscape is dominated by the food of the Arabs. Hummus is everywhere, as is falafel, but searching for a *knish* in Israel is like trying to work out a peace deal in the region . . . heartbreaking, exhausting, and destined for failure.

But elsewhere successful, homegrown Jewish delicatessens do exist in several large Ashkenazi communities outside America. They have evolved along with local tastes and circumstances, in ways that are at once similar to, and radically different from, the American deli experience. In places like Montreal, Toronto, London, Belgium, Paris, and Krakow, the common roots of Yiddish cooking have produced very different versions of the Jewish delicatessen.

Your Number 14
When Called It's Your Turn For Service

Montreal: A Smoked Meat Kingdom

"You know if you had really, really been intent on entrapping me on my wedding night, you wicked woman, you would not have dabbed yourself with Joy, but in Essence of Smoked Meat. A maddening aphrodisiac, made from spices available in Schwartz's delicatessen. I'd call it Nectar of Judea and copyright the name." —from *Barney's Version* by Mordecai Richler

Though I was born and raised in Toronto, my parents are both native Montrealers, leaving for Toronto in the late 1970s like so many of their contemporaries, fleeing the unstable politics of Quebec's separatists. Though her childhood home was just steps from Snowdon Deli, one of Montreal's finest, Mom rarely ate delicatessen. Her Canadian-born parents, Evelyn and Stanley Davis, were the furthest thing from Bubbe and Zaide. Grandma cooked from a pantry stocked with cans and powders, often tossing together "concoctions" from leftovers. They ate every meal with a glass of milk. Though they were decidedly Jewish in religion and race, at the table they were basically goyish.

My deli genes came from my father's side. Though both his parents came to Canada when they were children, they retained the flavor of Romania and Hungary. Long after "Poppa" Sam Sax died at the hands of that fatal sandwich, Daniel and I would visit the apartment of our "Granny" Ella Sax and head straight for her kitchen. On the stove, pots of sweet and sour meatballs bubbled. Our favorite treat waited in the oven: her baked rice pudding, a family secret made without any dairy. We'd douse it with maple syrup and chew on the crispy bits of rice while hot raisins burst in our mouths like juicy bombs. Dad would often drive us around his old haunts downtown, through the city of "Poppa" Sam, a garment worker who toiled in Montreal's schmatte business with limited success, and dressed his kids "sharp as a matzo ball."

Dad initiated us into the rituals of Montreal Jewish manhood, like the way to ask for the hottest hand-rolled bagels, fresh from the wood-fired oven at St. Viateur Bagel Bakery. It was my father and his best friend, Stephen Rothstein, who first brought me to Schwartz's Hebrew Delicatessen, Dad pointing out the piled white slices of *speck* in the shop's window, saying, "This is what killed Poppa Sam," while Rothstein correctly demonstrated the way to eat *karnatzel*, a long, thin Romanian beef salami that Montrealers hang to dry until it literally snaps. Rothstein took a single slice of rye, painted it with yellow mustard, and rolled it around the dark stick of meat. It was the first time I ever ate mustard, and I recall how its sour tinge perfectly offset the garlicky beef.

Even after all the great delicatessens I've visited around the world, nothing matches Montreal. It is nirvana for deli purists. Visiting New Yorkers remark how much Montreal's delis remind them of all that their city has lost. Montreal's delis have remained stubbornly original in their decor, food preparation, and menus. If the deli is to be saved, a large part of the solution lies in the mysterious Montreal smoked meat.

Smoked meat first appeared in Montreal around 1890, when a Romanian immigrant named Aaron Sanft opened Montreal's first kosher butcher shop. A large percentage of the Jews who came to Montreal were Romanian, and Romania's Jewish food traditions specialized in spicing and smoking. For nearly a century, the accepted tale of the smoked meat sandwich's origins lay with Ben Kravitz, the founder of Ben's Delicatessen, who had arrived in Montreal from Lithuania in 1899, with fifteen dollars and a bullet wound in the heel, courtesy of a Polish border guard. His wife, Fanny, opened a small fruit stand and candy shop in 1910, and Kravitz claimed to recall the method Lithuanian farmers used to cure and smoke briskets. He pickled the meat in brine and smoked it over hickory bark in the small backyard of the shop, then sliced it, and served it on rye bread with mustard. The smoked meat sandwich was born, so Ben's legend went.

This was taken as gospel until a local historian named Eiran Harris uncovered a potential predecessor, Herman Rees Roth, who had owned a deli in New York until 1908, when he moved to Montreal and opened the British American Delicatessen Store, where he served smoked meat sandwiches, predating Ben's by over a year.

While Montreal smoked meat's origins may lie in Romania, Lithuania, or even the Lower East Side of Manhattan, it is now Montreal's own. Outside the city it is always referred to as Montreal smoked meat, but in Montreal, it is simply called smoked meat or *le smoked meat* and is eaten with religious devotion. When I spoke about it in the United States, deli lovers gravitated toward each word. "I gotta get my hands on this stuff," they'd say, to which I sadly informed them that shipping it across the border was impossible. They had to go to Montreal; few did. But when people asked me what, exactly, smoked meat was, I had no satisfactory answer. I found it at Schwartz's.

Schwartz's Montreal Hebrew Delicatessen. Schwartz's Charcuterie Hebraique de Montreal. Schwartz's. Chez Schwartz. Across Canada, the mere mention of Schwartz's brings to mind smoked meat, and the words *smoked meat* trigger the name Schwartz's. Schwartz's seats sixty very cramped customers crammed six abreast along the left wall, separated by a narrow aisle from half a dozen seats along a counter. It is tiny, barely larger than a tractor-trailer, perhaps one-tenth the size of Katz's. There are no *knishes* at Schwartz's, no egg creams, chopped liver, soups, or coffee. You cannot get your smoked meat sandwich on anything but seedless rye, and it is always served with mustard. The menu exists on thin paper placemats and faded backlit photos. Though broiled rib steaks were the draw in the deli's first four decades, it is smoked meat that has made Schwartz's arguably the most famous restaurant in all of Canada. Schwartz's is the only deli enshrined in both a book (*Schwartz's Hebrew Delicatessen: The Story* by Bill Brownstein) and a documentary film (*Chez Schwartz* directed by Gary Beitel).

Reuben Schwartz opened his restaurant in the heart of the garment district, along Main Boulevard, in 1928. Though Schwartz was supposedly a horrendous boss, gambler, philanderer, and businessman (he lost Schwartz's just four years after opening), the recipe he brought with him from Romania lives on. Montreal smoked meat is the bastard child of pastrami and corned beef. If pastrami is spiced, smoked navel and corned beef is pickled, boiled brisket, then Montreal smoked meat (listen carefully) is a combination of the two: a brisket cured and smoked like a pastrami, with slightly different spicing.

Schwartz's legendary smoked meat is now under the stewardship of Frank Silva, the delicatessen's affable manager, who has worked at Schwartz's most of his life, like his father did. Calm, casual, and always sporting a toothy grin from behind a goatee,

Silva explained the smoked meat process. Raw briskets from Alberta are rubbed with a mixture of coarse salt, cracked pepper-corns, and Schwartz's secret spice mix, which involves much less sugar than a New York–style pastrami, with more pepper and fewer aromatic spices. Briskets are then cured in plastic barrels for a period of a week.

Once the briskets are suitably pickled, they are ready to enter the smokehouse, a small brick room perhaps four feet wide by six feet deep and nine feet high, like a tiny back alley stained with burnt fat and old spices. Silva claimed this caked-on residue was part of the Schwartz's secret, as if the oven itself were pickled. The smokehouse was jammed with dozens of partially smoked briskets lazily dripping their fat onto low blue flames. The briskets smoke from five to seven hours, without wood. It didn't look like it, but Silva said the smokehouse could accommodate up to 160 briskets at a time, with an average of two loads smoking during a typical day, three during summer, and four around Christmas, when Schwartz's also smokes turkeys, ducks, and geese around the clock.

Cooked smoked meat is hauled through the deli by a busboy, who squeezes past a charcoal broiler spitting orange embers, wedges himself into the minuscule space where the counter begins, and deposits a few of the briskets into the small steam box. The rest are piled high in the deli's refrigerated front window—a grease-stained sidewalk display case tempting passersby. The smoked meat will then steam for up to three hours, until cutter Joao "Johnny" Goncalves hauls out a brisket.

Johnny is Schwartz's top cutter, a role that demands tremendous physical and mental stamina. A Portuguese immigrant to Montreal who still speaks English and French with an Iberian bounce, he has twelve years' experience as a cutter, plus an additional twenty-four working in the deli. He is a stoutly built man with ruddy cheeks and a cheerful pudge, who squints when he smiles. With the knife in his thick right hand he can dispatch slices off a smoked meat in a flash, piling them with some of the spicy scraps onto small disks of rye, which a second counterman to his right will finish off by placing a mustard-slathered piece on top at a perpendicular angle (a Montreal trademark).

An elastic brace around Johnny's elbow attests to the strain that years of hand-cutting have taken on his body. He has acquired a condition similar to tennis elbow. The pain is numbing and intense, something that Silva shares as well, as do many cutters in Montreal . . . a slow-motion battle wound earned on the wooden duckboards of the smoked meat trenches. However, the presence of hand-cutting at almost every deli in Montreal is one of the key reasons behind the city's deli greatness. A dry cured smoked meat retains little moisture except for the fat. Schwartz's steams the hell out of its smoked meat, resulting in buttery sandwiches that you could chew with your gums. By the time the knife hits the meat, it's ready to disintegrate. Cutting a Schwartz's smoked meat on a machine would be a disaster. You'd basically get a mess of shavings.

While the circular blade of a machine offers uniformity and convenience through measurements, gears, and electricity, hand-cutting is an intimate art, dictated by a man's intimate experience handling the flesh of another animal. It is imperfect, results in more waste, costs more, and takes a physical toll, but hand-cut sandwiches taste better. The two best pastrami sandwiches in America are at Langer's and Katz's for a reason.

"These guys are artists," Silva said, his hand resting on Johnny's back as he cut. "No matter how hard or how soft, they can cut it." Most of the time Johnny is the only cutter working the tiny counter. Silva claimed that Johnny could make a sandwich in five seconds. With fifteen sandwiches in an average brisket, that translates into one brisket every minute and fifteen seconds. During lunch one day, I closed my eyes and listened to the *ding* "Medium!" *ding ding* "Lean *et* Medium," as Johnny shouted orders and slapped his little bell on the counter. Montrealers can custom-order their sandwiches cut according to levels of fat. "Lean" slices have a thin layer of fat along the top, but are so dry they require tsunamis of mustard. "Lean" is

for prude Torontonians. The vast majority of Montreal's deli customers order "Medium." "Medium" looks very similar to "Lean," but
a closer look reveals that each grain of brisket fiber is held together
by strands of glistening translucent fat, retaining the unique texture
that blends dry and wet. The ultimate decadence, reserved for a
hearty few, are the "Medium/Fat" slices and finally the "Fat," which
is a spice-adorned sandwich of hot white lard. "Fat" is almost as
insane as "Lean"—an indulgence that flirts with the devil himself.
This is where the *speck* that killed "Poppa" Sam Sax came from—the
brisket's deckle, dusted in paprika and cayenne, re-smoked and
sliced cold. Sadly, *speck* is no longer available at Schwartz's.

Eating at Schwartz's is intense. Once customers pass the bottle-
neck at the door, an odor assaults them like tear gas. They squeeze
into chairs that seem tailored for runway models, crammed next to
complete strangers with whom they then share a meal. In a space
already filled with salt, pepper, mustard, ketchup, and steak sauces,
descends a stick of *karnatzel*, a bowl of sweet vinegar coleslaw, a
crisp whole sour pickle, a Cott's black cherry soda, and a bowl of
freshly cut french fries.

Finally the waiter deposits the *pièce de resistance*, a smoked meat
sandwich barely holding itself together, the fat strips of steaming
meat hanging over the edge of the bread that defies the urge to
collapse against all of Newton's laws. The meat is a wild mess of
carnivorous beauty: at parts black and sticky, at points a light rose,
mostly a meaty maroon. Weighing in at roughly five ounces, it's
at the smaller end of the deli sandwich scale, though you'll never
leave Schwartz's hungry. Half of the smoked meat sandwich is
drawn to the mouth, where a bouquet of whole peppercorns and
coriander seeds and faint hints of brown sugar rise up from the
meat, through the nose, and into the brain. This is a taste of
smoked meat in its purest, finest, and most famous form: a touch
spicy, a bit salty, always fatty, and foremost tender. The sandwich
disappears in eight bites, a glorious, debauched, greasy invocation
of pure animal savagery. Heaven.

Astonishingly, this handheld banquet is ridiculously cheap. A smoked meat sandwich costs less than five dollars, fries less than two dollars. For the price of a sandwich alone at most New York delis, two can eat like kings at Schwartz's. In a world where delicatessens are pricing themselves out of the market in order to survive, Schwartz's is serving what could be the best deli sandwich anywhere, and still giving the customer value.

How the hell do they do it?

Schwartz's current owner, Hy Diamond, implies that the deli's success has come from resisting modernization. A Jewish Montrealer in his sixties who was previously the deli's accountant, Diamond purchased Schwartz's in 1996. "There's only so much to do here," Diamond told me. "If I can keep customer satisfaction level, I've done my job." He prefers to call himself a curator rather than an owner, a title that underlines his commitment to preservation. Even so, Schwartz's business has increased in the time Diamond has owned it. Though he receives nearly daily offers to franchise and sell Schwartz's smoked meat across Canada, Diamond has refused them all.

"You can't commercialize this operation. . . . " he said. "If I did, it would dilute it. If you have the opportunity to be the owner of something unique, what do you do? You'll never get the same sandwich twice because it's natural meat here. It's the opposite of McDonald's. Every brisket is different, so every time you eat a sandwich it's different. And sometimes," he said, with the pronounced excitement of a winemaker discussing his cellared vintage, "you'll get one that just melts in your mouth." In the fall of 2008, Diamond buckled slightly and converted the property next door to Schwartz's as a takeout-only location. The original thankfully remains untouched.

There's a stubborn adherence to the old ways in Montreal, and this, more than anything, is the secret to its great Jewish delis.

The circumstances that created this environment are unique to Montreal's delicatessens, and exist for three key reasons.

1. *L'effet francophone:* The east end of Montreal is predominantly French, while the west side is mostly English. The de-facto dividing line remains boulevard St. Laurent, previously known as Main Boulevard, home to Schwartz's, the lesser known Main Deli, and Moishes Steak House. The Gallic passion for food is just as prevalent in French Montreal today as it is in Paris. While Anglo-Canadian cuisine reflects its bland British influence, Francophones are gaga over fat, salt, garlic, herbs, and strong flavor.

With the exception of a few delis in predominantly Jewish neighborhoods, every deli owner I spoke with confirmed that the majority of their clients were French Canadian. Frank Silva estimated that 80 per cent of Schwartz's clients were French. "Without their business," he said, "we wouldn't exist." Robert Beauchemin, a food critic for the French-language newspaper *La Presse*, identifies with smoked meat as much as, or more than, a Jewish Montrealer. In his opinion, there's a historic synergy in Montreal between French Canadians and Jews. "When delis [were] first opened at the start of the century by poor Jews, it was affordable food that served the people who worked in those neighborhoods and in the garment trade, namely French Canadians and Jews." Like Jews, French Canadians are family-oriented and religious, celebrate around food, and are prone to outward expressions of emotion. "Anglos," Beauchemin says, "have a plug in their ass."

In French neighborhoods of Montreal, you'll find places like Le Roi du Smoked Meat serving smoked meat sandwiches along with smoked meat pizza and smoked meat spaghetti. The largest smoked meat operation in Quebec is Nickels, a chain of retro diners founded by Quebecois musical diva Celine Dion. Yes, her. The very same waif who belted from the deck of the *Titanic* started a chain of smoked meat restaurants in 1990. Smoked meat can be found anywhere in Quebec. Even in remote rural towns where Jews are a rare and mistrusted presence, you can still get a decent smoked meat sandwich.

"It is not clear whether Francophones register that deli is something Jewish," said Morton Weinfeld, a professor of sociology at Montreal's McGill University, whose class inspired this book. "It's an adopted cultural item. They can be eating smoked meat and completely disassociate it with Jews. Jews are the crazy ones in black hats, *les maudits juifs*, and they'll say it while eating a smoked meat sandwich."

Removed largely from Jewish influence, smoked meat and deli food thrive in far corners of Montreal. One of these is an unlikely spot called Smoked Meat Pete, a combo deli, BBQ spot, and blues bar in the distant suburb of Île-Perrot. Its owner, Peter Varvaro Jr., grew up in the deli business, the son of Peter Varvaro Sr., who owns the famous Main Deli. When he opened Smoked Meat Pete in 1996, dozens of miles from any Jewish neighborhood, people thought he was destined for failure. Instead, he packs them in.

Smoked Meat Pete is a short, energetic guy, whose mischievous grin conveys his twisted sense of humor. This man coined the slogan "You Can't Beat Pete's Meat." Seriously. He jokes about the few Jewish clients he gets, but he sells more chopped liver than most Montreal delicatessens—a dark beefy scoop of sweet purée mixed with chunks of rich egg and smothered in crisp fried onions. For a second-generation Italian owner of a Jewish deli, his smoked meat is superb. Dry cured for ten days, and hardwood-smoked for eight hours, it has a dark red crust that can only be described as devilish and tastes both sweeter and spicier than its counterparts in the rest of the city. I had it in a whopping sandwich larger than most in Montreal, and on top of a plate of smoked meat poutine, a sinful Quebec dish of french fries covered in cheese curds and gravy.

2. The *Schmatte* Business: Instrumental to the birth of delicatessen cultures in both New York and Montreal was the presence of the *schmatte* (garment) industry. But while entertainment, finance, and real estate quickly took over in New York, Montreal's *schmatte* trade remained the economic engine of the community. The city's garment trade was North America's second largest, and Jews were at the helm of almost every major clothing company. It was the *schmatte* business that defined the character of the Montreal Jew. Like my grandfather "Poppa" Sam Sax, the garment dealer (*garmento*) remains a larger-than-life character. He peppers conversations with a slew of Yiddish insults like *putz, prick,* and *shmuck.* The garmento deals strictly in cash, and never, ever, pays retail. Though he may be the second- or third-generation Montrealer, he keeps at least a few toes planted in the soil of the *shtetl*. It's all about Chutzpah with a capital C.

Even though the garment industry had declined, Montreal's delis remain tied to this culture. Delis were, and remain, the communal watering holes for garmentos. Nowhere can you see this more clearly than at Lester's Deli, in the Outremont neighborhood. Lester's has been around since 1951, though the Berenholc family has owned it since Eddie Berenholc, a cutter at Schwartz's, bought it in 1956. Eddie's son Billy Berenholc is the definition of a Montreal Jew. Tall, tan, and a good decade older than he looks, Billy talks with that classic Montreal Jewish inflection, drawing out his A's (*maaan*), addressing everyone by their last name, and abbreviating phrases, so that a "smoked meat sandwich with fries" becomes "a smoked meat and fry." As we sat outside the *shvitz* at the Jewish community center, Billy told me how he keeps Lester's going.

"We've boutiquized ourselves," Billy said. "When you sell a smoked meat sandwich, fries, coleslaw, and a drink, you're a boutique." Berenholc realized that his customers, many of whom were old-school garmentos, came to him for a specialty item. Lester's is too far from downtown to be a tourist destination like Schwartz's.

Billy's business is local, but with the decline in the schmatte economy, he has been forced to find customers elsewhere, so he's concentrated on the thing he does best. Billy has targeted the large community of Montrealers living in other cities, who simply have a craving for Lester's, but he's kept the taste traditional, because that's what they demand. Lester's is now shipping meat around the country. "My goal is to become the biggest Internet delicatessen in North America," Billy told me, "because if I wasn't doing my wholesale business, the store wouldn't be enough."

3. The Great Exodus: The departure of thirty thousand Jews from Montreal in the past three and a half decades (a departure that continues today) hollowed out the community to a shell of its former self. What was once a bustling population of 115,000, now hovers just over 80,000, half that of Toronto (a complete reversal). Like my own family, those who left were the young, successful, and mobile, while those who remained were mostly the elderly. It was only the adoption of smoked meat by French Canadians, largely in the late 1960s and 1970s, that saved Montreal's delis from total decline. For the entirety of the 1980s and much of the 1990s, Montreal endured a bitter recession. Two referenda on Quebec's separation, in 1980 and 1995, failed by the slimmest of margins, perpetuating economic instability and low property values. While economic conditions have recently improved, the hardship managed to kill Ben's, Montreal's biggest and oldest delicatessen.

Ben Kravitz, the man who certainly made smoked meat famous, worked tirelessly to build his deli business into an institution that rivaled the best in New York. Occupying a prime corner of downtown real estate, the ornately trimmed art deco cafeteria held hundreds of tables, filled around the clock. At its peak in the 1960s, Ben's served up to eight thousand customers a day and employed a hundred staff, churning out smoked meat sandwiches and other Jewish specialties. To many in Montreal it was an office, a temple, and a second home, and was fittingly where my parents' first date took place.

When Ben Kravitz died in 1956, the deli was taken over by his three sons, Irving, Al, and Sollie. They expanded the menu further and established a wholesale business, resisting the offers to franchise. But come the 1980s, the business began feeling the effects of the city's economic downturn. Most of the national banks and corporations had moved their headquarters to Toronto, sucking away a large part of the downtown lunch crowd. In 1992, Irving Kravitz died. Ownership shifted to his wife, Jean Kravitz, and her son Dr. Elliot Kravitz. According to former employees, including Brian Kravitz and Murray Kravitz (both nephews of Jean Kravitz), Mrs. Kravitz and her son (who lived in Toronto) let the deli fall into disrepair while raising prices. "They were only interested in squeezing blood from a stone," Brian Kravitz told me, resentment filling his voice.

Little by little, the grand deli was cannibalized. Fresh ingredients were switched for cheap substitutes. The paint began peeling. Bathrooms were filthy. There was no soap in the dishwasher. "Every time you wanted to cut a tomato you had to ask Jean Kravitz's permission," said Brian Kravitz. Toasters were broken. Replacing toilet paper in the bathroom required a written request. By the time I was living in Montreal in 1998, Ben's was an atrocity. The cavernous room was empty. The few waiters would grudgingly amble over, responding to requests with "We're out of that." The food was always a disappointment. Portion sizes shrank. The Kravitz family had even refused to fix the heaters and air conditioning, so Ben's was either hot as hell or freezing cold.

To counter this, Ben's employees did what so many in socialist Quebec do . . . they joined a union and in July 2006 went on strike. Their demands included an average raise of forty cents an hour, severance pay, and an improvement in working conditions. The strike went on into December, when Elliot Kravitz finally announced that Ben's would close for good. Obituaries and articles filled Canada's news media about the death of the country's oldest deli, just shy of its century anniversary.

I last saw Ben's in June 2007, just over a year before the structure was demolished and reportedly replaced with a hotel. Chairs and tables were pushed to the back wall. Looking in, I realized this was the first deli I had seen in the purgatory phase between death and destruction. It was sad, but in a perverse way somewhat beautiful. This was the raw death of a deli, and it filled me with a renewed sense of purpose.

Ironically, for many of the best delis in Montreal, low property values have eliminated the principal factor that has caused the death of the deli elsewhere . . . rent. Montreal's delis can afford to operate more cheaply than their counterparts in other North American cities. To see this in action, one has to look no further than Wilensky's.

Many have characterized Wilensky's interior as a museum, but I find shrine more suitable. Everything is perfect: the lime green paint on the wood-paneled walls, the strung-up letters W-I-L-E-N-S-K-Y hanging in the window like a smile, the nine wooden stools anchored in front of the Formica-topped counter, and the hand-painted mustard jar with a smiley face in the top right-hand corner that says "We Always Put Mustard On It."

The options at Wilensky's are limited to one: the Wilensky Special. It is a sandwich of such fine-tuned simplicity that the Wilensky family has distilled what was once a candy store, barber shop, and full-fledged delicatessen into a brief, intense ritual. When you first walk into Wilensky's, you lower your voice and sit at the counter. Asher Wilensky, his sister Sharon, or perhaps their elderly mother, Ruth Wilensky, wife of the late Moe Wilensky, who founded the shop in 1932, will ask "How many?" With the ease of seven and a half decades of repetitive motion, they will tilt back the lid of an electric sandwich press on the left, where the guts of the Special have been slowly warming. Invented by Moe during the height of the Depression, the Special is a pressed sandwich consisting of six slices of three different types of grilled beef salami topped by half a slice of baloney. Other delis have tried to duplicate it. Jewish caterers all over Canada have tried. My family has tried. Nothing comes close.

Mrs. Wilensky will take the warm meat, place it on the bottom of a specially baked, cornmeal-dusted *pletzl* bun spread with mustard, and transfer it to the other sandwich press. No mustard used to cost a nickel extra, but now they simply refuse. After a few minutes, the top is added and pressed down. The bread acquires a toasty crunch and is placed in front of you wrapped in a thin napkin. At this point you pay for the Special, regardless of whether you will have another. At $3.50 a pop, it may be the cheapest sandwich you've ever eaten, but it is also one of the most memorable. Biting past the scalding crust you reach a salty, greasy, and somewhat sweet multi-layered stack of Jewish sausage, all blending into one soft bite so hot you often burn your tongue.

A Wilensky Special takes less than two minutes to eat and leaves you with a powerful thirst, which is when Scott, the soda guy, will take an old-fashioned soda glass from the shelf and ladle in your choice of homemade syrup—orange, cherry, pineapple, chocolate, cola, strawberry, or cream soda—pull the lever, and stir until the bubbles rise just above the rim. To those whose tongues are accustomed to the over-carbonated, high-fructose-corn-syrup wallop of commercial soda, the Wilensky's hand-jerked concoction is pure ambrosia. Wilensky's isn't for lingering. It's an in-and-out type of place. You might spend a few seconds looking at the memorabilia lining the walls, including the framed obituary to Bernard Wilensky, who worked with his family until he tragically passed away in 2000. You notice this all in passing, for as quickly as you came in, you are out the door and into the street, awash with nitrates and nostalgia.

The Wilenskys own their building so rent is not a factor. But still, at $3.50 a Special, with perhaps $1.10 for a soda, and maybe $0.50 for a small nub of *karnatzel*, the average customer spends roughly $5.

For a restaurant that is open only during lunch hours and closed on the weekends, that meager sum is supporting five people, plus their families, all of whom live quite well. In any other city that would be impossible. "Ironically," said Sharon Wilensky, "the separatists have helped keep our business open since we can argue that they have kept the economy slow here. *Pure laine* [the racist philosophy of hard-core separatists] and pure baloney is an interesting mix."

The Wilensky family has gone the opposite route of delis in other cities. They used to sell eggs, salmon sandwiches, smoked meat, and salads. They dropped them all to focus on the Special. "Our philosophy has been the same," Sharon told me, out of earshot of her mother, "since my father's death we've almost clung to it . . . so there's more of a sense of nostalgia for when *they* come back, and we've kept things very special. We don't change it out of loyalty to *them*."

Them. The exiles. The ones, like my parents, who sit in their houses in Toronto, cheering for the Montreal Canadiens, listening to Leonard Cohen and reading Mordecai Richler novels. Returning to their favorite deli in Montreal is the best way for Montreal's exiles to reconnect to their past. "I know Jews who are originally from Montreal who come off the plane and take a taxi directly from the airport to Schwartz's," says sociologist Morton Weinfeld. "Nostalgia is more powerful in Montreal. Their identity is not toward the province of Quebec, or even the city of Montreal, but to Jewish Montreal." Everything else may have changed—their old neighborhood may be Lebanese and the street they grew up on has been renamed after a French saint—but the sanctity of their smoked meat sandwich remains thankfully intact. When Montrealer William Shatner sold his kidney stone on eBay for charity, a clause in the deal stated that the winner had to cater the *Boston Legal* set with smoked meat and bagels from Montreal.

"It's a prerequisite that every expat in Toronto gets their smoked meat and bagels," Abie Haim told me, as we sat at Abie's Delicatessen in the suburb of Dollard-des-Ormeaux, eating his fantastic house-cured smoked meat and grilled Romanian *meditei*: a homemade beef and garlic sausage. "It doesn't fail that every single weekend I have people calling in orders for vacuum-packed briskets for Toronto," said Haim. "I don't have one single friend I grew up with who lives in Montreal. All of them live in Toronto. In a way it's made those who stayed a tight-knit community. Maybe because our numbers are shrinking, it's why we keep our traditions together."

For each Montreal Jew who departs, the remaining community has grown closer. In the pockets where it remains, Jewish identity thrives in Montreal, but the saddest part about Montreal's deli culture is how little of it is directly connected to the Jewish community. Schwartz's, Wilensky's, and Lester's are all run by Jews but patronized by gentiles. The lone exception in Montreal is the Snowdon Deli.

The genesis of this book first came to me in 2001, when I was interviewing Ian Morantz for a term paper on delicatessen sociology. It astonished me how pessimistic the co-owner of Snowdon Deli was for the future of his business. Jews had left the city, the economy was stagnant, and his customers were dying off. Those questions led me back to his deli six years later. Opened in 1946 by Polish immigrants Abe and Joe Morantz, Snowdon Deli is now in the hands of Joe's son Ian, who co-owns it with John Agelopoulos, Snowdon's longtime Greek counterman. The Agelopoulos family is as much the soul of Snowdon Deli as the Morantz clan. In fact, Abe Morantz's daughter Cheryl co-owns and operates Toronto's Centre Street Deli with John's brother Sam.

No other Montreal deli carries the full range of traditional Jewish dishes that Snowdon does. In a city of delis serving only smoked meat, *karnatzel*, and rib steaks, Snowdon's stands out for its variety. They serve homemade *knishes*, *kasha varnishkes*, *kugels*, *kishke*, *latkes*, *kreplach*, and the cheese *bagelach*—a round, flat, cheese-filled sweet pastry. They bake bite-sized cocktail danish, sugar-dusted *rugelach*, almond *mandelbrot* (Jewish biscotti), and Snowdon's wafer-thin poppy seed *mohn* cookies, my mom's favorite.

Ian Morantz joined me at a booth and opened his shirt to reveal a zipper scar down his slender chest. "You didn't know that I nearly died?" he said, chuckling as he did the buttons back up. Gone was the morose pessimism that characterized our previous conversation. His young daughter Tobi was working with him now and doing a great job, as was John's daughter. "It hasn't gotten worse," Morantz told me of the business, which he'd previously predicted would end as his regular clients died out. "We're not coasting along here. But it seems to be more or less on a status quo." The deli had recently been featured prominently in *La Presse*, which wrote that Snowdon Deli was *"un classique aussi bon que chez Schwartz."* That article sent French Canadians well into the heart of Jewish Montreal for a taste of the goods. *Gourmet* magazine had also lionized Snowdon, and newspapers covered the deli's sixtieth anniversary.

Bearing the label of institution meant resisting regular offers to modernize for the sake of supposed productivity gains. "[Hand-cutting's] not the most efficient," Morantz told me, as we watched Johnny build a smoked meat sandwich. "In the USA nobody does it because in America money drives everything. There, you want to make it as profitable as possible, often to the exclusion of quality and tradition. It's formulaic, the exact opposite of how food should be." It dawned on me that the simple reason Montreal's delis tasted so incredibly good came down to this very central, very French ideal: food should first and foremost be about taste. Profit was important in order to survive, but those who ran delis like public companies couldn't taste their dividends.

"When you turn it into a formula it becomes cold, there's no human side to it and the human side is critical to the success of our business. It's where we excel. You have to give up something at one point. When the customer is on the phone and wants to talk about their kids, you don't let them go. It may cost you money to talk to them but *they are important.*" It was the way Montreal had been doing things all along, and the principal reason that the city exuded a certain character that Toronto openly envied. "Toronto is very much American," Morantz said. "The city itself is a financially driven place. But there's no *tam*, no culture. They make their money and buy the culture later."

As a native Torontonian, his words stung me, but they were true. I thanked Ian and picked up several boxes of *mohn* cookies for Mom. I drove to Schwartz's and grabbed a brisket, a smoked duck, and a pound of *karnatzel*, headed up to St.-Viateur Bagel and bought four dozen bagels for Dad. I drove to the Baron de Hirsch cemetery, tore a nub of *karnatzel* off, and went to find my grandfather's grave. Standing above Samuel Sax's plot I thanked the man who had given me this love of deli. I placed the *karnatzel* on top of his headstone and headed home.

Toronto: Home Bittersweet Home

When I was growing up, my family would visit Yitz's Delicatessen on Eglinton each Friday, where I'd take particular joy in pulling back the door handle, which was made to resemble a curved salami. We'd be greeted by Mrs. Bernice Penciner, wife of Yitz Penciner, though we just called them Mr. and Mrs. Yitz. Mrs. Yitz would beam a flashy smile when we walked in, her long skirts and high hairdo lending her a grandmotherly air. Dressed in slacks and a button-up shirt, Mr. Yitz cut a striking figure, with a thick head of precisely combed silver hair and a big set of spectacles perched on a formidable nose.

Yitz's menu was shaped like a sandwich, and on the back page Mr. Yitz's face winked at you. Without fail, we always started with *matzo* ball soup, dipping hard, sesame-covered breadsticks in the dark, salty broth with an ultra dense, almost meaty, *matzo* ball. Daniel and I would drink mugs of bright pink cream soda. Then we'd order our favorites; Dad a hot pastrami sandwich, Mom either a hot tongue sandwich or broiled liver, Daniel a salami sandwich, and me either corned beef or salami.

On our way out, Mom would stop at the counter and get provisions for the week: a salami and sliced meats for our school lunches (I probably ate deli every day from Grade 1 to 12), a loaf of sliced *challah* and one of rye, a tub of coleslaw, and if we were lucky, a box of sticky buns or crackling chocolate Florentine cookies. Finally we'd head to the register, where Mr. Yitz would say, "See you next week, Saxes." Yitz's Delicatessen was our home away from home, a Friday night tradition that, along with the Sunday night stalwart Real Peking, completed the culinary landscape of my childhood.

Despite warm memories, Toronto is the city where I worry most about the Jewish delicatessen's fate. It was where I first experienced the pain of delicatessens closing and the realization that delis could stray from the flock. Toronto was where I first heard about cholesterol and fat, where the words "Ewww, no way I'm eating deli, it's fatty and guh-ross" emerged from the lips of my friends. Toronto is where I first met Jews who had never once eaten at a deli. Toronto is where I saw delis shun corned beef sandwiches for avocado wraps, and where I first witnessed children begging their parents to please bring sushi to them on visitor's day at Camp Walden, instead of the deli we waited for in my day. Toronto is my hometown, and I love it dearly, but its deli legacy is bittersweet.

The history of Toronto's Jewish community can be traced up two streets, first Spadina Avenue and later Bathurst Street. Jewish immigrants mostly settled into an area known as Kensington Market, a tightly packed enclave downtown wedged between Spadina and Bathurst, where some sixty thousand lived, worked, and prayed. According to Ethel Rochwerg, her father's deli, Peter Wellts Delicatessen, was the city's first, opening after her family came up from New York in 1911. Smaller delis dominated Toronto's scene until 1922, when the Polish Shopsowitz family opened Shopsowitz Delicatessen, growing it into Toronto's landmark deli, Shopsy's.

It wasn't until the postwar years that Toronto's delicatessen business really boomed. With tens of thousands of Polish Holocaust survivors settling in Toronto, more than a few went into the deli business. In the decade that followed, Smith's Delicatessen, Becker's, Litman's, Shapiro's, Goldenberg's, and the Tel Aviv Deli all opened in the streets near Kensington Market. But by the mid-1950s new suburbs had sprung up along the northern reaches of Bathurst Street, and most Jews hightailed it uptown to bungalows in North York. Portuguese, Caribbean, and East Asian immigrants moved into Kensington Market, replacing kosher butchers with fish shops and Chinese restaurants. Many delis located downtown were fortunate enough to sell their properties for hefty profits. But for each new deli that opened up in neighborhoods such as Forest Hill or Bathurst Manor, there were perhaps two or three others that disappeared forever. Today, roughly half a dozen Jewish delicatessens exist in Toronto, down from several dozen a few decades ago.

Most of Toronto's Jews, who number roughly 175,000, live within walking distance of Bathurst, largely in its northern reaches. By the late 1980s, the common joke ran that when the fledgling Minsker synagogue in Kensington Market needed ten Jewish men to hold a service, they'd send a representative into Switzer's Deli. Shopsy's, which had been the anchor of the local deli scene, departed Spadina in 1983 for a downtown office building. Switzer's, the last Spadina deli, left in 1992. The only remnant of downtown's deli legacy is Silverstein's Bakery, maker of Toronto's stellar crusty rye breads. One day, when a developer offers enough, it too will likely leave downtown.

Many of these delis closed or moved just as Toronto received a population surge of deli fanatics from Montreal. When my parents first arrived in 1976, my father took my mother to a different deli every night. "After that week, I realized there was deli in Toronto and it wasn't as good as Montreal," Dad recalled. "I had trouble getting my mouth around a desire for corned beef or pastrami in lieu of smoked meat, and the biggest disappointment was that it wasn't hand-cut. Even if you asked them to cut it by hand, it never tasted the same because the meat wasn't cooked as tender." Toronto was a corned beef town—a less aggressive meat that matched Toronto's WASPY taste buds.

Suffice it to say, Dad did manage to put away his fair share of deli, machine-sliced and all, at long-gone downtown establishments like Mr. I's (owned by Izzy Shopsowitz, of Shopsy's) and Barney's. Though my parents settled upon Yitz's as their local deli of choice, most Montrealers felt lost without their smoked meat, and many hopeful deli owners attempted to bring Montreal smoked meat to Toronto over the years. Dunn's, a classic Montreal deli, has made several attempts in Toronto without much success. The smoked meat I recently ate there was terrible: tough and under-steamed, highly pumped, cut *along* the grain, and rubbery to the point of inedible. Same went with Mel's Montreal Delicatessen, which was actually the closest deli (in name alone) to my old apartment. To call their *matzo* ball soup "watery" would imply that it had some flavor other than water. Their smoked meat could have been carved by a chainsaw. Yet many Torontonians call it a "great deli" for some reason. A downtown deli called Reuben S's was the most recent hope, but it lasted all of two years. Since Montreal's Jewish exodus began, only one successful transplant has won over Toronto's smoked meat faithful.

Cheryl Morantz had no designs for the deli business when she moved from Montreal in the late 1980s, but she soon realized how well her family's Snowdon Deli could tap into the community of ex-Montrealers here. Her father was less enthusiastic. Cheryl knew nothing of the business, so Joe Morantz proposed a solution: he'd send his head counterman, Sam Agelopoulos, to help her. It was a chance for Joe to reward Sam with a real piece of the business, while ensuring Cheryl wouldn't get in over her head.

Centre Street Deli is now the most successful delicatessen in Toronto. Though Cheryl and Sam opened in a strip mall surrounded by empty fields on the northern fringes of the suburb Thornhill, the area is now the heart of suburban Jewish Toronto. On Saturdays, the lineup can snake into the kitchen. The place is big, bright, and sparkling clean, and the food is always on the mark. Their *kishke* dissolves away into soft bites of melting beefy mash, though the real draw is their hand-cut smoked meat.

Centre Street Deli uses the same meats from Lester's (a Montreal purveyor not related to the deli Lester's) that Snowdon Deli and most other Toronto delis use. They use the same Silverstein's rye as other delis and the same French's mustard. The secret rests in the touch of Sam Agelopoulos, whose nimble hands can carve a brisket as though he were Rodin chipping at marble. At least 80 per cent of Centre Street's clients were Montrealers in the beginning, and while the percentage has shifted, I still feel as though I'm at my parents' high school reunion. Some ex-Montrealers, like my friend Bryan Icyk's father, Henry, eat there every single day (he's also their accountant).

But it's the next fifty years that scare Cheryl and Sam more than anything else. Toronto is a city where pressure to shift away from the core of a Jewish deli is intense. "With all the demands that customers make," Cheryl said, "in general, you're [talking about] a food group that really is on its way out. . . . We used to make delicious herring, not just herring but *schmaltz* herring, I *love* herring, a fresh piece on rye bread, but nobody's eating it. Now if we're catering a funeral, they'll ask for herring, and say, 'My grandfather loved herring. Do you have any?' And we say, 'Your grandfather, rest in peace, was the last one to eat herring.' We don't even bother serving it anymore. So to answer your question about the future, in fifty years it's bye-bye," Cheryl announced.

"Especially doing something handmade. Slicing meat by hand," added Sam.

"It's bye-bye because it's a demanding business overall," Cheryl said, listing off reasons. "Bye-bye because eating habits have changed. Bye-bye because people's expectations have not. It's too bad, it's just not profitable."

Cheryl then said something to me that I'd heard repeated by Montrealers countless times: Torontonians didn't know deli. It wasn't an insult or a matter of civic pride, but a statement of fact. While smoked meat sandwiches are still very much a part of Montreal's Jewish culture, the same can't be said of corned beef in Toronto. Few, if any, of my friends eat deli. They'll indulge when visiting Montreal or New York, but I'm hard pressed to find any of them at Yitz's or Moe Pancer's. "Oh, you're writing a book on deli?" they'll ask. "Are there even any delis in Toronto?"

It breaks my heart that Toronto is a deli town with the potential for greatness, but with very little pride in its Jewish delicatessens. You'll almost never find Torontonians abroad bragging about their delis the way New Yorkers do. And while there is no marquee institution like Schwartz's or Langer's, I regularly taste greatness in my hometown. I would put some of Toronto's corned beef up there with the best on the continent. Yitz's corned beef, which is barrel cured in the deli's basement, is some of the most consistent, moist, and delicious corned beef anywhere. It is pink, ribbed with fat, and incredibly tender. One of the best corned beefs I've had anywhere was from the small Steeles Deli, run by Leslie Wong and his son Michael. Their briskets cure in a brine that is low in salt and contains such secret ingredients as brown sugar. The resulting corned beef, sliced translucently thin, is a wonder of gentle flavor, a sweetly tinged sandwich of candied, garlic-scented beef that liquefies the second you bite into it.

Toronto also boasts some of the finest hot pickled tongue anywhere. One of the best was from Coleman's, a deli run by Carol Silverberg and her daughter Jodi. Tongues are pickled in a solution similar to corned beef and then boiled until tender. During one of my visits there, Carol led me to the basement kitchen, where Coleman's cook, Joe, pulled a freshly cooked tongue still steaming from the pot, took a knife, and sliced a cookie-sized hunk off the fatty rear end of a tongue (the tip is leaner and, therefore, tougher). When I bit down, it just squished into salty velvet.

Toronto also serves a unique item, not found anywhere else in the deli world, called baby beef. In the 1940s, a Polish immigrant named Harry Eisen began dying veal briskets with red food coloring, passing them off as corned beef. Eventually the dye was banned, but Eisen renamed the product baby beef. Until recently, baby beef was a lightly brined brisket of milk-fed veal. When done properly, it is an unbelievably moist and supple product, a light appearance similar to corned beef with a creamy color and flavor. It is the most refined Jewish deli meat out there, a conduit for salt and garlic. I see it as the ultimate Toronto deli contribution: inventive, subtle, understated, yet undeniably delicious. Unfortunately, a lucrative export market in veal cattle has baby beef facing extinction in Toronto's delis. Though it is regionally as unique as Montreal smoked meat, Toronto's baby beef may likely be a historical footnote by the time you finish this book.

Toronto also makes its pastrami different from anywhere else. Delis take a fully cured corned beef brisket, rub it with pastrami spicing, and bake it briefly with water, effectively braising it. Though I absolutely love New York–style navel pastrami, the unique method of preparing Toronto's pastrami creates a product that occupies a wonderful place on the spectrum of spiced, cured Jewish meats. Juicy and flaky like the brisket-derived corned beef, it nonetheless hits with the spicing of pastrami. The spices in Toronto pastrami tickle the taste buds without overwhelming them.

But despite this rich selection of delicatessen products, among my contemporaries deli simply isn't eaten, and the primary reason for this is supposedly health. Deli, Torontonians are told, is bad for you. Actually, as I was lectured time and again, it will surely kill me. So far as my friends are concerned, this book might as well be the story of a kosher-style *Supersize Me*. Perhaps in the long run they will be right. If my arteries succumb to the fat and the salt, I owe them all a posthumous apology. But the effect this fearful mentality has had on the deli business in Toronto reflects that of cities all over the continent. Toronto's Jews are avoiding deli like the plague.

When you walk into Wolfie's, a small deli in North York covered in Coca-Cola memorabilia, a faded, grease-stained sign declares, "Our Meat is Always Lean. If You Want Fat you Have to Ask For It." It wasn't always this way. When he opened in 1975, Dave Gelberman served juicy briskets and pastramis. Back then, 90 per cent of his customers were Jewish. Today, the proportions are completely opposite; gentiles make up 90 per cent of Wolfie's clientele, with elderly Jews hanging in the minority.

"I must be the only shmuck in the deli business who just keeps trimming his meat until there's nothing left," Gelberman said. "I used to carry tongue, baby beef, and chopped liver that my mother-in-law made forty pounds of every single Friday. We used to have a lineup out the door for that stuff . . . it was gold." Wolfie's is now doing two-thirds the business it did a number of years ago, and the deli has cut back on its hours. To Gelberman, young Jewish Torontonians hardly factor into his business at all. "They come in as often as they go to shul!" he said. Which, believe me, is not often.

The supposedly healthy appetites of my contemporaries have migrated elsewhere. Their Jewish food experience is now based on whole wheat bagels and tofu cream cheese. Israeli food has replaced deli, ostensibly because hummus and salads are indeed lower in saturated fat, salt, and preservatives. Moreover, while deli is the food of nostalgia, Israeli cuisine is the food of pride. Young Jews today know the past of Jewish Europe mainly from the Holocaust. But when they eat falafel, they are engaging in a solidarity of sorts with their brethren in the Middle East. They are indulging not in the memory of a lost time and place, but of a proud, courageous, sexy nation. A generation ago, ethnic foods were the occasional treat for Toronto's Jewish stomachs. Today, it is a safe bet that on most nights of the week the food of Tuscany will feed far more of the Jewish households of Toronto than that of nineteenth-century Polish Galicia. At Jewish weddings and bar mitzvahs you'll find more sushi than salami.

At delis around the city, the client base has become decreasingly Jewish, something that more than a few places consider a positive development for business, though not always taste. Take the case of Shopsy's, once considered the top delicatessen in Toronto. In 1971, Sam Shopsowitz sold the family business to Lever Brothers, the Canadian arm of the Unilever soap conglomerate. Many in Toronto mark that very moment—when our most beloved, family-owned Jewish deli passed into the hands of a publicly traded corporation—as the beginning of the end. Over the years, ownership of Shopsy's has passed from Unilever to the burger chain A&W, to private equity buyers, and mutual funds. It is currently owned by a family of local Irish pub magnates.

Successive owners have removed many of the Jewish items from the menu, replacing them with diner fare and baby back ribs. Shopsy's brand corned beef, bologna, and even Shopsy's bacon sell in Canadian supermarkets. The company has opened several locations, attempted to franchise, and failed repeatedly. With each change of hands, the food's quality has declined, as new owners have attempted to squeeze more profit out of a fading brand name. No one who seriously appreciates Jewish deli even acknowledges the existence of Shopsy's. It is the fallen one, guilty of selling out so blatantly that calling it a Jewish deli is an insult to those who keep the tradition alive.

Other delis in Toronto have tried to emulate the path of Shopsy's expansion in one way or another, with varying success. Over the years, their rival Switzer's opened a dozen different stores, eventually selling them off one by one. Today, what remains of Spadina's last deli is found on an industrial road just north of Toronto's airport. Hy Beck, Switzer's owner for over half a century, is still slicing meat, along with his daughter and co-owner Charise. "Expansion is a bad thing," Charise Beck told me, handing me slices of their garlicky beef salami. "Your ass can't be in two places at once."

Several have learned this the hard way. Dave Gelberman attempted to open a second, more lavish Wolfie's in the past and failed. In 2000, Mr. Yitz sold his business to Barry Silver, a local businessman who had grown up in the appetizing business. Though the food at Yitz's always remained good, Silver had grand designs. In 2006, after much planning, Silver opened a second Yitz's in the suburban development of Thornhill Woods. It lasted a year. According to those who briefly worked there, it was staffed with inexperienced employees. "Owner-operated is the secret of original delis," Mr. Yitz told me. "It's hard to franchise because delis are only successful when the owner is there."

When I talk about saving the deli, it is based on the worry that these trends toward expansion and franchising, fat phobia, and diluting deli menus are going to eventually corrupt all of Toronto's remaining delicatessens to the point where they are unrecognizable. I say this because there are many in the city that look to one former deli named the Pickle Barrel, see its financial clout, and salivate.

When it first opened back in 1971, the Pickle Barrel raised the bar on Toronto's deli trade. Created by wealthy developers and headed by an experienced Deli Man (Jerry Wiseblatt) and restaurateur (Sam Firestone), it brought big, Michigan-style suburban deli to Toronto. Throughout the 1970s and 1980s, the Pickle Barrel was the place to be seen on a Sunday night. Half the menu was strictly Jewish, and two-thirds of sales came from delicatessen sandwiches. But the Pickle Barrel changed around 1990, when one of the financial backers told Wiseblatt that he wanted to move away from deli because customers were becoming more interested in healthier food. Wiseblatt soon left, opening the small New Yorker Deli downtown with his wife, where he still serves classic deli fare.

Into his position stepped Peter Higley, a former busboy at the original Pickle Barrel, who worked his way up to the president's office. Well-dressed, fast-talking, and forward-thinking, he makes no bones about where the chain has gone and what it left behind. A few years back, Pickle Barrel dropped the word "Delicatessen" from all restaurants and menus. The smiling pickle mascot in a top hat also disappeared. One of the business models Higley has actually emulated is Jerry's Famous Deli. "I like what Jerry's have done," Higley told me. "They've sexed up deli, made it nice."

The newly refurbished Pickle Barrels now have more in common decor-wise with luxury condominiums. Halogen lights and plasma screens abound. My friend Tracy's father has stopped eating there completely, because he finds the decor to be "pretentious," a family restaurant masquerading as fine dining. But the real shock always hits me when I pick up the thirty-plus–page menu and play *Where Has the Deli Gone?* With over three hundred dishes to choose from, you can now find only six deli items: cabbage borscht, *matzo* ball soup, pastrami, corned beef, smoked meat, and brisket. *Kishke?* Gone. *Kreplach?* Kaput. The new Pickle Barrel is all about multi-ethnic and low fat, and sorry folks, deli is not considered ethnic and is by no means healthy enough for their customers. You can, however, order Spanish paella, P.E.I. mussels, Asian nachos, or Alaskan king crab legs. There's also a five-hundred-calorie, nutritionist-approved menu.

As far as large chain restaurants go, the food at the Pickle Barrel isn't bad. But every time I end up there, I always wonder whether some Thai restaurant somewhere is serving Reuben sandwiches, or an Italian place has a chopped liver pizza. I doubt it. Jewish delicatessens might be the only ethnic restaurants where the very cuisine the business is based upon has been actively phased out by the owners. It is one of the clearest examples of a self-imposed culinary assimilation, and here's the thing . . . no one complains. In fact, many Jews in Toronto continue to view the Pickle Barrel as a deli.

Higley directed me to the company's Web site, where complete nutritional information for every menu item was listed. But what I found didn't necessarily justify the elimination of deli on the grounds of health. Cabbage borscht was only 80 calories, while a quarter-pound corned beef sandwich clocked in at 280 calories (34 per cent fat). Compared to the 920-calorie tuna sandwich it was a goddamned supermodel! Hell, you could combine a corned beef/pastrami sandwich, and still make it onto the 500-calorie menu.

It didn't make sense. This wasn't about lowering the calorie or fat count of menu items, it was about selling the idea that you were eating something better for you. "Rewind thirty years ago," Higley said. "You ate what you ate and enjoyed it. Today, everything you eat, you're second-guessing yourself. Health statistics and stories on the effects of nutrition are in the media all the time, and the Jewish people are very perceptive of this." It was the same logic that had people getting fat out of McDonald's salads, and it worked like a charm. If things progressed any further, a whole new generation would grow up thinking that Tex Mex Spring Rolls belonged in a Jewish deli.

Was this where the future of Toronto's delicatessen business was heading? Toward menus that read like novels, smartly dressed servers fresh out of high school, and watered-down quasi-Jewish food? Every time I went to the Pickle Barrel on the insistence of others, I came out flustered. Weighted down by a sense of dread, I'd invariably head up Bathurst, where I'd arrive at Moe Pancer's distraught and hungry.

"Heyyyyy *Duvid*," Lorne Pancer would say, beaming each time I came in, "welcome back, bud!"

I came to Moe Pancer's late in life, via my brother Daniel, but Lorne had been instrumental in helping me understand deli from the get-go. He was the first to teach me about the deli business. His veteran counterman, Wilf, taught me how to cut meat months before I went to Katz's. Whenever I craved that deli atmosphere—the intoxicating smell of steaming garlic and the tumult of crashing dishes—I'd head to Moe Pancer's, kibitz with Lori, the wisecracking waitress, and feast on Lorne's tender corned beef. Mostly, I'd sit down with Lorne and talk deli. The conversation would always start off the same: Lorne will tell me about the latest flack he took from a longtime customer—"Can you believe this?" he'd say, in his sweet sportscaster's voice. "I wanted to charge him for bread with his takeout meats, so he told me to fuck off." Then he'd unleash a wry smile from beneath the gray mustache, roll his eyes as though he were Bugs Bunny, grin out of the right side of his mouth, and sigh, adding, "What can I tell ya,' bud?"

Moe Pancer's was opened in 1957 by Lorne's father, Stan (son of Moe). As a Deli Man Stan Pancer was a staunch minimalist. "I am a deli," he was once quoted as saying, "not an 'and Restaurant.' I am seven meats!" Corned beef, tongue, pastrami, brisket, baby beef, turkey, salami. These were the Pancer's canon. When Stan died in 1999, Lorne stepped in, leaving his previous job as a stock trader. "To the Pancers, it's a life sentence, baby," Lorne joked. Looking at the photos of Stan, the resemblance between Lorne and his father is uncanny: the same high, gray hairline, the same broad shoulders and smile.

Places like the Pickle Barrel influenced the demands of Pancer's customers. They want more, for less, and they expect Lorne to conform. But while change may work for others, it's the first step down a long and dangerous path that could end by tacking the words "and Restaurant" onto Pancer's sign. "If you want to fill to the masses, you have to feed the masses," Lorne said. "I'm not going to water this place down for anything in the world. There's tradition and there's money. The questions I have to ask are how comfortable am I, and how comfortable do I need to be? We're just trying to stick with what has made our lives. Yeah, it's hard to stay loyal to a small client base and a small range of products, but it's the honorable thing, *Duvid*. What would my zaidy have said? It's not broken, and who am I to fix it? I'm a humble person taking on the traditions of two generations before me."

Which is why I was so crushed, when, two years after writing down those words, Lorne told me in fall 2008 that he and his siblings were selling Moe Pancer's Delicatessen. Each day he commuted nearly an hour to the deli, and he wanted more time with his family. Soon after, Coleman's Deli closed up suddenly. For me, it was the ultimate blow for my hopes to save the deli in Toronto. Short of a savior, I feared that deli in my hometown was indeed doomed.

YOUR
NUMBER

16

WHEN CALLED
IT'S YOUR TURN
FOR SERVICE

London: God Save the Deli

I had tried London's Jewish delicatessen some years ago, on a cold night with my parents and our elderly cousin Betty. On Betty's insistence we went to the famous Bloom's Delicatessen, in the solidly Jewish enclave of Golder's Green. Amid the peeling walls and the grumbling waiters, I ate one of the more appalling deli meals of my life. I remember cold soup, horrid bread, and *latkes* that could have been used as shells during the Great War. At one point, Betty, a fiery old broad in her nineties, upbraided the waiter when the Manischewitz wine didn't meet her expectations. He shrugged with such indifference I suspected his head would disappear into his torso. The meal was memorable only in its awfulness, and I quickly concluded that Britain's culinary atrocities had poisoned the Jewish kitchens of London.

But that was before John Georgiou held out what looked like a fried doughnut hole. "Allo there," he said as I stepped into the B&K Salt Beef Bar some years later, "you must be David. C'mon then, 'ave a lovely bite." I was greeted with the taste of mashed potato and sweet fish, kind of like *gefilte* fish married with fish and chips. John was the progeny of Bambos Georgiou, a Cypriot immigrant who had arrived in London in the 1950s and went on to become one of the most sought-after Deli Men in London, working in the Nosh Bar, Phil Rabin's, Carol's, The Stage, Ranch House, Leslie's, and the Brass Rail. When his wife, Katarina, died in the mid-1960s, leaving Bambos with six teenagers, he bought a struggling delicatessen and turned it into the B (for Bambos) and K (for his late wife) Salt Beef Bar. Bambo's sons John and Michael now ran the place. Though not Jewish, they were Deli Men through and through.

"It's real simple, yeah," John told me, as we sat at one of the eight tables in the small wood-paneled room. "We stick to what we know and don't try to be clever or greedy. You can actually taste the same food we're all eatin,' yeah? We look after the customers, don't take the mickey, pure, wise, and that's that."

John certainly didn't take the mickey on B&K's chopped ox liver, served as a dark brown scoop amid a mountain of loosely chopped egg and onion. It was stupendous. I had known chopped liver to have bits of egg mixed in, but left in a rough pile, the cool bits of egg mellowed out the powerful bite of the creamy, bitter liver, all sharpened by sliced shallots. When I headed over to the small counter to watch John hand-carve salt beef and steaming ox tongue, I nearly fell on my knees and swore allegiance to the Queen. John carefully drew his long knife against the grain of the brisket to produce sturdy, equally matched slices. As for the tongue, this was the first time I had seen a full one sliced by hand into thick ovals. Each time he pulled his knife back, it was like I was watching the sushi chefs at Nobu disassemble a side of Ahi tuna. None of the click-clack rapid-fire mess I'd encountered at Katz's or at Schwartz's. This was a master's work. I asked John if anyone in London used a machine to cut salt beef. "Well they shouldn't," he replied, without looking up. "As my dad said, there are a very few carvers, quite a few cutters, and a lot of butchers. They know how to cut, but they don't know how to carve the meat or handle a brisket."

John pickled his salt beef and ox tongues the same way his father did: in barrels with a low-salt cure, but without sugar or garlic, for two and a half weeks. Two and a half weeks! The longest curing I'd heard was half that, and only for pastrami or smoked meat. But John claimed that the slow, low-sodium cure imparted a gentler flavor than quicker pickling methods, to say nothing of commercially pumped products, which he detested. After pickling, the briskets and tongues were boiled in plain water, without additional spices. "If the beef is high enough quality, you don't need to flavor the water," John said. The secret was grass-reared Scotch beef, one of the finest breeds on earth, resulting in salt beef that was crumbly yet undeniably moist. It tasted like a steak with the aroma of the ocean's waves. The tongue was even better. Hot pink in the center and more rosy on the edges, it melted away quickly, but left a subtle sugary aftertaste, as though millions of blades of sweet grass from the Highlands lingered on the taste buds.

I'd come to London expecting poor substitutes for Jewish delicatessens. I'd been looking for the bland and pasty so stereotypical in British food. But here, in this small Greek-run deli on the edge of London, I saw that British delicatessen could be as good as, if not better than, its North American counterpart. Even the conversation was sufficiently Jewish, though wrapped in British gentility.

"Oh, I'll tell you, dear," an older woman said to her mother at the table next to ours, "I'd much prefer to have a colonoscopy than an endoscopy any day."

———

Jewish Britain is a complex community made up of 300,000 individuals, two-thirds of whom live in London, which is equal in number to the Jewish population of Canada in a country twice as populous and a fraction of the physical size. It is one of the few European countries where Jews have lived the longest without anti-Semitic violence, yet British Jews still endure the subtle prejudices of the upper-class establishment and the kicks of working-class skinheads and Muslim immigrants.

Jews first came to Britain with the Romans, though Ashkenazi Jews arrived from France with William the Conqueror in 1066. They lived in relative prosperity for a century until King Richard's crusades unleashed anti-Jewish riots and all sixteen thousand Jews were expelled to the European mainland. Jews did not return to Britain until the middle of the seventeenth century, when the Inquisition drove thousands of Sephardic Jews out of Spain and Portugal. German Jews followed, though in smaller numbers, and the first Ashkenazi synagogue appeared in London in 1692. But like elsewhere, the great surge in Anglo-Jewry came in the 1880s with the arrival of refugees from the Russian Empire, who settled into London's tightly packed East End, a dense, Dickensian neighborhood.

Delicatessens began as butcher shops, but soon blossomed into small kosher takeaway places with a few stools. Salt beef and pickled ox tongue predominated, though pastrami wasn't as popular, possibly due to the low numbers of Romanian Jews in London. Before World War II there were perhaps several dozen Jewish delicatessens in the East End, ranging from the small and simple, such as Kahn & Botsman, to the more ornate, like Barett's, which served the court of Queen Victoria. The most famous East End Jewish deli was Bloom's, which was opened in 1920 by Lithuanian immigrants Morris and Rebecca Bloom. It was by all accounts a loud, smoky, somewhat dirty place known for salt beef sandwiches, larger than life characters, and a reputation for the "rudest waiters in all of London." The Bloom family opened a second restaurant in the northern suburb of Golder's Green in the 1960s, and in 2007 they branched out in Edgeware, close to B&K Salt Beef Bar.

The British government closed the doors for Jewish immigration in 1909 until after World War II. Life in the East End gradually began to change, as more residents moved to emerging Jewish neighborhoods in the West End. During the war, the East End was struck hard. Wedged between the military targets of the docks and the city's financial hub, Nazi bombs and V2 rockets rained down on the tightly packed neighborhood, killing tens of thousands and destroying synagogues, shops, and delicatessens in the area. After the war, few Jewish residents returned.

Today, the East End is a mixed working-class and artistic neighborhood, inhabited mostly by Bangladeshi and other South Asian Muslim immigrants. There are no more Jewish delicatessens. The Whitechapel Bloom's closed in 1996 amid a scandal over health inspections and the loss of kosher certification. The only taste of Jewish food in the East End can be found at the far end of Brick Lane, in the beigel shops.

The Brits spell bagel as *beigel*, which I've been told is actually more faithful to the original Yiddish pronunciation. But the *beigels* are nevertheless the real deal: rolled, boiled, baked, and rather dense. At night, crowds of hungry hipsters pack into the blindingly lit Brick Lane Beigel Bake, where tough-talking counterwomen dish up overstuffed beigels with hot, juicy salt beef, spicy Coleman's English mustard, and garlicky pickles for just £2.60, with a generous helping of Cockney wit.

I asked Jo, the woman in charge, if they made their own salt beef. "Oh yeah!" she said, barrel-rolling her eyes like F-16s. "We raise 'em, we kill 'em, we slaughter 'em, and we cook 'em!"

Brick Lane Beigel Bake is actually only three decades old. There are no tables and the kosher salami is served with butter, but from the perspective of eating salt beef in the East End, this is as close as it gets. The steaming meat is hand-cut thick and heaped onto soft beigels. It's tender and not overly salty, with a strong, rare roast beef taste to it.

Jewish delicatessen has remained a limited ethnic specialty in the U.K. "Delicatessen here just simply isn't the same as it is in New York, where many of the classics [of Jewish deli] are firmly in the mainstream, and not just for the Jews," remarked Jay Rayner, the food critic for the *Observer* newspaper. We were sitting among the lunchtime masses at The Brass Rail, a "salt beef bar" in the sumptuous food hall of Selfridges and Co., the luxury Oxford Street department store. With plates of juicy salt beef and splendid, fatty tongue stuffed in our cheeks, we ate surrounded by Britain's upper crust. "America is an immigrant culture in all regards and everything permeates this culture," said Rayner. "Although we [British] are supposed to be officially multicultural, it's still a white, Protestant, homogenous culture. If there is an interest in salt beef, it's because of reverse Americana, without regard to its Jewish roots."

In London's Jewish delis today, you will find more references to New York's Lower East Side than you will to the East End of London. The Web site of The Brass Rail proudly proclaims, "There's something so New York about a salt beef sandwich, and something equally reminiscent of the Big Apple about The Brass Rail." I found this funny, because The Brass Rail, with its white toque–topped chefs and settings fit for royalty, would never, ever fly in Manhattan. Imagine the Carnegie setting up shop inside Saks Fifth Avenue, and you get an inkling of how characteristically New York that would be. No one calls salt beef "East End style." It is implied that the food is Jewish, but any explicit connection in writing to Jewish tradition is generally missing. This is a direct contrast to New York, where playing up the nostalgic aspect of a Jewish deli is common. In London, nostalgia may exist, but it is hidden, like much of Yiddish culture.

When Jewish immigrants began arriving in large numbers in the 1880s, East End schools became a battleground between Yiddish greenhorns and the Anglo-Jewish establishment. Wealthy Jews like the Rothschilds insisted that institutions they funded, such as the Jews Free School, served to anglicize immigrants as quickly and fully as possible. Having themselves worked to break into the heights of British society, they loathed the idea of uneducated, "foreign" Jews ruining it for everyone. Students at the school were made to dress like proper Englishmen and engaged in gentlemanly sports such as cricket and rowing. On school grounds, they were forbidden to speak Yiddish and were instructed to "avoid the thickness of voice and nasal twang at all times." This wasn't the voluntary country club assimilation of 1950s suburban America. This was a directed effort by the established Jewish community to make Eastern European Jews as British as possible, to "humanize them" and eradicate any flavor of the *shtetl.*

The ramifications of this are still being felt to this day. Jonathan Freedland, a London-based journalist and author who is actively involved in the Jewish community, compared the divergent Jewish experiences in the United Kingdom and United States to that of the gay community. In the United States, he said, Jews were "out," their Jewish identity proudly displayed. "Here, we're very much still in the closet. I'll even give you an example. I've been in Jewish delicatessens where two people are talking and one will say, 'Oh, Gwyneth Paltrow? I didn't know she was [Freedland mouthed the word 'Jewish'].' We can't even say it out loud in a Jewish restaurant. What does that tell you?"

While working-class roots are a source of pride in the United States, the rigors of a monarchy-based upper class in Britain place a greater emphasis on one's lineage. While the Hollywood studio executive can rhapsodize about his childhood in a Brooklyn tenement, the same cannot be said of the peer from the House of Commons who grew up on Brick Lane. This affected how London's Jewish delis evolved.

"Possibly because of the intense pressures of assimilation from within the Jewish community itself, you would only have found Yiddish culture inside the house," remarked Claudia Roden, a celebrated cookbook author and food anthropologist who lives in the heavily Jewish suburb, Golder's Green. Anglicization was pushed on the diet of Eastern European immigrants from the beginning. "Class mattered very much," Roden told me. "The first Jewish cookbook here was anonymously written by Lady Judith Montefiore, and it had all grand upper-class French and Victorian dishes, though it was kosher." This, and a later book called *The Economical Jewish Cook*, featured hardly any dishes considered traditionally Jewish. Perhaps because of this, Roden surmised, delis in Britain never became the great social gathering space that they were in the United States.

But the flipside of this is interesting. While delis in the United States and Canada are now serving mostly gentile clientele, those in London remain solidly Jewish. Many have a customer base that is 95 per cent Jewish, an almost unthinkable number in North America. Having stayed close to the taste buds of the Jewish community, the salt beef, *matzo* ball soup, and other traditional delicacies retain a faithful flavor. Very little of it is packaged or processed, and most of the dozen or so Jewish delis operating in the United Kingdom are either glatt kosher, kosher, or kosher style. When I say kosher style, I don't mean in the California sense of the word (Hebrew National hot dogs and Jimmy Dean pork sausages). I mean no milk with meat and no shellfish or pig on the menu at all. For those who love a greasy, cheesy Reuben sandwich, this may be a detriment, but for a delicatessen purist such as myself, this is always a welcome sign of respect. Most London delis cure their salt beef and ox tongues in barrels of salt and spices, without artificial preservatives, and every London deli cuts its meat by hand.

My one criticism of London Jewish deli lies with the rye bread, which is the worst on earth. It's basically white bread with caraway seeds. I don't think a grain of rye flour has ever neared it. I pray for the day when some bakery maven from London takes a course at

Zingerman's Bakehouse. Thankfully, the fighting lion of hot English mustard offsets the disastrous rye. It packs a serious wallop, which initially overwhelmed me, because I tend to douse my sandwiches with mustard. I often had to stop eating for two full minutes because it felt like I'd just inhaled a clump of wasabi.

London's deli menus are basic. Sandwiches are either hot salt beef, hot ox tongue, kosher salami, or chopped liver. There is a requisite chicken soup with *matzo* balls (referred to as the Yiddish *kneidlach*), *kreplach*, or *lokshen* (noodles). *Gefilte* fish is prominent and popular, especially the hot, fried variety. Each deli serves *latkes*, and all pride themselves on the quality of their *lokshen* pudding. Overall, the portions are good, about five to six ounces of meat per sandwich, though everything comes à la carte, which gets pricey. A salt beef sandwich alone can cost the equivalent of twenty dollars.

London's delis tend to be rather upscale, with cloth napkins, heavy silverware, and modern decor. While deli customers in North America want their delis down, dirty, and cheap, London's delis have adapted to the city's refined opulence. Only in London could you have The Brass Rail directly across from a counter selling white truffles at £1,000 a pound. Up the street from Selfridges is Reuben's, a kosher deli in surroundings rich with black marble and halogen lighting. Walking the restaurant with Tam Hassan, a tall, thick young man in his early twenties whose father, Az, owns Reuben's, I soon learned how the trappings of opulence have actually benefited the taste of the deli here.

The chopped liver sold at Reuben's comes plain, on china embossed with the restaurant's name, but it is nevertheless indicative of Tam's skills (he studied at the Cordon Bleu). There are actually two chopped livers. The "Paté" is a sweet ball of chopped chicken liver, loaded with caramelized onions, and served with beet-sweetened horseradish, known as *chrain*. It glides down the throat, cool and creamy, with a subtle candied aftertaste. Its cousin is the chopped liver of veal, served with a grating of chopped egg. The flavor of the veal's liver is stronger than chicken, though milder than that of ox or beef liver, and is also eased down by a generous dollop of *schmaltz* in the glistening mix. Once I tasted the chicken soup I could see why *schmaltz* was so liberally used at Reuben's. The shallow bowl glowed like the jewelry of the Saudi princesses who shopped at Harrods. The *matzo* balls were golden down to the core. Liquid decadence.

No one has married Jewish London's food traditions with the trappings of class more than caterers Kenneth and Susan Arfin. Their high-end kosher restaurant, Bevis Marks, is connected to Britain's oldest synagogue, in London's East End. Arfin's family were originally butchers in nearby Petticoat Lane, and though the menu is fusion-heavy, there are contemporary nods to deli roots. At Bevis Marks you'll find *matzo* ball soup, as well as chopped liver with spiced fig compote. There's a traditional salt beef with horseradish relish, but they also do a Thai salt beef, fried in green chili sauce. "We mustn't forget our traditions," Kenneth Arfin said to me; he was dressed in an impeccable three-piece pinstripe suit. "Once we lose our traditional foods we inevitably lose other things. And then what actually are we?" he asked. "Jews by name perhaps?"

Stately delis don't necessarily translate into civilized clients. At Harry Morgan's, London's best-known Jewish delicatessen in the posh St. John's Wood area, owner Mitchell Tillman recounted with amazement how he walked back to the kitchen one crowded Saturday, heard the usual argument for an empty table, and emerged minutes later to see chairs, food, and bloody fists soaring through the air. Most of the time, Tillman just fields the standard complaints from his loyal customers, however ridiculous, like when a diner said his *lokshen* pudding was served upside down (there is no right side up). Young, tall, and elegantly dressed in a wool suit with cufflinks, Tillman hardly presented the image of a Deli Man. But he is an energetic and dedicated owner who hopes to take Jewish delicatessen out of obscurity in Britain.

Harry Morgan's was opened in 1948 by an East End butcher and his wife, Ray, along the High Street of St. John's Wood. After Harry dropped dead of a heart attack in the middle of the store, Ray continued to run the business from her perch behind the register. Inside one found an intersection of shady gangsters and East End bookies. "I remember Harry Morgan's as a kid," Tillman recalled. "They had curtains on the windows and big *Sopranos* type guys who could really shovel in a salt beef or chopped liver sandwich. All these guys had eaten their whole lives was fried food, and of course they all lived to a hundred! I remember you used to have to fight the smoke back. Today it would be closed by the health department." Later, Ray Morgan relinquished much of the business to a young Israeli manager, who subsequently gambled away the restaurant.

Tillman took over in 2000, backed by his restaurateur father. At age twenty-four, the graduate of restaurant and hospitality school successfully transformed Harry Morgan's into one of the few London Jewish delis with broad appeal. Before Tillman, Harry Morgan's clientele was almost exclusively Jewish. Now it was only 65 per cent Jewish. Out went the smoke and the curtains. In came a bright café with an adjoining takeout area. Tillman had opened additional locations: a smaller outlet right off busy Oxford Street, a kiosk in the swank food hall at the luxury Harrods department store, plus licensed Harry Morgan's branches in several office towers throughout London, supplied by a commissary. Harry Morgan's also sold merchandise at Harrods, including prepared foods and a set of dishware embossed with the names of deli foods. There was a delivery service, plans for additional units around England, and yes, offers from Las Vegas.

"We've even been approached by a food-service company in Dubai," Tillman said, adding how the success at Harrods sparked an Arab interest in Jewish delicatessen. A big part of his weekly business now came after Friday services let out down the street at the London Central Mosque, the largest in all of Britain. His meat wasn't kosher, but interestingly enough, it was halal, and Muslim customers were a growing part of the business. Tillman had done what no one in Britain had managed to do before; he'd successfully taken delicatessen beyond the Jewish community.

"When I took over the business, delis in London were disappearing," Tillman said, as we both tucked into large bowls of gorgeous chicken soup, loaded with fat strips of white meat, peppery *matzo* balls, and dense *kreplach*. "Our clientele was dying off . . . it was all old people. So we refurbished the restaurant to a great extent, to make it more modern. If you don't entice your younger customer you won't have a customer. Sure, it irked some of the old regulars, who said, 'Vhy did you do this? It was nice as it was,' but now they say it's better, and none of them have left."

Tillman had recently brought in a chef from the legendary Ivy restaurant, just to ensure the kitchen was staying faithful to tradition. The *gefilte* fish balls were perfectly round spheres, fried to a dark, crisp brown, which puffed out steam when bit into, revealing loosely chopped whitefish and garlicky mashed potato. A plate of sliced pickles, ranging from green to sweet and sour to old dills (which they call a *heimeshe* pickle), were arranged like a vertical tasting of wines. Hand-cut tongue, soft and gooey, was sublime, while the *latke* was airy and piping hot. And naturally, the salt beef sandwich was wonderful. Hand-carved by Nick, Harry Morgan's counterman for three decades, it was streaked with just enough soft fat to bless each bite.

Why couldn't the rest of Britain learn to love this? Tillman didn't think that it would ever become as popular as it had in the United States, but he clearly had proved that deli could appeal outside of London's Jewish community. In deli, Tillman saw something that Britain needed, which no other restaurant could deliver.

"Deli is great because you'll get George Michael or Minnie Driver coming in here, but also regular people," he said. "One day we had Roman Abramovich in here [the Russian Jewish oligarch and the world's fifteenth-wealthiest man]. He was sitting at a table, with two bodyguards nearby and two outside. At the opposite table were two people who probably couldn't string two pounds together, and they had no idea who he was . . . I don't think you'll find that mix of people anywhere else in London."

In the ultimate class-based society, Jewish deli turned out to be the great equalizer. Despite the efforts of London's Jewish aristocracy to anglicize Yiddish culture, the proletarian charms of a hot salt beef sandwich united Britain in the end.

YOUR
NUMBER
17
WHEN CALLED
IT'S YOUR TURN
FOR SERVICE
BY TICKET CO.
PRINTED IN U. S. A.

The Fine Art of Jewish Delicatessen
in Belgium and Paris

"Do you have something like pastrami?" the American Jewish community representative loudly asked Nadia Benisti. "You know, something more like *traditional deli*?" The gentleman, who proudly boasted that he was a big shot in Cleveland's fundraising circles, was visibly confused. His Belgian counterparts had told him they'd be lunching at Brussels' finest Jewish delicatessen. After a long day of meetings, this man was deeply looking forward to a corned beef sandwich piled to the ceiling . . . just the sort of thing he'd eat at Jack's. He wanted to sit and kibitz, rub elbows in a little *schmutz*, and loosen his tie for the first time since he'd arrived in Europe's bureaucratic capital.

Instead, he found himself in an opulently restored room, with turn of the century frescoes. Lounge music played softly over delicate conversations between stylish Orthodox businesspeople. People sat on Philippe Starck's iconic Louis Ghost Chairs and ate off linens. I saw his face and sensed what he was thinking: "They've got it all wrong. These Euros don't know what a deli is supposed to be like!"

When I walked into Chez Gilles, with its air of continental civility and displays of neatly prepared gourmet foods, I initially thought the same. The owner, Nadia Benisti, an elegant woman who ran the place with her husband, Gilles, brought my friend Christopher Farber and me a warm basket of *pletzl* (onion roll) and a small plate of sliced *broust*, also referred to as smoked pastrami. The portions were small, immaculately presented, and resembled only faintly the deli back home. But as we began smearing whole-grain mustard on pieces of warm *pletzl* and applying the meat, our apprehension evaporated into exclamations of pleasure. Smoked by Gilles Benisti himself, the meat was shaved transparent. It tasted of peppery roast beef with a subtle hint of applewood. There was no dripping grease, no salt rush to the brain; just the regal interplay of fluffy bread, wine-scented mustard, and cool meat. It was upscale, refined, and utterly gastronomic. I'd entered the age of European deli enlightenment.

Sweet, decadent Europe. Luxurious, fashionable, handcrafted land of five-week vacations, small cars, and intellectual snobbery. Historically obsessed on one side, cutting edge on the other, the Continent beckons with its gilded finery. It is a place in love with American and Jewish culture and yet a land where anti-Americanism and anti-Semitism flourish. For eaters, Europe offers the opposite of the North American diet: food carefully produced using timeless, traditional methods, in small, very rich portions. Through this gourmet filter, the Jewish delicatessen has emerged in Europe as a high-end version of its North American cousin.

The day after that initial meal at Gilles, my friend Chris and I took the train to Hoffy's, a wood-paneled glatt kosher delicatessen in Antwerp's Hasidic diamond district. The halogen lights were dim, and the tables were dressed with fresh linen napkins and polished silverware. Moishe Hoffman came over to greet us with pickles, a basket of fresh challah rolls, and a plate of artfully arranged meats spread out like the petals of a flower—an asparagus tip and a single fanned strawberry resting atop a small bulb of chopped liver. Were I at a delicatessen in Long Island and a strawberry appeared on my plate of meat, I'd surely walk out. Here it seemed rather tasteful.

Hoffman, a soft-spoken man with wire-framed spectacles, a thick black beard, and a warm, Yiddish-inflected Flemish accent, treated his dishes as precious gems. His father was a fishmonger from a *shtetl* in Hungary, and after the war he opened a fish shop in Antwerp. When Moishe Hoffman opened Hoffy's in 1986 as a small takeout delicatessen, his father warned him, "You either do it properly or not at all." So Hoffman went to a top culinary school where he adapted classical recipes with kosher ingredients and reopened the renovated Hoffy's, which he ran with his brothers.

The fruits of Hoffman's labor were apparent on that initial plate. Bursting with enough garlic to wipe out Transylvania, the crunchy pickles made North American "full sours" seem like those flimsy things on McDonald's burgers. The meats, each one exceedingly tender and trimmed lean, were nonetheless moist and delicate, the highlight being the veal, which was a creamy pink and tasted almost sweet. Chris and I savored each lithe slice, rolling the flavors around on our tongues. Eating deli in this way—slowly, carefully, contemplatively—felt like rediscovering the love of your life halfway through a neglected marriage.

Often, Hoffman would receive requests from visiting Americans for New York–style deli sandwiches. A few years back he thought it would be a good idea to feature them at Hoffy's. So he created towering sandwiches loaded with pastrami, coleslaw, mustard, and other fillings similar to what he'd tasted in the United States. They didn't take off. "People didn't want to eat so much," Hoffman said. "Imagine that I had a hundred or a hundred and twenty people eating here in a day. I didn't sell but ten of them."

Hoffman really loved serving gentile Belgian customers, who came from all over the country to experience Jewish cooking. When two plump, ruddy-faced women walked in, Hoffman greeted them warmly in Flemish, took them through a tour of the dishes in the display case, and sat them down. Walking behind the counter, he grabbed a large plate and began scooping, shaping, and slicing a whole variety of tapas-sized portions. When he finished, Hoffman held up what looked like a gourmet Seder plate.

"For these women I don't even let them look at the menu," he said, beaming with pride. "See? We have all the major Jewish foods represented here." Packed on the plate were two-bite portions of apple *kugel*, *gefilte* fish, vegetarian pâté, a miniature cabbage roll, chopped liver, pastrami, and spicy eggplant salad. "I'll go over now and explain to them what this is and I promise you the next time they will come back with six people."

Hoffy's business increasingly relied on gentile clients to supplement Antwerp's shrinking Jewish population. Since the 1970s, Jain Indians had established themselves as low-cost players in the diamond industry, moving much of it overseas. This, combined with an increasing atmosphere of anti-Semitism in Belgium from both immigrant Muslims and white supremacist groups, caused many of Antwerp's Jews to move to Israel or the United States. Hoffy's was one of the few kosher restaurants remaining in Antwerp, and Moishe Hoffman knew that his future was up in the air. Across Europe, the situation was similar, though nowhere was it more dramatic, or visible, than in Paris, home to Europe's largest Jewish community.

The only time I had spent in France was when I was nine. Between museums, my family packed in a quick visit to Jo Goldenberg's deli and restaurant. My parents explained that it was a deli, like Yitz's, but I couldn't see any resemblance. Goldenberg's was creepier, with worn wood and miserable waiters. The only things I recall about the meal were the terrific *matzo* ball soup and the rat that scurried overhead. Nearly two decades later my parents were in Paris, but when they got to Jo Goldenberg's the grates were pulled over the windows of an empty deli. Jo Goldenberg's had apparently closed for renovations toward the end of 2005 and never reopened.

The Franco-Jewish story closely mirrors that of Jews throughout Europe, with communities settling and establishing themselves under protection from friendly monarchs (such as Charlemagne), until being massacred by the next ruler who came to power (Philip Augustus). French Jews were expelled from the kingdom in 1182, recalled in 1198, exiled in 1306, brought back in 1315, and kicked out again in 1394. In the early thirteenth century, the Jews of Paris, banned from the city, settled in a swampy area called Le Marais just outside Paris's walls. It was only with the ascension of Napoleon Bonaparte as emperor in 1804 that French Jews became full citizens.

Le Marais was resettled in large numbers from the 1880s onward, as Jews fled persecution by the Russian empire. Poor and unwelcome in the cultured society of established French Jewry, they crammed into tenements, recreating an urbanized version of *shtetl* life in the heart of Paris. At the center of this was a short, narrow street, the Rue des Rosiers. By the 1930s, the area was home to twenty thousand Jews, concentrated into several square blocks. When the Nazis invaded France, and the collaborative Vichy government began deporting Jews to the concentration camps, Le Marais was hit particularly hard. Of all of France's Jewish communities, Le Marais suffered the highest losses during the Holocaust. After the war, refugees began to trickle back into Le Marais, joined by a large population of Sephardic Jews expelled from Arab colonies following the creation of Israel. They brought to the Rue des Rosiers their own traditions and foods.

Jo Goldenberg's had been founded as a kosher butcher shop in the 1920s by an immigrant from Russia. His sons, Joseph and Albert, opened the restaurant later on, and though the Nazis murdered most of the family, the deli's owners survived. Goldenberg's went on to become the best-known Jewish restaurant in Europe, serving French interpretations of Ashkenazi dishes in a bustling atmosphere. In August 1982, terrorists led by the notorious Palestinian Abu Nidal attacked Jo Goldenberg's with machine guns and grenades, killing six customers and wounding dozens. After the attack, Goldenberg's became a gathering spot for defiant Holocaust survivors. But it was neither Nazis nor terrorists that put an end to Jo Goldenberg's. In the end, Paris's best-known deli went out of business from a host of reasons not too dissimilar from those plaguing New York delis.

Over the past decade, the Rue des Rosiers and Le Marais have become a haven for much of Paris's fashionable gay community. Synagogues now sit next to the most coveted boutiques in France. Rents have shot up, as bourgeois bohemians and foreign millionaires scooped up apartments along the charming Rue des Rosiers. The street, which stretches several short blocks, exists as a bright, bustling, cross-section of Jewish life, where Israeli falafel vendors and Hasidic barbers (whose signs say "The Moschiach is coming, so you'd better look good") mix with Jewish-themed book stores, art galleries, jewelers, bakeries, butchers, and delicatessens. It's as though the whole of the Jewish world has been buffed and polished with a dreamy Chagall aesthetic.

For lovers of Jewish food, the shops along the Rue des Rosiers are a dream. At the Murciano bakery, the gilt-edged marble shelves are equally split between Ashkenazi treats, like velvety squares of light cheesecake, and Sephardic specialties, such as rosewater-flavored Cornes de Gazelle. Panzer Dimitri (a distant relative of my friend Lorne Pancer) most resembles a North

American–style deli, with bright white tiles throughout and barrels of dill pickles by the door. Down the road, the Ukrainian and Russian women inside Sacha Finkelsztajn, "*la boutique jaune*," pile fillings on the French equivalent of deli sandwiches: slim slices of pastrami, tongue, or *pickelfleish* (corned beef), on a warm *pletzl*, topped with chopped eggplant caviar, roasted red pepper salad, half sour pickle slivers, ruby tomato slices, and hot Dijon mustard.

I had gone to Paris after Belgium with Chris, where we'd met up with my old friend Daniel Steinberg. I'd wanted to find out more about the story behind Jo Goldenberg's, but the family was uncooperative, and after exhausting my leads, I found myself somewhat lost. Not sure what to do next, I wandered across the cobblestones of Rue des Ecouffes and when I looked up, the most beautiful sight greeted my eyes from behind a storefront window. Sausages and salami of every shape and size were illuminated as though they were sculptures in the Louvre. Some were big as base-ball bats, covered in chalky white mold, while others were studded with checkered patterns from the webbing that held them. There were linked salamis in huge clusters, fat as potatoes, and giant tor-pedoes of meat over a meter long. I'd seen sausages like this back home, in Italian and German delicatessens, but never in a Jewish deli. To me, the options for Jewish sausage were processed salamis, hot dogs, and Montreal's *karnatzel*. Then, I stepped back and read the script on the glass . . . *Maison David* . . . David's House.

In the few feet Chris, Daniel, and I could stand between stocked shelves and the cool glass of the display case, our eyes struggled to take it all in. Meats of every description hung from hooks on the ceiling or waited behind the refrigerated glass in neat little trays. A fashionable woman was busy ordering from the proprietor, a man wearing a white butcher's jacket, with a thick black mustache and eyebrows that rose and fell as he spoke, betraying expressions on his shiny bald forehead.

"Ahh *madame*," he said in flirtatious French, "if you only knew the joy I could bring you and your family with an entrecôte," and with that proffered a gorgeous piece of dark aged beef for her inspection. Each time the lady seemed to be ready to conclude, the butcher's eyebrows would ascend his forehead while his mouth opened and inhaled quickly, as if he'd just solved a great mystery. Then he'd dart into the back of his tiny shop, emerging with something else for her feast. One time he came out rocking a duck stripped down to its pink flesh. "Look at this beautiful baby," he said, practically cooing. The Madame laughed, ordering until she'd spent four hundred euros. Within seconds of her leaving, the butcher laid down three transparent slices of creamy-colored cold cuts on the glass top of his counter and gestured with his hands to taste.

"What is it?" I asked him in grade school French, but the merry butcher of Le Marais just zipped his fingers underneath his mustache and smiled surreptitiously.

"*Allez*," he said, eyebrows gesturing for us to taste.

We laid the meats down on our tongues and savored the familiar texture of roast turkey or chicken, only more complex—fattier, richer, with a stronger flavor.

"Turkey?" I guessed. The butcher shook his head.

"Beef?" said my friend Daniel. The shakes again.

"Pork?" Chris ventured, which brought "*tsk tsk tsk*" from behind the mustache.

"*Non, non, non, mes amis!*" he said, shaking his bald crown disappointedly. "This one's duck and this one goose." Over the course of the next two hours, the butcher, Michel Kalifa, took us on an edible roller coaster of Jewish delicatessen that stretched the limits of our imaginations. We ate tiny dried nubs of *veguilly* salami the size of a fingertip, which burst like fat bonbons under the teeth, and thin, cigar-sized *cognacs*, smoky and glistening after having dry cured for three whole months. Kalifa would nod with a knowing smile and pluck more treats from the refrigerator with great ceremony, peeling off the yellow fatty casing of a salami, cleaning away the goose or duck *schmaltz* in which it was preserved, then running the meat under the deli slicer. Out would come the most wonderful salamis I'd ever tasted, the fat and meat coarsely ground into burgundy and white flecks. One was interlaid with fiery white peppercorns, another with whole chestnuts, while a third, which he called *krakovi*, was a salty and impossibly rich salami of duck fat and preserved duck meat. With each new treasure Kalifa would lecture us further on the art of kosher *charcuterie*. His words melded history, cuisine, religion, and philosophy, in the great tradition of Parisian intellectualism.

"Everything we eat well in Ashkenazi cuisine is made with things that we found in the *shtetl*," he pronounced. "With the same ingredient they made ten dishes. The goose and the duck, these were the meats of the *shtetl* . . . but what you see before you, well, these are creatures of the culinary imagination. It was a poor man's food, made from the bits left on the carcass that Jews were allowed. Now, today, it has become a noble product."

Though Maison David had existed as a butcher shop since 1917 (opened by Polish immigrant David Cohen), Kalifa himself was Moroccan-born and joined the shop in 1976, after studying economics and law. He had trained as a master butcher, *charcutier*, and wine authority, applying gourmet techniques to elevate the simple foods of Jewish tradition. After all, he remarked, it was French Jews in Alsace who were so instrumental in bringing foie gras to France, taking the *gavage* force feeding they'd seen the Romans apply in Israel and using it to produce fatty goose and duck livers.

Kalifa beamed with pride and laced his discourse with a French air of culinary superiority. When I called a slice of *pickelfleish* corned beef, he once again shook his head and *tsk tsked*. "*C'est pas New York, David,*" he admonished me, "you have to call things by their proper name. We French, you know, are purists." Clients, he said, could not rush their experience in Maison David. For him, they needed to pass two hours talking and tasting, to share a moment and appreciate the pleasure of his work.

On he went, slicing a *pletzl* into thin pieces, and spreading generously from plastic tubs. The first was *foie hache*, or chopped liver.

This was incredibly moist, literally glistening with *schmaltz*, with tiny flecks of meat, eggs, caramelized onions, and rich chunks of foie gras. There was a caviar of eggplant and other roast vegetables, and a pink spread, peppered with bright red buds. When finally prodded, Kalifa admitted that it was a pâté of salmon roe, the creamy spread kicked up by little pops of salty fish eggs.

Kalifa led us through a wonderland of gourmet deli, a kind of Jewish Willy Wonka. After hundreds of similar deli meals in America, Canada, and England, I saw then and there in Paris that I'd been experiencing only one half of Ashkenazi food's journey, the Anglo-Saxon half, and like a Talmudic scholar who happens upon a revelatory text, whole new worlds of possibility appeared before my eyes. This wasn't American deli reinterpreted in France. This was a Yiddish extension of the great French gastronomic tradition.

"It relates to the entire European concept of food and life," Kalifa said. "I strongly believe that this type of cuisine cannot and should not be industrialized. What we French eat, we must love as well. Sure, you came here, you bought, you tasted, but," he paused, "you didn't suffer. You didn't love. People today, they don't want to learn this art. It takes time. I'm thirty-five years in the business and I am still learning. I learn every single day!" He stopped and held up his finger for pause, and when our silence was assured he posed the question, "Do you feel how light it is? It's not how it tastes," Kalifa went on, "or how it looks . . . it's how you digest it. If it's a pleasure, it must also be a pleasure in the stomach. . . . Look, there is no international body of Yiddish cuisine ensuring quality. It's a mosaic of particularity. Each community assembles it and makes a foundation of Jewish culture in the world. This food is a history of the Diaspora in the mouth. The problem with Yiddish cuisine is that you can't eat it now and then, you have to *live it*. You have to eat it at least once a month, it has to be regular, not seldom. One's stomach cannot be Jewish during the holy days alone, it's a year-round affair. I'm not talking about a question of kosher or religion, but of an edible culture."

In all my travels before and since, Kalifa was by far the most creative, passionate, and talented Deli Man I would encounter. His encyclopedic knowledge of Yiddish cuisine came in bite-sized manifestations brimming with intense, complicated flavors. One didn't nosh in Maison David. Instead, Kalifa piloted a sensual voyage of culture. At one point, he unwrapped a small baking pan and sliced into a brown, gelatinous substance. Gently doling out domino-sized pieces, he told us to place them upon our tongues and wait. I felt the cool jelly slowly dissolve and release intense aromas of garlic, then boiled eggs, then sharp onion until it finally tasted like rich beef stock. Kalifa had given us *p'tcha,* a dish of jellied calves feet, which had all but disappeared in North America's Jewish kitchens.

Perhaps the beleaguered North American deli could use someone like Kalifa. His artisanal meats could provide the antidote for cheap corned beef in Las Vegas casinos. Deli owners in North America owed it to themselves to pay a visit to Maison David, if only to see the infinite possibilities of their creative potential . . . not by looking outward at fusion with other cultures, but by looking inward at Yiddish food. Kalifa hoped they'd come soon, because he wasn't sure how much longer Maison David would last.

The Jewish character of Le Marais was facing extinction, Kalifa told us in dire tones. The city had recently implemented a plan to turn the Rue des Rosiers into a pedestrian mall, closing it down to automobile traffic. Paris said the work would further preserve the look and feel of the neighborhood, while opening it up to tourists, but Kalifa and other local Jewish residents suspected differently. "This was a lovely community," he said, indignant, "but they have ridded it of Jews. [The city] doesn't want anything here but fashion boutiques and franchised bistros. It's become a tourist area, a little Jewish Disneyland. A tourist, he lives in a hotel. He's not going to buy a steak or get a haircut."

Rent was soaring. More than two dozen small Jewish butchers, bakeries, and shops had closed in just two years—including Jo Goldenberg's. The street construction had disrupted business.

Kalifa said his own sales had declined by 80 per cent in just two years. To fight it, Kalifa had formed a neighborhood association. It was an uphill battle.

"It's going to be very difficult for all of us to survive," he said, sadly. "This is a symbol of the Jewish community in good times and bad. It's just terrible. These were the streets where the victims of the Holocaust walked. This is where generations of French Jews have lived. But when I raise it with the city, they just laugh and say we're being hysterical. The reality is, in 2003 there was a strong Jewish quarter that was full of life. Now, there's hardly any Jews living here. It's a facade . . . a false street. The real neighborhood, *c'est mort*."

On the ticket: YOUR NUMBER 18 WHEN CALLED IT'S YOUR TURN FOR SERVICE

Krakow: Heartburn from Poland's Tortured Past

My glasses fogged as I stared down at what was once the most important dish in Yiddish cooking, *cholent,* traditionally eaten as a Sabbath lunch. A rich stew thickened with a few bits of brisket, cubed potatoes, bursting red beans, and white pearls of barley, the sprinkling of chopped parsley on top did little to disguise the heft of this dish. It was said that its ingestion required an extra day of prayer for the stomach to recover. I took a bite, expecting perhaps some profound revelatory connection to this place, the cradle of Ashkenazi Jewry for eight centuries. Instead I pushed the bland, sticky *cholent* around the plate. I'd already fought my way through the Jewish Style Carp, a firm, cold carp steak heaped with sweet, almond-flavored jelly, and my stomach was protesting audibly.

I was eating in Klezmer Hois, a restaurant in the Kazimierz section of Krakow that featured traditional Jewish food and music from the historic region of Galicia. It was a low, dark, curtained place meant to evoke a vanquished era. A band emerged, made up of a bored bassist, a young accordion player, and a stout older woman who led the trio on violin. With all the joy of a Chinese military band, they struck up their repertoire of old klezmer numbers, Jewish wedding tunes, and other Yiddish musical standards. The rest of the diners in the room were British high school students, here on a class trip. After a song or two, a couple of the kids got up and started dancing. The stern-faced violinist stopped and refused to play, pointing at the teenagers with her bow. She said something to the teacher, who instructed his students to sit down. The band left shortly after.

"I'm sorry," the teacher said, approaching my table, "but I feel as if we've done something culturally offensive. Was it wrong to dance to that type of music?" I didn't see why not. The music was hardly sacred. In fact, the song the children were dancing to was "If I Were a Rich Man," from the Broadway musical *Fiddler on the Roof*, about as sacred and reverent a song to Jews as the Village People's "YMCA." The band members, for their part, probably didn't know what they were playing. The musicians weren't Jewish, but they clearly felt that Jewish music should be somber. I was the only Jew in the room. In fact, at this time of the evening, I was the only Jew in the building. They were all just trying to play their roles in Krakow's confused Jewish present, guided by the whiffs of history, but without the actual presence of living, breathing Jews.

———

In Poland, the Ashkenazi Jews truly blossomed. From the eleventh century onward, Jews were encouraged to settle in Poland by royals who saw benefit in their economic activity. Still forbidden from owning land, Polish Jews formed a new merchant middle class. When the Church pushed hard for their persecution, Polish leaders such as Kazimierz IV increased protection for Polish Jews throughout greater Poland, including Lithuania and parts of the Ukraine. Kazimierz IV himself established a special town for Jewish Poles, built just outside the walls of Krakow, which still bears his name.

Following the Spanish Inquisition, Poland became the religious, political, and financial center of Jewish Europe. By the mid-sixteenth century, some 80 per cent of the world's Jewish population lived in Poland, a figure comparable today to the combined Jewish populations of both Israel and the United States. In Poland, the scope of Ashkenazi cooking grew and evolved, shaped by geography, history, and local flavors. Though some specialties, like the German frankfurters or salamis, or the Romanian pastrami, come from lands outside Polish territory, the bulk of what we eat today in a delicatessen has its roots in greater Poland, including the bagel, originally from Krakow.

But a series of wars and invasions over the course of the seventeenth and eighteenth centuries left Poland to be annexed by the Russian and Austrian Empires. Those who fell under Russian rule were forced to live within the Pale of Settlement, a specific rural territory stretching from the Baltic Sea to the Black Sea. It was during this period of imperial domination that *shtetl* life developed. Driven from cities and prohibited from joining professional associations, Jews were forced into poverty. *Shtetl* life turned inward, and as a consequence more religiously orthodox. By the late nineteenth century, czarist persecution and pogroms drove millions to flee to America.

After World War I, Polish autonomy was briefly restored, and Krakow reemerged as a major center for Jewish political, religious, and intellectual life. Poland still boasted the largest Jewish population in Europe, numbering close to three and a half million.

Though Krakow's Jewish population of 68,000 was significantly less than that of Warsaw (which, at just under 400,000, made up a third of that city), it was nevertheless significant. One out of four Krakow residents was Jewish. They saw themselves as Poles in the same way that New York Jews see themselves as Americans.

At the outbreak of the Nazi invasion in September 1939, the Polish Jewish community was the second-largest in the world, after the United States. More than 90 per cent of Poland's Jewry died during the next six years. Tens of thousands perished fighting the Nazis and Soviet invasion. Hundreds of thousands died of starvation and disease in the ghettos of Warsaw and Krakow from 1940 onward. More than a million were gunned down by roaming *Einsatzgruppen* death squads in the early years of the war, while twice that number perished in the death camps later on. Jewish Poles made up half of all the Holocaust's victims and half the Polish citizens killed during the war.

Upon invading Krakow, the Nazis looted Jewish businesses, distributed yellow Star of David armbands, and desecrated synagogues. In 1941, the entire community was marched into Krakow's newly formed ghetto. In 1942, the Nazis began transports to Belzec, the first death camp. Belzec was open only for eight months, but out of six hundred thousand only two individuals survived. In March 1943, Krakow's remaining Jews were packed into cattle cars and sent to Auschwitz, some fifty kilometers away.

Just six thousand Jews from Krakow survived the Holocaust. Of these, more than a thousand were saved by the German businessman Oscar Schindler, who had set up his factory in Krakow for its Jewish slave labor, but soon spent his own money rescuing Jews. While the actions of righteous Polish gentiles saved many during the Holocaust, there were also bitter memories of collaborative anti-Semitism. After the Kielce pogrom in 1946, when thirty-six Jews returning to their hometown were lynched, most survivors realized that after eight centuries of peaceful coexistence, Poland was no longer home.

Under communism, Polish Jews weren't allowed to associate with Jewish organizations worldwide. Following Israel's victory against Soviet-backed Arab forces in the Six-Day War, the Polish communist party closed down Jewish schools, youth groups, and clubs. Official government anti-Semitism forced the emigration of half the remaining Jewish community. The rest buried Jewish life underground. Today, the organized Krakow community has a mere 150 members, most of whom are elderly and alone. If you were to count unaffiliated Jews, or those with a Jewish parent or grand-parent, the total Jewish population in Krakow could be as high as five hundred. After eight hundred years as the cradle of Jewish civilization in Europe, Krakow's Jewish residents have been reduced to the lunch crowd at Katz's.

The story of Jewish Krakow could have ended there, until all that was left of Jewish life in Krakow were the ruins of synagogues and crumbling gravestones. But as the Soviet Union collapsed, something remarkable occurred. With the veil of oppression lifted, intellectuals and artists began organizing lectures on the "blank spots" of Polish history,—subjects that were previously taboo. Central to this was the Jewish question, including the real nature of the Jewish loss in the Holocaust, as well as the Jewish contribution to Polish culture. Against the monochromatic back-drop of decades of communism, Judaism was exotic. Studying Jewish culture was a way of expressing yourself at a time when doing so was like gasping for air after drowning your whole life.

Though the neighborhood was a crime-ridden slum during com-munism, Kazimierz turned out to be the best-preserved Jewish quarter in all of Eastern and Central Europe. Students played klezmer music in smoky bars, and shot slivovitz, a Passover plum brandy. In 1988, a Polish intellectual named Janusz Makuch and a friend organ-ized a small seminar on Jewish films, which drew more than two hundred people. Today, Makuch's Jewish Cultural Festival in Krakow is an annual nine-day summer party that draws more than twenty-five thousand people, mostly non-Jews. There's art, cooking, dance, and music by local klezmer groups and international musicians. With its huge outdoor concerts, it has been dubbed a "Jewish Woodstock," and though various Jewish individuals participate, it is run entirely by Polish gentiles like Robert Gadek.

"My parents talked about Jews in the past," Gadek told me, as we sat in the festival's office, drinking cherry tea to ward off the damp November cold. "They were an extinct, abstract group of people. To me, *Jew* was simply an empty word." As Gadek discovered Poland's Jewish history as a student in the 1990s, he became convinced that resurrecting it was the right thing to do. "Those from the start of the Jewish revival said, 'Jews are no longer here, and in the absence of Jews we have to be in charge of that culture. Not necessarily to protect the Jews, but because it is *our* culture as well!'"

Among those in the fold of the revival were so-called New Jews—Poles who had grown up secular or Catholic, but who later discovered Jewish ancestry. Maltgosia Ornat, the woman who founded Klezmer Hois in 1993, was one of them. Tall and blond, Ornat's neat, dramatic eyebrows and deep blue eyes resembled those of countless Polish beauties. At eighteen, she learned that her mother had been Jewish, but had converted. "It was not a kind of shock," Ornat told me, "more of an interesting tidbit. But it stimulated me to finding out about Jewish culture."

As Kazimierz grew in popularity, Jewish-themed businesses emerged. Most of these are concentrated on Szeroka Street, a square with two historic synagogues and a Jewish cemetery. The first of these businesses was a place called Ariel, a Jewish art gallery that opened in 1991 and soon turned into a restaurant. With no Jewish chefs left in Krakow, old cookbooks were unearthed and recipes were gleaned from the surviving seniors in the Jewish community. Ariel became a popular hangout during the early years of the Kazimierz revival. Someone who knew nothing about Jews could eat a Jewish meal, listen to Jewish music, and buy Jewish art. Most importantly, Ariel offered a unique culinary experience in a city that under communism hadn't had any private restaurants.

Kazimierz's big boost came in 1993, when Steven Spielberg filmed *Schindler's List* there, sparking renewed interest worldwide in the Holocaust and Kazimierz. Wealthy philanthropists refurbished synagogues, built museums, and opened up cultural centers. Tourism blossomed. More Jewish-themed restaurants opened up in Szeroka Street, while the old ones expanded into 200-seat dining halls with adjoining hotels. Jewish bookshops appeared. You can even buy the *2nd Ave Deli Cookbook* near the very land where Abe Lebewohl (a Galician Jew) was born.

My first Jewish restaurant in Kazimierz was Ariel, the pioneer of Krakow's Jewish food revival, and the one that advertises itself most blatantly as Jewish (though its owners are not). Above the gate to the courtyard patio was a giant wrought iron candelabra, below which the restaurant's name was welded in Hebraic-style lettering. On either side of this elaborate signage were two stately stone lions, presumably Lions of Judah. Short of a neon Star of David, it practically screamed J-E-W.

The restaurant was split into two rooms, each with low ceilings and dark wooden beams. The walls were covered with paintings of Jewish life, though exclusively of Hasidic scenes: men in dark suits praying or deep in contemplative study. Among the dishes on offer were *matzo* ball soup, *gefilte* fish, chopped herring, fried *kreplach*, *borscht*, *kasha*, cabbage rolls, and *blintzes*. I was more interested in trying the dishes that were once common in Poland, but couldn't be found in North American delis.

I started with the waiter's recommendation of Berdytchov soup, a dish that was supposedly typical of the town Berditchev, currently in Northern Ukraine. Though the broth was laced mostly with cabbage, cubed potatoes, carrots, and microscopic pieces of beef, it was the overwhelming sweetness added by honey, cloves, and cinnamon that gave the soup its characteristic flavor—like dumping spiced cider into canned vegetable soup.

I ventured on to the menu's most traditional *shtetl* dish: stuffed goose necks. Though goose was to Yiddish cuisine what beef is to the New York deli, in North America only Montreal's Schwartz's serves goose anymore. Ariel's version stuffed the skin of a goose neck with chopped chicken liver and rice-sized dough dumplings. The stuffed neck was fried until it resembled a stubby crackling sausage. They weren't the most appetizing sight, but the prospect of fatty liver, wrapped in fatty skin, and then deep-fried (in fat!), was tempting. Of the two necks, one was overdone, with tough, chewy skin and gamey, bitter liver. But the other was an artery-slaying taste sensation. The outer layer of crisp, oily skin gave way to a creamy membrane of sweet fat, which bathed the smooth, earthy liver in an undercurrent of richness that was almost unfathomable.

My head swimming with goose *schmaltz*, I headed out, pausing for a few moments in Ariel's gift shop. It featured some CDs of klezmer bands, a few books, and Hasidic figurines in glass cases. These, I would soon discover, are common all over Poland, sold to tourists and locals alike. Most are wooden carvings of Hasidic men playing instruments. One of these caught my eye. His skin was pale and ghostly. His eyes were black, with dark, heavy bags underneath. His nose was huge and bent in the most perverse way. He held a tightly clutched bag of money and a large gold coin. I was staring at a classic anti-Semitic portrayal of a penny-pinching Jew, for sale to tourists in a Jewish restaurant owned by Polish gentiles, a mere hour from the ovens of Auschwitz. Not the thing you want to see when you're trying to hold down greasy fried goose necks.

Kazimierz inevitably provokes strong feelings from anyone who visits it, especially if they are Jewish. On the one hand, you have the sincere rehabilitation of a lost Jewish culture that's driven, financed, and run by Polish gentiles. Theirs is a heartfelt attempt at reconciling the troubled events that occurred on Polish soil. To see these people enthusiastically nourishing Jewish culture is touching. Their work has helped eradicate negative stereotypes, both of Jews in Polish eyes, and also of Poland in the eyes of Jews. Many Holocaust survivors have returned to visit Poland for the first time because of the work that people like Robert Gadek have done.

Yet the same emotions that make the Kazimierz revival so powerful also render it extremely volatile. While elements of it are touching and genuine, there is a certain streak of opportunism and exploitation. Kazimierz is first and foremost a tourist destination, and the business of tourism, whether a Times Square delicatessen or a restored Jewish quarter, will always sacrifice altruism in the name of profit. Sometimes it takes on the feeling of kitsch, such as the *Fiddler on the Roof* songs played at Klezmer Hois, while at other times it seems like something out of the world of *Borat*.

In Kazimierz, I found poor taste present, though not prevalent. Some Jewish restaurants advertised traditional "Jewish" dishes on their menus like pork loin and other blatantly *treyf* foods. Some restaurants have dressed their waiters and musicians in "Jewish" costumes, including fake beards and skullcaps. When Jews abroad hear about Kazimierz, many express outright disgust. Poland to them is the world's largest Jewish cemetery, and the idea that people are profiting from Jewish memory is blasphemy. Staring at that little Jew figurine, I imagined what Native Americans must feel when they stumble into a souvenir shop in Wyoming and see the pow-wow dolls for sale.

The common criticism leveled at the Jewish revival in Krakow is that it is not Jewish-led. When I asked Robert Gadek about this, he gave an exasperated sigh. "We need to ask: 'Who shall organize Jewish culture in Poland so that it's sufficiently Jewish? Does the office staff have to be Jewish? Does the audience have to be Jewish? Do all the foods have to be kosher?' Maybe. It can be done. But for what? Because I'll tell you, if it is only for Jews, by Jews, we'll have fifty people out there, instead of twenty-five thousand. Poland is the perfect place for this, because of its Jewish history, and yes, because of the Holocaust. . . . It belongs here to show these people what they lost. If you don't know what was lost, and what this culture could have been, you don't understand what the Holocaust was. You only get numbers."

On my second day in Kazimierz, I finally met Jews. The city's small Jewish community center is found just outside Kazimierz, where twenty or so elderly Jews come to eat kosher meals that are cooked daily. On Monday nights the cook even makes "pickle meat," essentially corned beef. She told me that it was cured there over several days, then boiled, and served with potatoes and a sauce made from horseradish. When I asked her if it was ever served as a sandwich she burst into laughter. Apparently the very concept of a corned beef sandwich was simply ridiculous.

In fact, the Polish Jews I met found the whole idea of North American delicatessen strange. While in the Senior's Club, a social spot where the older members of the community met daily for coffee and Hebrew lessons, I looked through a translated Jewish cookbook. The woman whom I sat with remembered foods such as pickled beef (which she'd boiled with wine and pepper) and *matzo* brie. But when we came to the page that had a Reuben sandwich on it, she tried to explain that it was named so because it was Reubenesque, after the painter who did colorful portraits of plump women. She even did a little outline of a curvaceous figure with her hands.

Krakow's remaining Jews dined at the Jewish-themed restaurants only on special occasions. What really mattered to them was the creation of a group called Czulent (the Polish spelling of *cholent*). Czulent is a youth group formed in 2004 by students who had discovered some Jewish heritage in their families. Because the orthodox rabbis wouldn't accept these New Jews as so-called kosher Jews (without documentation, they need to undergo conversion), they banded together, discovering their identities in their own way, especially through cooking. Gathering Jewish recipes from seniors or the Internet, they cooked dinner for the community in the synagogue each Friday night. Dr. Zosea Radzikowska, an elderly and vocal lawyer, called Czulent "our hope for the future."

One of the principal members of Czulent was a young woman named Ishabel Szatrawska. Food, she told me, remains part of the Jewish identity, even if the formal association with Judaism has been severed for several generations. This was her experience. Her family was the only one she knew of that made chopped liver. Even though they ate pork, her grandfather could not bring himself to eat a sandwich with butter on it. Though Ishabel didn't know why, as a kid she was never allowed to eat at anyone else's house. Only later did she realize that it was because they were Jewish.

And though my Ariel experience left a bitter aftertaste, this wasn't the case with Alef. Owned by Janusz Benigier, another New Jew, the restaurant had recently moved out of Szeroka Street, into a newer hotel. Instead of the dark, somber spaces that the other Jewish restaurants occupied, the dining room at Alef was flooded with natural light. Two large murals depicted historic Kazimierz and historic Jerusalem, and the walls were jammed with old portraits, some of Jewish figures and rabbis, another of Mozart and famous Polish poets. There were no display cases filled with scary figurines.

The menu at Alef looked basically the same as the other restaurants, but I was intrigued by an appetizer called Goose Liver Soufflé. The soufflé was basically a terrine of cooked goose liver, mixed with *matzo* meal and some other ingredients, resembling a slice of meatloaf. Its texture was surprisingly light and soft, with a subtle touch of gamey flavor that was enhanced greatly by a bright red sauce, the most amazing beet-sweetened horseradish that was creamy, sugary, and fiery (in that succession). It was easily the best dish I ate in Poland and remains a Jewish food I've yet to find elsewhere.

To cap off my lunch I ordered the *kreplach* in broth. During the preceding year I'd eaten dozens of *kreplach* in soups from Los Angeles to London, so my expectations weren't too high. Out came a bowl of consommé the color of bourbon, darker than most chicken soups, with the flavor of onion and some beef marrow.

Every other *kreplach* I'd come across had been some variation of a shapeless blob. But these were neat little empanadas of thin dough, crimped artfully around the edges as though Alef's chef had spent his formative years making dim sum in a Hong Kong hotel. Inside I found minced brisket with strong overtones of peppercorns and freshly chopped garlic.

On my last night in town, fighting my *cholent* and watching the solemn band at Klezmer Hois, the sad truth about Krakow's revival appeared a bit clearer. Here I was, supposedly eating authentically Jewish food, surrounded by Jewish art and artifacts, listening to traditional Jewish music, in a building that had been a part of Europe's Jewish legacy centuries before any delis came to New York. But no matter how faithful Klezmer Hois, Alef, or Ariel were, they lacked a Jewish soul. There was no *tam*. I felt at home at most North American delis, or even the British, French, and Belgian delis from the moment I walked in, but I never felt that in Krakow's Jewish restaurants. When the violinist upbraided the students for dancing to a Broadway show tune, I realized that no matter how carefully the Poles recreated this world, it would never be sufficiently Jewish.

"It's not real because there are no Jews," Klezmer Hois' owner, Maltgosia Ornat, told me. "This place is a monument because it is not authentic. Different activities happen, but it's not real. There's no continuation of Jewish life."

On my last afternoon in Poland I stood in the driving rain of Birkenau, the Nazi's largest death camp. As far as the eye could see, long wooden barracks stretched to the horizon. Two hours earlier I had been a few miles away, in Auschwitz, the Polish army base used by the Nazis as a political prison and eventually a death camp for Poles, Gypsies, Soviet POWs, and Jews. Despite the electrified barbed wire, the wrought iron *Arbeit Macht Frei*, and the small gas chamber and crematorium, Auschwitz felt like a museum. Inside each of the buildings were exhibits depicting the atrocities committed on these grounds. Though barbaric, I felt a certain sense of detachment. I'd seen these same images, films, and artifacts dozens of times before, and I felt like I could have been at any one of the Holocaust memorials I'd visited in my life.

But Birkenau was different. It was the physical manifestation of Hitler's "Final Solution," specifically built as a factory of death. Its gas chambers dispatched twenty thousand lives each day, and its scale was simply staggering. I stepped into one of the dark barracks, alone. I inhaled the worn cedar of the bare bunks. There was no smell of humanity, no trace of the four hundred souls who had once awaited death here. I closed my eyes and thought back to one of the exhibits in the Auschwitz museum: a vast pit behind glass where thousands of cooking pots and pans were heaped into a pile. You had to remind yourself that every item represented a Jewish family. Each pot once simmered on a stovetop in Krakow, Odessa, or Amsterdam, filled with chicken, onions, garlic, dill, and perhaps a marrowbone for extra flavor. Each pot had belonged to a mother, who cooked for her family and friends and community. Some had been *cholent* pots, which had stewed in *shtetls* that were now empty fields. Others were used to pickle briskets in Paris, make fricassee in Bucharest, or cabbage rolls in Hamburg.

Six million lives.

Each family with a pot.

What had been lost?

How many recipes were gone forever?

In that moment, sheltered from the driving rain in that quiet barrack, amid a field of death scattered with the incinerated remains of three generations of European Jewry, I thought back to the journeys I had taken that year: to New York, across North America, to Europe. Each deli began with one member of one family who had left Poland or Russia and settled in America,

Canada, England, or France. The Jewish delicatessen as we know it may have manifested itself in lower Manhattan, but the Ashkenazi heartland of Eastern Europe was always its source. It was the well from which deli drew its Yiddish flavor, and I was standing where that well had been drained.

Out of the six million dead, how many potential Deli Men went into those ovens?

Tens of thousands? Hundreds of thousands?

How many Jewish delicatessens had been smashed and burned across Europe?

Hundreds? Thousands?

How many Yiddish cooks had perished feet from where I stood? One million? More?

I remembered the golden corned beef *knish* prepared by Rose Guttman outside Detroit, and the bubbling blueberry *blintz* that I'd eaten with David Apfelbaum in San Francisco. Both Rose and David had been in this place. They'd lost their families here, but had miraculously survived, going on to own dozens of successful Jewish delis. They were just two individuals spared by fate, and they had fed deli to millions in the decades since. Had this place never existed, how many more Jewish delicatessens would the world have known? Would I still be on this mission to save the deli?

In the flames of the Holocaust, the Jewish world lost more than lives. It lost an entire culture, which survives now only in fragments. In America, every other immigrant group will always have a source for their authentic flavors. So long as a billion and a half Chinese live in China, there will always be a family in Fujian willing to move to America and open another Chinese restaurant. Jewish delicatessens don't have that option. Theirs is the food of a partially destroyed people, three generations or more removed from its source. Delis are cooking from the fading memories of a time and place that no longer exist. No more Jews from Poland are coming to New York to open up a delicatessen.

For all the reasons that the delicatessen was endangered and in need of saving—economics, demographics, assimilation—all of them were presaged by the Nazi destruction of the Yiddish world. The source of all Jewish delicatessen had been systematically extinguished, wiped off the face of the earth forever. This, above all else, was the reason that the deli was dying.

Epilogue
Deli's 2nd Coming (Just off 3rd Ave)

Though the windows were papered over and the sign covered, the door was unlocked. Inside the bright new delicatessen on this mid-December night, contractors scurried around making last-minute adjustments. The slicing machines were still wrapped in plastic, and many of the refrigerated cases sat empty, though behind sections of the glass I spotted trays of chopped liver, coleslaw, and pickles. Packages of unopened kosher hot dogs were ready to sizzle on a grill that wasn't yet hooked up to the gas line.

"David Sax!" It was Steve Cohen, the former manager of the 2nd Ave Deli, a huge smile across his face. "Welcome," he said, "welcome to the 2nd Ave Deli."

Out from the back of the deli, where sixty brand-new seats were filled with friends and family on this Friday night, barreled Jack Lebewohl. A huge goofy grin was splashed across his face as he snared me in a big embrace. "I gotta tell you something, David," he said, holding my arm. "It's great to see you here." From behind Jack appeared Jeremy, his youngest son, who would reopen the 2nd Ave Deli in just over forty-eight hours.

I was standing in a narrow restaurant on 33rd Street, just west of Third Avenue, ready to experience the rebirth of one of New York City's most famous Jewish delicatessens. Everything I had been working on for the previous year and a half seemed to come alive in that very moment. Part of me simply expected to wake up, as if it were all a glorious, impossible dream. It wasn't. "Come," Jeremy said to me, "let me show you my deli."

The new 2nd Ave Deli occupied a small footprint in the neighborhood of Murray Hill, twenty-three blocks uptown from its original East Village location. It was not in a particularly Jewish area of Manhattan, nor was it in a tourist area, though it was close to the long-standing Sarge's Deli and Yeshiva University's city campus. You entered into a small vestibule, where a painting of the vibrant street scene that was in the original 2nd Ave Deli hung behind glass. Once inside, there was little space between the wall and a tall, long display case packed with food. Beyond the deli counter, across from the cash, was a small bar with four seats. A narrow passage led back to the dining area, which was split into two sections by dark mahogany dividers topped in glass etched with the deli's logo. Removed from the street and the hubbub of the takeout counter, the dining room already felt warm, intimate, and inviting. This was a space tailor-made for *fressing*.

Jeremy took me downstairs, into the cramped prep kitchen, where bags of potatoes and onions seemed to fill every available space. "I still have a few weeks until my commissary is ready," he said, "so until then we're crammed in." Jeremy opened one of the small walk-in refrigerators and showed me the crown jewels: wrapped Empire National pastramis, and large metal vats where Empire National's corned beef pickled further in the 2nd Ave Deli's special brine.

"Do you know what this is?" Jeremy asked, holding out a metal tray.

"Is it *p'tcha*?" I asked, seeing the elusive dish for the first time since France.

"Ahh," said Kathy, a slim veteran waitress from the old delicatessen, eyeing the *p'tcha* as we returned upstairs. "So this is the famous garlic Jell-O."

When the original 2nd Ave Deli closed down, all of the deli's employees drifted to jobs at various delicatessens around New York. What was amazing about the 2nd Ave Deli's reopening was how many of the original staff had returned. Managers Steve Cohen and Tony Sze came back. Four of the old waitresses, including Faye and Linda, did too, though Ida Berger and Diane Kassner did not. One new waiter had owned a kosher deli in Queens while another had been a trader at Goldman Sachs. Several of the cooks were back in the kitchen, and only three countermen were missing out of a dozen.

Mohamed, a young-looking Egyptian counterman with a goatee, had returned to his native Cairo and opened a falafel shop when the deli closed. But when he heard that the 2nd Ave Deli would be reopening, he called Jack Lebewohl. "I never feel like I'm working for a boss here," he told me, explaining why he'd left Egypt to return to the Jewish delicatessen trade. "I've had the same customers for twelve years. They are hugging us like they are happy to see us." The other countermen on that night—Louie, David, and Mahmoud—all felt the same way. The 2nd Ave Deli was family.

Jeremy and I split a square of *p'tcha*, which was lemony yellow in color. Chunky, with a bubbly, almost champagne consistency, fat hunks of garlic, eggs, and flakes of flesh greeted my mouth as I watched Jeremy inhale his piece. When Jeremy Lebewohl was a kid, he would hang around the deli with his uncle Abe and eat anything that was put in front of him. One time, Abe wanted to introduce bull's testicles to the menu after tasting them in Israel, and for a week young Jeremy ate bull's balls.

"David?" Jack asked, appearing above me at the bar. "Have you tried the *g'fish*?" The what? "The *g'fish* . . . the *gefilte* fish? Can I tell you something?" he asked. "This *g'fish* here is the best I've ever had. It's even better than we had on 10th Street, and it's the same cook!" Jack went behind the deli counter and came back with half an oval of *gefilte* fish. "It's so good," he proclaimed, "you don't even need horseradish." Flecked with grated bits of carrots, it was the color of oatmeal. A fountain of juice spurted in my mouth. It was like eating freshly steamed whitefish, each bite surging with the torrent of the stream the fish had swum in. I'd never tasted *gefilte* fish so full of life before.

"Here, you're not just eating deli," Jack said, as he passed me silky-smooth chopped liver spread on rye. "How many places make *gefilte* fish today? What restaurant makes *p'tcha*? No one even eats it, and we won't make any money off it, but that's what makes the 2nd Ave Deli." The new 2nd Ave Deli, like the old one, was going to be a cultural center for Yiddish cooking. Jeremy Lebewohl, just twenty-five years old, was already committed to expanding the traditional items the deli offered. On each table, the waiter deposited a small dish of *gribenes*, which are bits of chicken skin, fried to a golden crisp. Jeremy called them "Jewish popcorn." Sprinkled over the chopped liver, they gave off a greasy crackle that was like a kosher pork rind.

As I took my seat for dinner, I beheld a cross-section of familiar faces. Sitting at my table was Ted Merwin, the Jewish studies professor and my fellow deli historian, plus my cousins Stephen Lack, a veteran Lower Manhattan artist, and his son Asher, an East Village musician. Across the aisle from us, the comedic actor Robert Wuhl shared meatloaf with Drew Nieporent, the powerful restaurateur behind Nobu. Sitting right behind me were Karen and Eddie

Weinberg, the owners of Brooklyn's Empire National. When we last spoke, Eddie had been resigned to the death of the industry, having lost his largest account when the 2nd Ave Deli closed. But tonight the meat merchant with the muscular physique of a bull had a smile that dynamite couldn't have chipped away.

"It's great to have them back," Weinberg told me, as he folded slices of his own dark, burgundy pastrami onto rye bread. "It's great for the whole industry . . . a little optimism. This carries weight. I'm hoping they're going to be a great success and being hand in hand we'll be a great success together."

Why, I asked Eddie, did this one deli's reopening make any difference? I mean, delis closed and opened all the time in New York, and the 2nd Ave Deli was by no means the first to rise a second time. "Yeah? Well, the Yankees create more interest than the Kansas City Royals do, but they're both just baseball teams, right?" he said. "Listen, even other delis are happy about them opening. When a place like this is missing, it weakens the rest of them, makes them feel less significant."

Each time the waiter slowly poured out the chicken soup from a metal dish into a ceramic bowl, the faces around the cozy room would light up. Then they would take their first hunk out of the baseball-sized dumpling, soak up the rich, golden liquid, inhale for one rewarding second, and bring themselves right back to the corner of 10th Street and Second Avenue. The *matzo* ball was the perfect density; you could hold it on your tongue and it would stay intact, but if you applied just enough pressure it would fall apart. The soup itself was another wonder—dilly, light, and completely clear.

The corned beef was also sensational. The deli's extra curing had somehow improved on Eddie Weinberg's work, so that it was at the point of crumbling, but still dotted with veins of lubricating fat, with a sweet aftertaste. The waiter brought us dessert—the most sensational *rugelach* I'd ever eaten. Each dense little cookie was bristling with cinnamon sugar. Finally, the meal concluded with a new touch of Jeremy Lebewohl's: shot glasses of Bosco chocolate syrup with soda. It was a chocolate phosphate slider, and the sweet fizz of the bubbles was the deli's answer to champagne.

Each individual seemed absorbed in his own equivalent of Proust's madeleine moment. The small room brimmed with joy . . . pure, unsullied, genuine joy. It was the type of euphoria you feel when your hometown team wins the championship, the type of intravenous happiness that makes you want to hug every single person around you, which I, and everyone else, pretty much did that night. As the evening wore on and the vodka appeared, stories and jokes began flowing freely. An old customer pulled out a crusty bottle of half-finished mustard from the original deli, which he'd been saving in his freezer for two years. Though he knew in his heart that the 2nd Ave Deli would somehow reopen, when his faith was in doubt, he'd pull out the jar, hold it tight, and pray.

After the shock of the original deli's closing faded, Jack and Jeremy Lebewohl began discussing the future. Jack loved the deli, but he took over because of Abe's murder, and it was not the life he wanted to lead. Joshua, Jack's oldest son, was starting his career as a lawyer, and none of Sharon Lebewohl's children were interested. Jeremy was selling bagels wholesale, and so the torch of the deli was his. By the summer of 2006 he began looking at properties, and by the end of that year he and Joshua were the proud owners of 162 East 33rd Street. This time, rent wouldn't force anyone out of business.

I first heard about the deli's reopening in January 2007, the very first day I began my journey across the United States. As the deli's debut grew closer, Jeremy and I spoke regularly, mostly about the logistics of the business and when he hoped to open. First it was early October, then before Thanksgiving, then after Thanksgiving, until it finally came down to the week before Christmas. People rightly called it the hottest restaurant debut in New York that year, if not the decade, and the buzz was deafening.

Now we were sitting in Jeremy's deli, at the end of his final preview dinner, on the eve of the Jewish Sabbath. Tomorrow he would rest, on Sunday the staff would train, but come Monday morning the doors would open at six, and they wouldn't shut as long as Jeremy Lebewohl kept the 2nd Ave Deli in business.

"My goal is to open up a classic deli," Jeremy said. "I'm not a chef, but I can guarantee I'm a perfectionist." Still, he knew that his was a different narrative from New York's Deli Men of the past. Jeremy was young, was fairly wealthy, and had graduated from NYU. He dressed not in beaten white aprons, but in designer jeans. "I've never been a dishwasher. I've never worked my way up. People will hate me for it, but that's who I am. It's not the classic immigrant story, but I'm proud of my time and my generation."

Jeremy saw in his contemporaries a burning desire for something real, very much in line with the resurgent movement toward traditionally made, slowly prepared foods. Raised on chain restaurants and prepackaged products, young consumers wanted more than just another concept. They wanted food the way their parents remembered it, without shortcuts, and they were ready to pay for it. The food at the 2nd Ave Deli would be healthy in the sense that it was soulful, freshly cooked, and faithful.

The 2nd Ave Deli brought a recognized brand and established customer base, but it also carried with it a tremendous burden. Expectations for the deli's reopening were astronomical. As one longtime customer wrote me in an e-mail:

"Basically, everybody and their Aunt Tillie is waiting for the 2nd Ave Deli to reopen, and everyone has said the same thing to me. They are going to walk in, order their favorite thing and take ONE BITE. That's all, just one. And if it is not how they remember it they are going to let out a blood-curdling scream and throw the money on the table and walk out. Never to return again."

In reopening the deli, Jeremy had placed himself in the shadow of Abe Lebewohl, possibly the most revered Deli Man of the twentieth century. How did Jeremy plan to meet those expectations? "Impossible. Impossible," he replied emphatically, as the table raised shots to Abe's memory. Abe was Abe. No one could fill those shoes. Jeremy would have to earn the respect of his customers. "My goal is to open the doors Monday morning and have the people who want me fail to say, 'Hey, this is terrific!'"

The original title of this book was *The Death of Deli*, and it was very much a swan song. Everywhere I looked delis were dying. Their numbers, which had been so high in the early twentieth century, had fallen steeply in almost every city I visited. This was as true in Chicago as it was in Paris, but nowhere was this more obvious than New York, a city that once boasted thousands of delis and now had a few dozen. The reasons were well established: a shift in Jewish demographics had replaced the close-knit traditional communities where delis thrived, as Jews moved out to assimilated and disparate suburbs; a change in eating habits, exacerbated by diet fads and shifting warnings about fat, carbs, salt, or meat, had demonized Jewish deli food; the changing landscape of the restaurant industry, with the economics firmly tilted on the side of large chains, made operating family-owned Jewish delicatessens nearly impossible. Everywhere I turned I saw delis closing, delis abandoning their Jewish roots, or delis selling out their very souls for a shot at corporate success. If things continued along this road, the Jewish delicatessen would soon be gone.

I never intended to try to help save the deli; I honestly never thought it was possible. The phrase came about by chance, when I was trying to register domain names for a blog. Deli.com, delicatessen.com, jewishdeli.com, and pastrami.com were taken, but savethedeli.com was available. But the more I visited delis around the world, the greater my sense of hope that the Jewish deli could indeed be saved.

I saw it in New York, in the camaraderie of the countermen at Katz's, and in the late-night love affair between New Yorkers and their pastrami. I saw it in the tourist crowds at the Stage and Carnegie delis, where people came from all over the world to eat a gigantic sandwich. I tasted it in Brooklyn; at Gottlieb's, a glatt kosher deli operated by Yiddish-speaking Hassidim; but also in the sweet potato *knishes* at Adelman's, a kosher delicatessen on King's Highway owned by Mohamed Salem, a devout Egyptian Muslim.

I felt hope in Detroit, where Sy Ginsberg showed me there were people who would do almost anything to help delis, whether behind bulletproof glass in the inner city or at Zingerman's, where sustainable thinking showed a new way forward. I saw it in Chicago, a city that had basically given deli up for dead and was now experiencing a downtown revival. I found hope along the road west, from fading traditionalists hanging on in Missouri to diehard New York deli owners in Denver. I tasted possibility at Jimmy and Drew's 28th Street Deli in Boulder, which proved that great deli could happen anywhere. I witnessed it in San Francisco, in a gourmet deli movement by the Bay, and in Los Angeles, a city with the strongest delicatessen families anywhere.

I saw hope for the deli in Las Vegas, not in the casinos, as many did, but in the local spot Weiss Bakery and Delicatessen, which served wholesome deli meals. I felt it in the new frontiers of Arizona, and in Texas, where a veteran New York Deli Man like Ziggy Gruber could sell a traditional, *haymish* delicatessen as though he were operating on the Lower East Side. I tasted it in New Orleans, where tough delis outlasted tough times, and yes, even in Florida, where the demise of delis at the hands of corporations did nothing to temper the love of the food among the state's aging Jewish residents.

I beheld deli at its purest in the uncompromising smoked meat sandwiches of Montreal. I beheld dignity in London's well-manicured salt beef bars, in the gourmet meats at Antwerp's Hoffy's, and Michel Kalifa's small Parisian delicatessen, an experience that opened my eyes to the limitless culinary possibilities of this food. Even in Poland, I witnessed traditional Jewish food rise up from the grave against all odds.

Best of all, I finally witnessed salvation back home. In June 2008, a young Toronto cook named Zane Caplansky installed himself in the unused kitchen of a dank tavern downtown and began selling hand-cut smoked meat sandwiches. Inspired by Schwartz's, Zane had cured raw briskets from scratch, smoking them over hardwood for ten whole hours, resulting in a heaven-sent blend of Montreal smoked meat and Texas BBQ brisket. Deli lovers all over Toronto emerged from hibernation, and within two days of opening, Caplansky's Delicatessen had sold out of meat. Caplansky's has been packed ever since. When the growing crowds have occasionally eaten through Caplansky's entire supply of meat, Zane, ever the purist, simply closed shop for a day or two until his next batch of briskets have cured. Sure, he could order a replacement product or farm out his production to purveyors (he's had countless offers), but his respect for deli's purity is so strong that he'd rather turn away diners than cut corners. My hopes for deli's preservation in Toronto were buoyed even further when, six months after telling me he was going to sell, Lorne Pancer, owner of Moe Pancer's deli, had a change of heart. He took his grandfather's delicatessen off the market and got back to slicing sandwiches. "How could I let anyone else own this?" he said with a smile, acknowledging that the negative reaction to the sale on my website was a factor in his decision. Between Pancer and Caplansky, Toronto's legacy and its past were in good hands.

What I saw, heard, and ate in these places represented a slight but significant shift in the history of the Jewish deli. A change was in the air. The delicatessen had come so close to death that even normally complacent people had finally taken notice. I had encountered a small, passionate group of people who were ready to stand up and fight for the very survival of the Jewish delicatessen. There was an appetite for a new type of Jewish delicatessen, one that blended the traditions of the past with the ideals of the present. This new breed of deli would come from a different generation of Deli Men unbound by age, sex, nationality, or even religion, but who possessed the fearlessness and creativity that could bring the Jewish delicatessen into the twenty-first century, while staying faithful to the flavors of the nineteenth. I encountered this in several places, but nowhere did I feel this more than at the reopening of the 2nd Ave Deli.

———

At 9:00 a.m. on December 17, 2007, the perky hosts of the morning shows, wire services reporters, and newspaper photographers all filled the 2nd Ave Deli, descending on the few eager customers eating pastrami sandwiches for breakfast like they were celebrities. I sat down with Jack Lebewohl, who ordered me lox, eggs, and onions—a fluffy, plate-sized pancake filled with salty flakes of smoked fish.

"Jeremy has a certain knack," Jack said. "He got it from Abe. That's why Abe had a special affinity for Jeremy. In many ways he's just like my brother; his relationship with employees, the way he talks to vendors, his feel for the food. . . . The secret is that you're willing to try something new, like the *gribenes* or chocolate soda, and if it doesn't work you go back. It's a certain kind of fearlessness. But Jeremy also has a certain intelligence to know how to reverse course."

At 11:00 a.m., the assembled press corps gathered outside for the official opening, and the 2nd Ave Deli's sign was unveiled. Jack and his wife, Terry, Jeremy and Joshua Lebewohl, Steve Cohen, and a few other staff officially opened the deli by cutting a long string of small kosher salami links. Flashbulbs popped, a small cheer went up, and then everyone went back inside for lunch. At the deli's rear table, I happened upon my friend Joshua Wolf Shenk. "I couldn't be there when the Berlin Wall came down," he said, "but this I wouldn't miss." Joshua had ordered a combination pastrami/corned beef sandwich. The thin slices of the pink corned beef and the dark red pastrami spilled over the crust of the rye bread, leaving a trail of meat scraps and peppercorns on the plate. He generously applied spicy brown mustard, shut his eyes, and bit in. "Ummmmpppphhhh!" His eyes rolled back into his skull, and he reclined into the vinyl. After ten seconds or so he swallowed, and opened his eyes, looking as though he'd emerged from a trance. "I really forgot how good it tastes," Joshua said. He took another bite, closed his eyes, and nodded. Inside his brain, Joshua's neurons were firing away in sharp sparkles, his grin verging on the post-coital. "This is fucking dynamite! Usually the anticipation is greater than the experience, but this is a fucking incredible meal!"

Jeremy came up to us. "David, come with me outside—the lineup is down the block and I need help handing out chopped liver." We donned coats and walked out the front door, to a crowd of thirty-odd people and growing that snaked down the street. The food disappeared in ten seconds, with elderly women in fur coats literally licking up the greasy scrapings from the parchment paper. Soon, every seat was filled. The small space between the door, the takeout counter, and the cash became packed with bodies. The slicing machines were humming, orders were being shouted, and dishes were clanging. Above it all rose a symphony of chatter, smacking lips, drained drinks, and the guttural utterances of happy customers. Once again, the 2nd Ave Deli was alive.

Then, through the throngs of people, I saw Sharon Lebewohl. When I last spoke to her she was broken-hearted and very much at odds with her uncle Jack. The closing of the original deli, plus the pain of her father's murder, had amplified any rift they'd felt. When I contacted her weeks before, she sent me a brief reply:

"I would love to speak with you but I'm not involved with the new deli at all. I doubt that I will be there for the grand opening."

Now she was standing in front of me, looking simply radiant, her face flushed with color. Jeremy walked up and gave her a big hug. "Thank you for coming, Sharon," he whispered into her ear, "you have no idea what this means to me." Jack came over and wrapped his arms around her, and once again, the Lebewohl family was whole. "It's her father's place," Jeremy told me out of earshot, "and for her to be here means the world to me."

We sat and ate, Jack, Sharon, and I. We had mushroom barley soup, made with dried shiitake mushrooms and beads of barley that held the sweet, woodsy flavor of a forest floor. Sharon thought it was actually an improvement on the original. Next came the stuffed cabbage, which had a hint of cinnamon that lingered in the mouth after the tender beef was devoured. Then I ordered something that I'd never had before: a rolled beef sandwich. Rolled beef was once a staple of New York delis. Basically butterflied navel, peppered on the outside, it is then rolled and tied with string so the slices come out in large rounds. Empire National was the only purveyor who still made rolled beef, and they sold it to a handful of old-school delicatessens on an irregular basis. Now I stared down at rounds of pink meat streaked with white tributaries of creamy fat, rimmed with the slightest hint of pepper. It was mild and rich, cool and slick, sweet and spicy.

When Jack left to help Jeremy, I asked Sharon why she'd changed her mind about coming. "I thought it over and I just woke up this morning and felt I needed to be with my family," she said, tears of joy welling up in her eyes. "Everything that happened . . . it was nobody's fault. When I first heard they'd be reopening, I thought it was a mistake. I thought restaurants and delis didn't last long, and I was afraid it would hurt the name my father built. I couldn't let go of the old. This is a great testament to my father, and if anyone was going to do great it'd be Jeremy. . . . It feels like a continuation. I feel my father's presence, and this would have had his blessing. My father was so proud of his family. Even if he were alive, Jeremy would be doing this."

A young busboy came over and looked at a cartoon hanging on the wall. It was from the days after Abe Lebewohl's murder, and it showed the Deli Man ascending on a cloud to heaven. The angels looked on with glee at the food he was bringing to the Pearly Gates. The busboy's face changed to a frown. "Awwww. . . " Sharon just smiled.

All afternoon people kept streaming in the door. At four o'clock Ariella, Jeremy's recent bride, came in for a quick hello, while Jeremy ran around putting out fires. The deli was running out of *challah* bread and chicken soup, and there hadn't been a quiet moment to mop the floors. The phone rang nonstop with orders, questions, and even people applying for jobs. Added to this, New York deli customers were doing what they do best . . . argue. A man and a woman had staked a claim on the same seat, and each was pleading their case to the assembled crowd.

"Excuse me, lady, but I gotta eat quick, because I have a sick son in the hospital!"

"Oh yeah, well if he's so sick you should be in the hospital with him, not here!"

The computer system kept crashing, and people trying to pay for their takeout orders waited nearly an hour. The whole time in line they *kvetched* and on their way out really let Jeremy have it. "That's when I don't envy his job," Ariella said, as she got up, kissed Jeremy, and returned to work. Still, not a single person I met complained about the food, which was uniformly acknowledged as excellent.

"When I walked in I got tears," said Jeff Jacobs, a longtime customer, as he waited for takeout. "I don't see corned beef, I see my family celebrating occasions. I see my mother getting pink flowers from Abe on Mother's Day. This is Jewish culture living. This is my family's heritage living on."

By seven o'clock the crowd wasn't letting up, and I had to leave to meet friends. "Come," Jeremy said, "let's have a beer." We headed down to the basement, into the small manager's office packed with supplies. He'd been up for fifteen hours straight and probably had another five to go before he could even begin to contemplate going home. His forehead had broken out, and bags appeared under his eyes. He sucked back the beer and breathed deeply. "This is the first time I've sat all day," he said. "I'd love nothing more than to sleep, but this is my newborn baby and there's no way I can leave it now."

I looked at Jeremy Lebewohl and saw in that young man's drained face the future of the Jewish delicatessen. I didn't tell him though. Of all the things he needed to hear on that first day of the rest of his life as a New York Deli Man, that wasn't one of them.

We finished our beers and headed out into the cold, dark

street. The lineup was still halfway down the block and growing. There were college kids, millionaire bankers, and poverty-stricken Holocaust survivors. There were families and singles, Jews and Asians, blacks and Hispanics, New Yorkers, Americans, and foreigners. All of them were standing in the freezing cold, in a constantly replenishing lineup that wouldn't die down for weeks. I wished Jeremy Lebewohl all the luck in the world. Then I walked away, confident that at least one deli was safe.

Afterword to the Paperback Edition

The Schmaltz Strikes Back: Deli's Future Returns to Its Roots

In the spring of 2008, shortly after I'd finished most of the writing and editing of this book, I received a brief e-mail via savethedeli.com from a guy named Zane Caplan. He stated his intention to cure his own smoked meat and sell it in Toronto, and though his budget was lean, he boasted that deli was "in his blood". To be honest, I kind of shrugged. I got e-mails like this all the time and never heard from the majority of these dreamers again. My roommate at the time, Adam Caplan, looked over my shoulder and remarked, "I think that guy's my cousin."

If there was ever an unlikely savior for deli in my hometown, Zane Caplan was it. He grew up in a political dynasty, surrounded by well-known parents and siblings who held prominent posts in Canadian government. Zane fell into that life, running campaigns and working in related businesses, until a difficult divorce sent him across the world on a bout of soul searching. He lived for a number of years in India, working in and running small restaurants for travelers. Cooking was his passion, and when he returned to Toronto after a few years abroad, he began catering to film sets and managing a pizzeria.

Deli held a special place in Zane's heart. He had grown up eating at Switzer's with his grandfather, who was in the garment business, and later held court at Moe Pancer's, Yitz's, Coleman's, and other stalwarts of the Toronto deli scene. Inspired by his frequent road trips to Montreal for Schwartz's smoked meat, Zane began tinkering around in his home kitchen, trying to replicate a decent alternative so he wouldn't have to drive five hours each time he wanted a sandwich. He dry cured raw briskets with pickling salt and a dozen heady spices (including mustard seed, fennel, and Kashmiri chili powder he'd procured in Little India) for two weeks, then smoked them over hickory in his backyard. He served it to friends. They loved it. "You should open a deli," a few said.

Why not a deli? People loved the barbecue and charcuterie restaurants that were popping up on every corner, and wasn't smoked meat a marriage of the two? Young Jewish families and retiring baby boomers were returning to downtown Toronto, which boasted a vibrant Jewish cultural scene, but most of the Jewish restaurants remained in the suburbs. Wasn't it time the delicatessen returned as well? Zane saw his life's mission taking shape before his eyes. His great-grandfather was one of the first kosher butchers in the city, and this would be a continuation of the family legacy. He would name the deli after his family's original name, and to make his commitment official, Zane went and legally changed his last name back to Caplansky.

Though Zane didn't have the money to start a restaurant from scratch, he caught a lucky break. Sitting in the Monarch Tavern one day, a Little Italy dive bar he frequented, Zane began discussing his plan of opening a deli with the owner. The owner pointed to a small kitchen beside the bar, which hadn't been used in years, and suggested he start up his operation there. Zane could use the kitchen to prep and sell his sandwiches, and he could keep all the profits from what he sold. The bar would sell the drinks, increasing business during their quiet lunch hour. All Zane would have to pay was a couple hundred bucks a month in rent . . . peanuts compared to the thousands most landlords wanted for a restaurant, not to mention the tens of thousands in construction costs and legal red tape needed to open his own place. It was a no-brainer.

Two weeks before he was going to open, I met Zane at the Monarch Tavern. He had a baby face, a loveable pudge, artsy glasses, and salt-and-pepper curls that flopped to the side. Though we'd never met, when he started talking about deli, I knew there was something special brewing in this soul. "I'm putting the Star of David on my menu as a way of identifying this as an authentic Jewish deli," he told me, proudly. "I hope that the smell of smoked meat will awaken the nascent memories of the Jews who live downtown and have forgotten about this food."

In the tradition of Montreal's great delicatessen temples, Caplansky's was going to be spartan. The meat was cured in barrels in the tavern's basement and smoked in a small electric smoker on site. Fries were fresh cut to order and double fried in the tiny kitchen, which was about the size of a compact car. Smoked turkey would be available on occasion, as well as borscht and coleslaw, but not much more. He figured that business would slowly grow over the summer, starting with one or two sandwiches a day for the first month, as word slowly spread. Zane would leisurely slip into the role of deli man after a drawn-out learning period. He planned to have enough free time that he'd spend his afternoons taking sailing lessons.

Thanks to advanced press (some of which I contributed), Caplansky's had a sizable crowd waiting for him on opening day. The smoked meat was nicely salted, cut thick by Zane's own hand and tenderized with ribbons of melted fat. It boasted a complex spicing that was entirely unique, a subtle prickle of heat with whiffs of Texas BBQ smoke. As I left, every table was occupied, and customers were still coming in the door. Zane had widely underestimated the chord he would strike. Word was spreading via phone calls and blog posts that Jewish deli was back in downtown Toronto, and deli lovers flocked to the Monarch for a taste. The next day, within ten minutes of opening, Caplansky's delicatessen had completely sold out of meat.

Zane now faced a choice: order some pre-pickled meat from a

purveyor and keep the momentum going, or close down the deli, get back to curing, and wait for a week until it was ready. That Zane went the latter route—closing his business, handing out two-for-one coupons, and waiting for his briskets to cure—is more than just an indication of his overnight success. Most deli owners would have opted for the pre-pickled product in a heartbeat, which is easier, cheaper, and more consistent than anything made by hand. Most would have seen a week without business as disastrous, a still-born start for a brand new delicatessen. But Zane Caplansky was just *meshuga* enough to have the courage to hold off on the fear and stick to his guns.

To Zane, the integrity of his meat came before anything else, and serving someone else's product was simply unthinkable. In this mindset, he is part of a small but growing cadre of deli men whose greatest goal isn't so much progress as regress, bringing Jewish deli back to the way it was done a hundred years ago. They look to the greenmarket for inspiration as much as to Katz's, and manage to successfully balance traditions with current tastes. This is the Jewish delicatessen's own roots movement, and it is producing the most promising future for deli lovers since pastrami first met rye.

Across North America, the buzzwords amongst foodies, restaurateurs, and chefs for much of the past decade have been "local," "seasonal," "organic," and "in-house." What began with Alice Waters in Berkeley, California, some forty years earlier has become the hallmark of quality eating across much of the continent. Sure, your fast-food chains and your conglomerates like ConAgra are still expanding our waistbands with refined corn and microwavable fajita pockets, but for serious food lovers, it is all about the slow, the handmade, the authentic. Part of this has to do with a social consciousness. Local, slow food (so its advocates preach) is said to be better for the environment and ourselves.

This is certainly the philosophy driving Karen and Peter Levitt, the owners of Saul's Delicatessen in Berkeley, who have been spearheading the Jewish deli's back-to-the-roots movement for over a decade. They've made sustainable deli their hallmark, sourcing products locally, often to the protest of loyalists who want to know why the Dr. Brown's Cel-Ray has been replaced by a no-name variant made nearby. But they've gained the support of local food gurus like writer Michael Pollan, who is to this vanguard of eaters what Warren Buffett is to your Wall Street trader.

Sustainability is also what drives much of the philosophy behind Ari and Paul at Zingerman's, where the sourcing of ingredients is as important, if not more so, than the recipe behind the *challah*, or the *blintz*, or the *knish*. The reason they do this is for the flavor. Food made the old-fashioned way, without preservatives, has a flavor that's positively alive. To the roots delis, the best thing you can do in the kitchen is turn back the clock, because among all the advancements in production we've made, a lot of the taste has been sacrificed.

"[The deli business] has been stuck in a late-twentieth-century model," said Nick Zukin, co-owner of Kenny and Zuke's Delicatessen, in Portland, Oregon. Zukin consistently bemoans the homogenization of the Jewish deli's flavors in favor of better margins. "Everything after World War II was about efficiency. But a hundred years ago there *had* to be more variety in the products and the way things tasted in the deli."

In 2006, Zukin, a solidly built local food blogger with a baby face (who wears shorts every day), contacted Ken Gordon, a boastful restaurant owner originally from the heart of Queens, New York, with a proposal. There was no good pastrami in Portland, which has a relatively small Jewish population, but an active and vibrant food scene. Gordon had a great smoker at his restaurant and regularly did BBQ nights. Was he interested in a little pastrami experiment?

The duo set to work curing briskets in salt, sugar, and spices, rubbing them with cracked pepper and coriander, and smoking them for eight hours over oak. They rented a booth one Sunday at a local farmers' market and at 10 a.m. slapped their first steaming pastrami on the cutting board. Within ten minutes all their briskets were gone. A week later, they doubled their batch. That sold out in fifteen minutes. People were literally trying to buy half-eaten sandwiches out of customers' hands. The two realized that they were onto something special, and Gordon and Zukin soon began offering a Saturday delicatessen brunch at Gordon's popular restaurant, Ken's Place. They made corned beef and tongue, pickles, *knishes, rugelach,* freshly baked bagels, and rye bread, all from scratch. Lines would snake around the block for over an hour. It was so successful that by late 2007, Gordon shut Ken's Place, and the two opened Kenny and Zuke's Delicatessen.

A visit to Kenny and Zuke's, located in a sun-drenched space below the boutique ACE Hotel, offers a taste of the Jewish delicatessen's hopeful future. Windows reach nearly two stories high and wrap around the bright yellow interior, which is minimally decorated and retains the original hardwood flooring. The people who work there are young, idealistic, and enthusiastic. Each morning, a trio of hippies turn on the tunes, hand-roll bagels, dip them in malted water, and bake them for breakfast. The night before, Matt Scaletta, a shaggy-haired twenty-five-year-old who grew up canning fish in Alaska, preps and smokes the pastrami over solid chunks of oak that he splits with an axe in the deli's basement.

What emerges is a dark red brisket with an intense, brackish tang, hints of peppery spice, and a pronounced smokiness that melts perfectly into the rich marbling. The meat is steamed for close to three hours, hand-carved thick (because, like Caplansky's, they believe their meat should never be thrown on a slicing machine), and placed atop Kenny and Zuke's own house-baked rye bread. Studded with caraway seeds and baked to a malty brown, it is dense, sourdough fragrant, and a far cry from the homogenized loaves of white bread that most delicatessens pass off as rye.

"I can buy other rye cheaper," says the cherry-nosed, salt-and-pepper haired Gordon, "but damn, ours is good! Are we going to put our pastrami on a lesser rye? I don't think so." Behind Kenny and Zuke's refusal to compromise is a fiercely independent streak common to these new delis. They ignore the accepted wisdom of the deli business, especially the maxim that all roads must lead through New York. That may seem foolish, but cleaving themselves from the New York deli mindset is the first step Jewish delis need to move forward. There are far too many delis scattered around the world that bring in meats, breads, and other products from New York, when there's great stuff in their own backyards. They decorate their interiors like some compressed version of a Times Square souvenir shop—a Statue of Liberty at the entrance, taxicab murals, Broadway posters galore. The problem is that these places compete with the dead, and no matter how hard you try, you can never make a sandwich that's better than the one you ate with your Uncle Lou fifty years back in Flatbush, Brooklyn.

At Kenny and Zuke's, you won't find a single reference to New York on the menu or on the walls, despite Gordon's proud roots there. "We have never billed it as a New York deli," he says emphatically. "Never, ever! And we never will." Kenny and Zuke's bills itself as a Jewish delicatessen, just as Caplansky's does. In an era where many deli owners outside New York are still afraid to identify too loudly as Jewish, these new ones exhibit a refreshing streak of cultural pride.

Although their food may be rooted in what took shape in the late nineteenth-century Lower East Side, by taking a local approach to sourcing, ingredients, and handmade preparation, they're moving deli food forward while looking back. Instead of bringing in frozen *knishes* from Long Island, they use a recipe from a local blogger, filled with creamier, garlic-infused mashed potatoes and topped by a glistening crown of caramelized onions. Scaletta even cures the deli's thinly sliced *gravlax*, which practically melts atop the chewy bagels with nice, large holes. The result is food that's at the top of the deli game: puffy *latkes* with a fresh ginger applesauce, sashimi soft pickled tongue, and a noodle *kugel* that tastes like a creamy cinnamon bun. The tastes are probably closer to what people in New York were eating at delis a century ago.

While most delis make an egg cream soda with U-Bet chocolate syrup, Kenny and Zuke's makes theirs with Dagoba organic chocolate, an upscale brand from Oregon. When they first introduced this, many of their transplanted East Coast clientele threw up their arms, protesting that "you can't make an egg cream without U-Bet!" One local food writer accused them of "gentrifying the egg cream." But one sip demonstrated the superiority of Kenny and Zuke's interpretation. Their egg cream was deeper, richer, and more full of cocoa than any I'd tasted before, with a cap of foam on top that almost looked like a cappuccino.

The point, Ken made sure to tell me, was that the food they served at Kenny and Zuke's had their unique fingerprint on it. Anyone could make an egg cream with U-Bet syrup, pastrami sandwiches with Hebrew National meat, and *matzo* ball soup with frozen stock, and hundreds of delis did just that. But you could only get a Kenny and Zuke's egg cream and sandwich at one delicatessen in Portland, Oregon. It defined their deli as a destination, a place where people had to come to taste what they were up to. But it also sent a message: that the taste of Jewish deli food wasn't defined by any standard parameter. It could be as creative and diverse as the deli owner could make it.

"Why should there be just one type of pastrami?" Ken asked me, frustrated that the field was so narrowly defined. "Why shouldn't there be as many varieties of pastrami in America as there are of pizza?" Nick echoed, "Pastrami flavor is so uniform, people say, 'That isn't how pastrami tastes' when they try ours, because it's different than what they expect. But it's interesting to look at hundred-year-old recipes for pastrami and see how unique it was back then, before it all got homogenized in the 1950s, when price was all that anyone cared about."

Kenny and Zuke's pastrami, and indeed much of their food, demanded an opinion. It wasn't middle-of-the-road. It took bold risks, and often they paid off, but just as often brought up criticism from dedicated deli lovers. But they didn't shirk away from this. They sought it out, and challenged the status quo.

The same philosophy had worked for Zane Caplansky, whose tremendous success after a year in the Monarch Tavern allowed him to open his own restaurant. The new Caplansky's Delicatessen found its home at the entrance to Kensington Market, Toronto's historic downtown Jewish enclave, in a building that had housed delicatessens in the 1950s and '60s. Zane expanded the menu to include homemade *kishka* with real *schmaltz*, pickled tongue, and several variety of *knishes* in a strudel dough, with homemade mushroom and smoked meat gravies.

On many weekends the lineup snakes out the door, and the makeup of Caplansky's crowd belies Zane's crossover success. There's always a core of middle-aged Jews (my parents included), many of whom only returned to deli eating when Caplansky's opened. But you also find a cross-section of downtown Toronto, with Chinese university students, American tourists, and Portuguese construction workers filling up the tables and relishing in the *haymish* food. Caplansky's has ignited a mini deli fever in my hometown, which is starting to rival Montreal in its passion. Several restaurants have begun featuring their own smoked meat and tongue sandwiches, each with its own taste fingerprint. Not only that, but veterans like Moe Pancer's have benefited from the Caplansky phenomenon, as deli is once again hot for Toronto's Jews after a long dormant period.

The roots deli movement isn't bound to these two examples. Out west, stalwarts like Canter's, and young upstarts in San Francisco and Los Angeles have been rolling out pastrami trucks and egg cream stands on bicycles, selling their goods at farmers' markets, concerts, or other events without worrying about framing it between four walls. They have injected the Jewish delicatessen with a spirit of innovation and excitement that had been lacking for some time.

But while it took root on the West Coast, and has made landfall in places like Chicago, Philadelphia, and South Carolina, there was one place where I was still waiting for this new movement to land: New York. The spiritual and cultural home of the Jewish delicatessen had seen the greatest decline in delis over the years, and its deli lovers were by far the most traditional, the most stubborn, the most resistant to change. When I'd tell deli owners in New York about Caplansky's or Kenny and Zuke's, they'd dismiss them offhand. "That would never work here," they'd tell me with a scoff. "You can't cure stuff yourself. It's too expensive. It's impossible." But I knew it was only a matter of time before the deli revolution made landfall in New York. And last summer, just months before *Save the Deli* hit bookshelves, I met the man who would make it happen.

Noah Bernamoff was twenty-seven years old at the time, a Montreal suburban Jew with fat sideburns, whose previous job was bassist in the rock band Lovely Feathers. He was now living in Park Slope, Brooklyn, two and a half years into a law degree, and engaged to be married. An avid cook and foodie, he'd spent the previous months tinkering with a recipe for smoked meat, which he'd desperately missed since he had moved to New York with his fiancée, Rachel. Bernamoff began curing briskets in his apartment with an experimental mix of over a dozen spices, and smoking them on the roof in a BBQ with whatever wood he could find. Friends were invited over. Beers were drunk. Sandwiches were sliced and served. Hushed silence followed. Bernamoff suddenly had a mission. Law school would have to wait.

The plan was to open a Montreal-style delicatessen in brownstone Brooklyn, where he'd serve smoked meat, Montreal bagels, and other treats inspired by his hometown. Everything would be homemade (except the bagels) in a tiny little kitchen. Bernamoff was already grinding, stuffing, and smoking his own salamis, as well as *karnatzel*. He was pickling pickles, baking cheese *bageleh*, curing salmon, and trying to perfect a Wilensky-style sandwich. All of this would go into a restaurant so small it could only seat twenty comfortably and twenty-five squished: about a quarter the size of Schwartz's, or the size of a few booths at Canter's. He'd name it Mile End, after a neighborhood in Montreal.

As word spread, and red tape delayed his opening from the fall of 2009 to early 2010, the buzz around Mile End built. There was a sense of anticipation that rippled through the city's deli lovers, both old and young, traditional and experimental. The roots deli was finally landing in New York. The city's deli owners remained skeptical, however: "A kid without any restaurant experience? Not a single day working at a deli? Forget it. He won't last a week." On top of that, this was a foreign deli coming into the delicatessen heartland, akin to a reform rabbi from Los Angeles showing up at the Western Wall in Jerusalem and reading a sermon. It simply wasn't done.

But when Noah and Rachel opened the door that cold January day, the doubters were blown away. The meat, which was made with dry aged briskets from select purveyors, then cured and smoked in the deli, was so tender it barely made it onto the bread. The flavor was inspired by Montreal, but more rounded, with notes of fresh garlic, paprika, and other aromatics like clove, which melded with the homemade mustard Bernamoff had provided. The salami was incredible, with a rough texture that worked perfectly when fried and tossed with loosely scrambled eggs and fresh greens. The silken lox were hand carved into translucent slices, which dissolved into the essence of salt, sugar, and dill. The cheese *bageleh*, wrapped in flaky pastry, were somewhere between a *blintz* and Balkan *burek*.

From the communal tables made of salvaged bowling lanes to the indie rock soundtrack to the smile of Rachel—who quickly became a natural hostess with her welcoming smile and vintage outfits—Mile End projected an immediate and cool intimacy that few other delis could boast. It felt very much of the moment, likely because the crowd was so young. In most delis, I walked in and felt like I was in an AARP commercial. Mile End felt like an American Apparel ad. It was a fun place to be. Everyone there, from the staff to the customers, was excited to be a part of it.

It also turned out to be the perfect fit for New York. Rather than present itself as a foreign challenger, questioning the supremacy of New York deli, Mile End became a complement to the city's unparalleled Jewish food universe. Considering that smoked meat came to Montreal by way of New York City, this was a repatriation of lost flavors that had disappeared from New York decades before. That brought in the old-timers as well, whose skepticism often disappeared after the first bite. Even one or two of the city's deli owners had checked it out and conceded it was "interesting," which was as big a compliment as you could ever wring out of that crew.

Over the decades that the Jewish delicatessen has been in decline, many have attempted to fix it, change it, or reinvent it in one way or another. They've brought in foods from different cultures, expanded menus greatly, and changed the taste of the classics depending on trends. Others have poured their money into the decoration, trying to make the deli look more fancy or more fun. None have had the desired effect: to save the Jewish delicatessen by rescuing its relevance. If anything, they've made it even more irrelevant.

Mile End, Kenny and Zuke's, and Caplansky's each began with a craving for deli, a recipe, and a backyard smoker. No one started with a concept or a business plan. They all originated with a brisket, some spices, and a firm desire to put out their own version of a classic. Each of these were begun by cooks and chefs who had gourmet skills, but who craved comfort food most of all. There's nothing gimmicky or glib about any of this. It's decidedly honest, and let's all hope it's a glimpse into the future of the Jewish deli as a whole.

Food and Yiddish Appendix

(for the goyim or woefully assimilated)

Soup (Go on, make it a meal)

Chicken Soup with Matzo Balls (a.k.a. *kneidelach*): The essence of all Yiddish life. Matzo balls are made from matzo flour, *schmaltz*, and seltzer. Can be either floaters, sinkers, or the rare, perfect mix. Your mother's are always the best, and your mother-in-law's are always the worst.

Mishmosh: Chicken soup fully loaded with matzo balls, kreplach, noodles, rice, chicken, and vegetables.

Cabbage Borscht: Some brisket, some cabbage, some beets, a little tomato juice . . . dinner for a month.

Berditchev Soup: Rare Polish vegetable soup with honey, cloves, and spices . . . think apple cider meets Campbell's. Served in vaguely anti-Semitic Krakow restaurants.

Mushroom Barley Soup: Rib-sticking soup, often made with beef stock.

Forshpeis (Appetizers)

Knishes: Baked or fried pockets of dough, filled with potato, kasha, spinach, and sometimes meat scraps from the deli. Served with gravy or from New York vendor carts.

Kishke (a.k.a. Stuffed *Derma*): Beef intestine stuffed with chicken *schmaltz,* matzo meal, and the traces of what were once vegetables. Smothered in gravy, to reach every last artery.

Kreplach: Little dumplings filled with minced beef and onion, fried or boiled and served with caramelized onions or added to soup.

Kasha Varnishkes: Buckwheat grains and onions sautéed in *schmaltz* and tossed with bowtie pasta. Served with gravy if you want it to taste like anything.

Tzimmes: Stewed carrots with prunes, honey, raisins, and enough sugar to kill a horse.

Hush Puppies: Hot dog wrapped in a potato knish. Like a pig in a blanket, but somehow puppies are more kosher than pigs.

Gribenes: Chicken skins fried in fat until they crackle. Jewish pork rinds.

Chopped Liver: Fried chicken (or beef) livers, chopped with eggs and fried onions. Loved by babies, despised by kids, rediscovered during pregnancy.

Schmaltz: Fat, most often chicken fat, rendered during the making of soup, cooled, and used for cooking, flavoring, or as an aphrodisiac to attract Jewish men.

P'tcha: Calves' feet and garlic boiled and then cooled into a jelly, set in a mold and sliced. What's not to love?

Gefilte Fish: Minced whitefish poached into a ball. Served with beet sweetened horseradish (*chrain*).

Coleslaw: Chopped cabbage, vinegar, sugar, spices, and for some (ugh) mayonnaise.

Latkes: Fried potato pancakes traditionally eaten at Hanukah. Served with applesauce and all too often a hockey stick.

Breads (a.k.a. Carbs)

Rye: Traditional Eastern European bread made with coarse rye flour and caraway seeds. The foundation of any deli sandwich. Best served double baked, ideally from Detroit.

Pletzl: Onion Kaiser. Also a nickname for Paris's Rue des Rosiers.

Challah: Braided, sweet egg bread traditionally eaten on Sabbath eve. Perfect with a *shmear* of chopped liver.

Bagel: That's a whole other book.

White Bread: Don't you fucking dare.

Deli Meats (The Holy of Holies)

Pastrami: Spiced, cured, smoked navel of beef. The pride of New York, though L.A. does it well too.

Corned Beef/Salt Beef: Pickled and boiled brisket of beef. Good cop to pastrami's bad cop. Best in the Midwest.

Salami: A sausage of minced beef trimmings, spices, fat, and enough salt to melt ice. Served cold, grilled, or fried with eggs.

Karnatzel: Romanian-inspired salami the width of a nickel. Only available in Montreal and best when hung to dry for a week or so.

Pickled Tongue: Like corned beef but with a big cow's tongue. An edible French kiss.

Rolled Beef: A navel butterflied, rolled, tied with string, then cured and smoked like pastrami and sliced paper-thin and cold. Carried by a handful of delis in New York on elusive days.

Baby Beef: Pickled and lightly smoked veal brisket, found only in Toronto. Disappearing rapidly.

Montreal Smoked Meat: Romanian-style spiced, cured, and smoked brisket. The best deli meat you've never eaten.

Roast Brisket: Simple oven-braised brisket. Bland but quite delicate.

Stuffed Chicken: Montreal specialty of minced chicken baloney. Made too often with pork!

Roast/Smoked Turkey: Why even bother?

Kosher Hot Dog: Because kosher-style hot dogs just won't do.

Knoblewurst: Large garlic sausage, eaten hot off the griddle.

Speck: Paprika-dusted, twice-smoked slices of pickled fat from a brisket. Deadly to Saxes.

Combinations (For true gluttons)

Reuben: Corned beef, sauerkraut, Swiss cheese, and Russian dressing on grilled dark rye. So goyish it's practically kosher.

Mains (. . . Now that you're warmed up)

Flanken: Boiled beef short ribs served in beef or chicken broth. The fattier the ribs, the better.

Fricassee: Stew of chicken parts (usually wings/drums) and perhaps meatballs in a tomato-based gravy. One of the more fun dishes to pronounce.

Stuffed Cabbage: Cabbage leaves stuffed with rice (vegetarian) or rice and ground beef, in a sweet tomato jus. Fart factory.

Tongue Polonaise: Sliced broiled tongue in a sweet raisin sauce. When in doubt, drown it in sweetness.

Charbroiled Romanian Tenderloin: Also known as a skirt steak, a thin, fatty cut of meat that drapes off the place and is consumed with fried onions by old Jewish gangsters.

Cholent: Slowly braised stew of beans, potatoes, and meat. Traditionally eaten on the Sabbath, it requires prayer to digest.

Desserts (Because the diet starts tomorrow)

Rugelach: Dense little cookies/danish seasoned with fruit, nuts, cinnamon, and buckets of sugar.

Lokshen Kugel: Egg custard made with egg noodles, then baked. Like a sweet lasagna omelet.

Cheesecake: Baked, chilled sweetened cream cheese cake in a graham cracker crust with fruit or chocolate topping. Should constrict throat first, arteries later.

Blintzes: Crepes stuffed with farmer's cheese or sweetened fruit and rolled like burritos. Served with applesauce, sour cream, and a bib.

Drinks (For digestion, of course)

Cel-Ray Tonic: Celery-flavored soda. Produced by Dr. Brown's, supposedly a cure-all.

Black Cherry: Libation of choice for deli drinkers. Dr. Brown's in the U.S., Cott's in Canada.

Seltzer: Bubbly water. Billed as "2 Cents Plain," costs $2.50. The nerve.

Tea: Best drunk out of a glass with lemon and spilled over half the table.

Coffee: Decaf only. Be sure to ask waitress ten times if it's decaf, then complain that it isn't strong enough.

Key Terms (So you don't sound like a schmuck)

Fress: To eat a lot. A big eater is a *fresser*. "He polished off two sandwiches and a knish. Quite the *fresser*."

Nosh: To eat a little. A nibbler is a nosher. "I'll stop by, but just for a nosh."

Bissel: A little bit. "Gimme a *bissel* of that chopped liver."

Chutzpah: Nerve. "You got a lot of chutzpah to ask for butter on that sandwich."

Gonif: A thief. "Sixteen dollars for a sandwich? Those *gonifs*!"

Meshugah: Crazy. "You've gotta be *meshugah* to pay those prices."

Kibitz: To joke. "Mel Brooks was in yesterday, kibitzing with everyone."

Plotz: To burst, explode. "I ate so much I could *plotz*."

Shonda: A shame. "They took herring off the menu . . . such a *shonda*."

Schmutz: Dirt. "There was so much *schmutz* there it was like eating in a bus station."

To Die For: The highest culinary compliment. "The rolled beef was to die for" or "The rolled beef: to die."

Zay Gezunt: Be in health. "See you next week. *Zay gezunt*."

Ess Gezunt: Eat in health. "*Ess Gezunt*. Enjoy that sandwich."

Shmear: To spread, though also a term for all spreads. "What kinds of *shmear* can I get with this bagel?"

Kvetch: To complain. Every diner's right at a deli. "She came in, ate, and then kvetched at me for twenty minutes about the soup's color."

L'Chaim: Cheers. "Is it cool to say *l'chaim* with Cel-Ray?"

Maven: A master. "Ziggy Gruber calls himself a deli maven."

Goyish: Gentile, or exuding a non-Jewish vibe. "That deli is really goyish. I mean, they serve lobster rolls."

Treyf: Unkosher. "I don't eat Reubens, they're pure *treyf*."

Haymish: Like home. "Such a *haymish* deli. His mother's in the kitchen."

Listing of Delis

Over the course of researching this book I visited many Jewish delicatessens around the world. Most of these made it into the book, but some did not for reasons having primarily to do with space and the flow of the story. These delis listed below are those that I specifically visited during my three years researching this book. It is by no means a comprehensive list of all Jewish delis, either past or present, but it's nothing to sneeze at.

Part I: New York

Chapters 1–5

Liebman's – Bronx
552 West 235th St
Bronx (Riverdale), NY 10463
(718) 548-4534
www.liebmansdeli.com

Loeser's – Bronx
214 W 231st St
Bronx, NY 10463
(718) 601-6665

Adelman's – Brooklyn
1906 Kings Hwy
Brooklyn, NY 11229
(718) 336-4915

Caraville Glatt/Essex on Coney – Brooklyn
1910 Avenue M (between 19th St. and Ocean Avenue)
Brooklyn, NY 11230
(718) 336-1206
www.caravilleglatt.com

David's Brisket House – Brooklyn
533 Nostrand Ave
Brooklyn, NY 11216
(718) 783-6109

Gottlieb's – Brooklyn
352 Roebling St
Brooklyn, NY 11211
(718) 384-6612

Junior's – Brooklyn – various locations
386 Flatbush Avenue Extension
Brooklyn, NY 11201
(718) 852-5257
www.juniorscheesecake.com

Mill Basin – Brooklyn
5823 Avenue T
Brooklyn, NY 11234
(718) 241-4910
www.millbasindeli.com

Kensington Kosher – Long Island
27 Middle Neck Rd #A
Great Neck, NY 11021
(516) 487-2410

Artie's – Manhattan
2290 Broadway
New York, NY 10024
(212) 579-5959
www.arties.com

Ben's – various in Manhattan, Long Island, and Florida
209 W 38th St
New York, NY 10018
(212) 398-2367
www.bensdeli.net

Carnegie Deli – Manhattan
854 Seventh Ave
New York, NY 10019
(800) 334-5606
www.carnegiedeli.com

Friedman's – Manhattan
75 Ninth Ave
New York, NY 10011
(212) 929-7100
www.friedmansdeli.com

Katz's – Manhattan
205 E Houston St
New York, NY 10002
(212) 254-2246
www.katzdeli.com

Noah's Ark – Manhattan
399 Grand St
New York, NY 10002
(212) 674-2200
www.noahsark.net

Pastrami Queen – Manhattan
Frnt 2
1125 Lexington Ave
New York, NY 10075
(212) 734-1500
www.pastramiqueen.com

Sammy's Roumanian Steakhouse – Manhattan
157 Chrystie St
New York, NY 10002
(212) 673-0330

Stage Deli – Manhattan
834 7th Ave
New York, NY 10019
(212) 245-7850
www.stagedeli.com

2nd Ave Deli – Murray Hill
162 E. 33rd St
New York, NY 10016
(212) 677-0606

Berger's on the Go – Murray Hill
2 E 39th St
New York, NY 10016
(212) 447-5052

Ben's Best – Queens
96-40 Queens Blvd
Rego Park, NY 11374
(718) 897-1700
www.bensbest.com

Part II: USA

Chapter 6 – Detroit: Motown's Deli Blues and Michigan's Suburban Jews

Zingerman's
422 Detroit St
Ann Arbor, MI 48104
(734) 663-DELI
www.zingermans.com

Steve's
6646 Telegraph Rd, at Maple in the Bloomfield Plaza
Bloomfield Hills, MI 48301
(248) 932-0800
www.stevesdeli.com

Ron's Bagel Deli
40270 14 Mile Rd
Commerce Twsp, MI 48390
(248) 960-3850
www.ronsbageldeli.com

Bread Basket – various locations
throughout Michigan
15603 Grand River Ave
Detroit, MI 48227
(313) 836-DELI
www.breadbasketdelis.com

Lou's – various locations
throughout Michigan
6 Mile
8220 W McNichols Rd
Detroit, MI 48221
(313) 861-1321
www.lousdeli.net

Tony's Embers Deli
3258 Orchard Lake Rd
Orchard Lake, MI 48324
(248) 683-3344

Star Deli
24555 W 12 Mile Rd
Southfield, MI 48034-1208
(248) 352-7377

Deli Unique
6724 Orchard Lake Road
West Bloomfield, MI 48322
(248) 737-3890

Stage and Co.
6873 Orchard Lake Rd
West Bloomfield, MI 48322
(248) 855-6622
www.thestagedeli.com

Chapter 7 – Chicago: Can Deli Return to the Windy City?

11 City Diner
1112 S Wabash Ave
Chicago, IL 60605
(312) 212-1112
www.elevencitydiner.com

Ashkenaz
12 E Cedar St
Chicago, IL 60611
(312) 944-5006
www.ashkenazdeli.net

The Bagel
3107 N Broadway St
Chicago, IL 60657
(773) 477-0300
www.bagelrestaurant.com

50 Old Orchard Center
Skokie, IL
(847) 677-0100

Manny's
1141 S Jefferson St
Chicago, IL 60607
(312) 939-2855
www.mannysdeli.com

Romanian Kosher Sausage Co.
7200 N Clark
Chicago, IL 60626
(773) 761-4141

Max & Benny's
461 Waukegan Rd
Northbrook, IL 60062
(847) 272-9490
www.maxandbennys.com

Kaufman's Bakery and Deli
4905 W Dempster
Skokie, IL 60077
(847) 677-6190
www.kaufmansdeli.com

**Chapter 8 – The Yucchuputzville Diaries
Part 1: Goy West Young Man**

Jimmy and Drew's 28th Street
2855 28th St
Boulder, CO 80301
(303) 447-3354

The Bagel
6439 East Hampden Ave
Denver, CO 80222
(303) 756-6667
www.thebageldeli.com

Deli Tech
Unit AA
8101 E Belleview Ave
Denver, CO 80237
(303) 721-6768
www.delitech.com

East Side Kosher
499 S Elm St
Denver, CO 80246
(303) 322-9862
www.eastsidekosherdeli.com

**Heidi's – various locations
throughout Colorado**
17th and Lawrence
1225 17th St
Denver, CO 80202
(720) 214-4728
www.heidisbrooklyndeli.com

New York Deli News
7105 E Hampden Ave
Denver, CO 80222
(303) 759-4741

Zaidy's
121 Adams St
Denver, CO 80206
(303) 333-5336
www.zaidysdeli.com

1512 Larimer St (Corner of 15th
and Lawrence)
Denver, CO 80202
(303) 893-3600

*

Protzel's
7608 Wydown Blvd
Clayton, MO 63105
(314) 721-4445

**New York Bakery and
Delicatessen (since closed)**
7016 Troost Ave
Kansas City, MO 64131
(816) 523-0432

*

Kosher on the Go
1575 S 1100 E
Salt Lake City, UT 84105
(801) 463-1786

**Chapter 9 – I Left My Kishkes in
San Francisco**

Saul's
1475 Shattuck Ave
Berkeley, CA 94709
(510) 848-3354
www.saulsdeli.com

California Street Deli (since closed)
3200 California St
San Francisco, CA 94117
(415) 922-3354

David's
474 Geary Street
San Francisco, CA 94102
(415) 276-5950
www.davidsdelicatessen.com

Miller's East Coast
1725 Polk St
San Francisco, CA 94109
(415) 563-3542
www.millersdelisf.com

Moishe's Pippic
425 Hayes St #A
San Francisco, CA 94102
(415) 431-2440

SF-NY Kosher Deli (since closed)
5 Embarcadero Center
San Francisco, CA 94111
(415) 788-0244
www.sfnewyorkdeli.com

Chapter 10 – Los Angeles: Hooray for Hollywood

Nate n' Al
414 N Beverly Dr
Beverly Hills, CA 90210
(310) 274-0101
www.natenal.com

Fromin's
17615 Ventura Blvd
Encino, CA 91316
(818) 990-6346

1832 Wilshire Blvd
Santa Monica, CA 90401
(310) 829-5443

Canter's
419 N Fairfax Ave
Los Angeles, CA 90036
(323) 651-2030
www.cantersdeli.com

Factor's
9420 W Pico Blvd
Los Angeles, CA 90035
(310) 278-9175
www.factorsdeli.com

Greenblatt's
8017 Sunset Blvd
Los Angeles, CA 90046
(323) 656-0606

Junior's
2379 Westwood Blvd
Los Angeles, CA 90064
(310) 475-5771
www.jrsdeli.com

Langer's
704 S Alvarado St
Los Angeles, CA 90057
(213) 483-8050
www.langersdeli.com

Pico Kosher
8826 W Pico Blvd
Los Angeles, CA 90035
(310) 273-9381

Brent's
19565 Parthenia St
Northridge, CA 91324
(818) 886-5679
www.brentsdeli.com

2799 Townsgate Rd
Westlake Village, CA 91361
(805) 557-1882

Izzy's
1433 Wilshire Blvd
Santa Monica, CA 90403
(310) 394-1131
www.izzysdeli.com

Art's
12224 Ventura Blvd
Studio City, CA 91604
(818) 762-1221
www.artsdeli.com

**Jerry's Famous – various locations
throughout California**
12655 Ventura Boulevard
Studio City, CA 91604
(818) 980-4245
www.jerrysfamousdeli.com

**Chapter 11 – Las Vegas: Luck Be a
Brisket Tonight**

Weiss Bakery and Deli
2744 N Green Valley Pkwy
Henderson, NV 89014
(702) 454-0565

Canter's (in Treasure Island)
3300 S Las Vegas Blvd
Las Vegas, NV 89109
(702) 894-6390

The Carnegie (in the Mirage)
Mirage Hotel
3400 S Las Vegas Blvd
Las Vegas, NV 89109
(866) 339-4566

**Greenberg's (in New York,
New York)**
New York, New York
3790 S Las Vegas Blvd
Las Vegas, NV 89109
(702) 740-6969

Harrie's Bagelmania
855 E Twain Ave, #120
Las Vegas, NV 89169
(702) 369-3322
www.harries.tripod.com

**The Stage in Caesar's Forum Shops
(since closed)**
3500 S Las Vegas Blvd, Ste G11
Las Vegas, NV 89109
(702) 893-4045

Zoozacrackers (in the Wynn)
Wynn Las Vegas
3131 S Las Vegas Blvd
Las Vegas, NV 89162
(702) 770-7000

**Chapter 12 – The Yucchuputzville
Diaries Part 2 : Schmaltz by Southwest**

Goldman's
6929 N Hayden Rd Ste C2
Scottsdale, AZ 85250
(480) 367-9477

*

**Loeb's Perfect New York
Restaurant**
832 15th St NW
Washington, DC 20005
(202) 371-1150

Morty's
4620 Wisconsin Ave NW
Washington, DC 20016
(202) 686-1989
www.mortysdc.com

*

**Goldberg's Bagel and Deli –
various locations throughout
Georgia**
1272 W Paces Ferry Rd NE
Atlanta, GA 30327
(404) 266-0123
www.goldbergsdeli.net

**New York Corned Beef Society
of Atlanta**
Twain's Billiards and Tap
211 E Trinity Pl
Decatur, GA 30030
(404) 373-0063
www.nycbsa.com

*

Kosher Cajun
3519 Severn Ave
Metairie, LA 70002
(504) 888-2010
www.koshercajun.com

*

Parkway Deli
8317 Grubb Rd
Silver Spring, MD 20910
(301) 587-1427
www.theparkwaydeli.com

*

Gleiberman's
5668-D International Dr
Charlotte, NC 28270
(704) 563-8288 OR (800) 849-8288
www.gleibermans.com

Leo's
1421 Elizabeth Ave
Charlotte, NC 28204
(704) 375-2400

*

Katz's
618 W 6th St
Austin, TX 78701
(512) 472-2037
www.katzneverkloses.com

Kenny & Ziggy's
2327 Post Oak Blvd
Houston, TX 77056
(713) 871-8883
www.kennyandziggys.com

**Chapter 13 – Florida: Where Deli
Goes to Die**

Mo's Bagel and Deli
2780 NE 187th St
Aventura, FL 33180
(305) 936-8555

**Too Jay's – various locations
throughout Florida**
3013 Yamato Rd
Boca Raton, FL 33434
(561) 997-9911
www.toojays.com

3G's Gourmet Deli
5869 W Atlantic Ave
Delray Beach, FL 33484
(561) 498-3910
www.3gsdeli.com

Pomperdale
3055 E Commercial Blvd
Fort Lauderdale, FL 33308
(954) 771-9830

Sage Bagel and Deli
800 E Hallandale Beach Blvd, #1
Hallandale Beach, FL 33009
(954) 456-7499
www.sagebagelanddeli.com

Arnie and Richie's (since bought by Roasters' and Toasters)
525 Arthur Godfrey Rd
Miami, FL 33140
(305) 531-7691

Bagel Bar East
1990 NE 123rd St
Miami, FL 33181
(305) 895-7022

Bagel Cove
19003 Biscayne Blvd
Miami, FL 33180
(305) 935-4029

Best Deli
1015 S University Dr
Plantation, FL 33324
(954) 472-0157

Myron's
1800 SW 3rd St
Pompano Beach, FL 33069
(800) 843-4753

Rascal House (since closed)
17190 Collins Ave
Sunny Isles Beach, FL 33160
(305) 947-458

Part III: World

Chapter 14 – Montreal: A Smoked Meat Kingdom

Abie's
3980 St. Jean Blvd
Dollard-des-Ormeaux, QC
H9G 1X1
(514) 626-ABIE (2243)
www.abiesmokedmeat.com

Chenoy's
3616 St Jean Blvd
Dollard-des-Ormeaux, QC
H9G 1X1
(514) 620-2584

Smoke Meat Pete
283 1st Avenue
L'Ile-Perrot, QC J7V 5A1
(514) 425-6068
www.smokemeatpete.com

Ben's (since closed)
990 de Maisonneuve West
Montreal, QC H3A 1M5
(514) 844-1000

The Main
3864 Boulevard Saint-Laurent
Montreal, QC H2W 1Y2
(514) 843-8126

Reuben's
1116 rue Sainte-Catherine Ouest
Montreal, QC H3B 1H4
(514) 866-1029
www.reubensdeli.com

Schwartz's
3895 St Laurent
Montreal, QC H2W 1X9
(514) 842-4813
www.schwartzsdeli.com

Snowdon
5265 Boulevard Décarie
Montreal, QC H3W 3C2
(514) 488-9129
www.snowdondeli.ca

Wilensky's
34 Fairmount Ave W
Montreal, QC H2T 2M1
(514) 271-0247

Lester's
1057 Bernard St W
Outremont, QC H2V 1V1
(514) 213-1313 OR 1-866-LESTERS
www.lestersdeli.com

Deli St. Laurent
2073 Saint-Louis Rd
Saint-Laurent, QC H4M 1P1
(514) 744-4113

Chapter 15 – Toronto: Home
Bittersweet Home

Shopsy's Markham
7240 Woodbine Ave
Markham, ON L3R 1A4
(905) 474-9333

Shopsy's Mississauga
6986 Financial Dr, Unit 5
Mississauga, ON L5N 8J8
(905) 812-4944

Switzer's
7310 Torbram Rd
Mississauga, ON L4T 3X2
(905) 671-0900

Coleman's
3085 Bathurst St
North York, ON M6A 2A3
(416) 789-1141
www.colemanscatering.com

Katz's
3300 Dufferin St
North York, ON M6A 2T5
(416) 782-1111

Wolfie's
670 Sheppard Ave W
North York, ON M3H 2S5
(416) 638-9653

Centre Street
1136 Centre St
Thornhill, ON L4J 3M8
(905) 731-8037
www.centrestreetdeli.com

Steeles Deli
180 Steeles Ave W
Thornhill, ON L4J 2L1
(905) 881-8366

Caplansky's
12 Clinton St
Toronto, ON M6J 2N8
(416) 500-3852
www.caplanskys.com

Dunn's
284A King St W
Toronto, ON M5V 1J2
(416) 599-5464

Moe Pancer's
3856 Bathurst St
Toronto, ON M3H 3N3
(416) 633-1230
www.pancersdeli.sites.toronto.com

New Yorker Deli
1140 Bay St
Toronto, ON M5S 2B4
(416) 923-3354

Pickle Barrel (various, including the following)
595 Bay St
Toronto, ON M5G 2C2
(416) 977-6677
www.picklebarrel.ca

312 Yonge St
Toronto, ON M5B 1R4
(416) 542-9471

Reubens' (since closed)
10 Bay St
Toronto, ON M5J 2R8
(416) 861-0175

Shopsy's
33 Yonge St
Toronto, ON M5E 1G4
(416) 365-3333
www.shopsys.ca

Yitz's
346 Eglinton Ave W
Toronto, ON M5N 1A2
(416) 487-4508
www.yitzs.ca

Chapter 16 – London: God Save the Deli

B&K Salt Beef Bar
11 Lanson House
London HA8 6NL
+44 20 8952 8204

Bevis Marks Kosher Restaurant
4 Heneage Lane
London EC3A 5DQ
+44 20 7283 2220
www.bevismarks-therestaurant.com

Bloom's (various)
130 Golders Green Rd
London NW11 8HB
+44 020 8455 1338

313 Hale Lane
Edgware, Middlesex HA8 7AX
+44 020 8958 2229

7 Montague St
Bloomsbury
London WC1B 5
+44 020 7323 1717

The Brass Rail Salt Beef Bar
400 Oxford St
London W1A 1AB
+44 800 123400

Brick Lane Beigel Bake
159 Brick Lane, Tower Hamlets
London E1 6SB
+44 020 7729 0616

Britain's First and Best Beigel Shop
155 Brick Lane, Spitalfields
London E1 6SB
+44 020 7729 0826

Harry Morgan
29-31 St. Johns Wood
High Street
London NW8 7NH
+44 020 7722 1869
www.harryms.co.uk

6 Market Place
Oxford Circus
London W1W 8AF
+44 020 7580 4849

Reuben's
79 Baker St, Marylebone
London W1U 6RG
+44 020 7486 0035

**Chapter 17 – The Fine Art of Jewish
Delicatessen in Belgium and Paris**

Chez Gilles
Rue de la Clinique 21
Anderlecht, Brussels, Belgium
+32 02 523 94 22

Hoffy's
Lange Kievitstraat 52
2018 Antwerpen, Belgium
+32 03 234 35 35

*

Chez Marianne
2, rue Hospitalières St Gervais,
75004
4th Arrondissement
Paris, France
+33 1 42 72 18 86

Dimitri Panzer
26, rue des Rosiers, 75004
4th Arrondissement - le Marais
Paris, France
+33 1 40 27 82 75

Florence Finkelstajn
24, rue des Ecouffes, 75004
4th Arrondissement - le Marais
Paris, France
+33 1 48 87 12 20

Jo Goldenberg (since closed)
7 rue des Rosiers, 75004
4th Arrondissement - le Marais
Paris, France
+33 1 48 87 20 16

Maison David
6, rue des Ecouffes, 75004
4th Arrondissement - le Marais
Paris, France
+33 1 42 78 15 76

Sacha Finkelsztajn
27, rue des Rosiers, 75004
4th Arrondissement - le Marais
Paris, France
+33 1 42 72 78 91
www.finkelsztajn.com

**Chapter 18 – Krakow: Heartburn
from Poland's Tortured Past**

Alef
31-071 Kraków, ul. wi tej Agnieszki 5
Krakow
+48 12 424 31 31
www.alef.pl

Ariel
31-053 Kraków, ul. Szeroka 18
Krakow
+48 12 421 79 20
www.ariel-krakow.pl

Klezmer Hois
Kazimierz, 31-053 Kraków, ul.
Szeroka 6
Krakow
+48 12 411 12 45
www.klezmer-hois.cracow.pl

**Afterword—The Schmaltz Strikes Back:
Deli's Future Returns to Its Roots**

Kenny and Zuke's Delicatessan
1038 Southwest Stark St
Portland, OR 97205
(503) 222-3354
www.kennyandzukes.com

Mile End Delicatessan
97A Hoyt St
Brooklyn, NY 11217
(718) 852-7510
www.mileendbrooklyn.com

Acknowledgments

It takes a lot of people to Save the Deli, so let's start rolling the credits. Thanks to Mitch Dermer for being insane enough to write a term paper on the sociology of the Jewish delicatessen business with me, and then being sane enough to head off to law school before it was too late. Thanks as well to Professor Morton Weinfeld at McGill for giving Dermer and me such a good mark. If we'd gotten a B, I'm not so sure you'd be reading this now.

I owe a debt to Rabbi Jon Moscowitz, who put me into the hands of Canada's premiere agent, Michael Levine, a true dynamo. Michael understood the idea right away, and within a day he had a pending deal with Doug Pepper. Pepper, a dapper deli lover at the helm of McClelland and Stewart in Toronto, deserves twelve ounces of mustard-slathered gratitude, not only for taking a chance on me by buying the book, but for seeing me through damn near three years of research and writing, and answering the endless questions of a first time author. Doug, you're not only a great publisher, but a good friend.

Infinite amounts of praise should be showered on Jenna Johnson, the editor at Harcourt (now Houghton Mifflin Harcourt) who brought this book to New York, deli's heartland. Throughout the long editing process Jenna never shied away from her opinions (not to mention her trusty red pen), and always asked the tough questions that needed to be raised. Ultimately, this is a stronger, more enjoyable book because of her brilliant direction at every step along the way. Someone ought to name a sandwich after her.

The other editor to whom I owe an incalculable debt is Jenny Bradshaw in Toronto, whose name should adorn each and every comma-and-hyphen in these pages. Jenny bore much of the heavy lifting during the later stages of editing and design. Her attention to detail, patience, and willingness to try anything is what editors everywhere should aspire to.

Thanks to Lori Glazer and Taryn Roeder at HMH and Ashley Dunn at M&S (and the respective sales and marketing folks at both) for your work in spreading the word, to Marilyn Biderman for selling the heck out of it, to the legendary Carolyn Hessel at the Jewish Book Council for putting me onto the Jewish book circuit, and to Roger Bennett and the Reboot Crew for every link in the chain.

I cannot express enough gratitude to all the deli owners I met over the past three years who sat down with me, piled a table with food, and let me into your lives. Meeting you all was the greatest benefit that came out of this process, and I sincerely thank each and every one of you for your help and generosity. I especially want to thank Lorne Pancer, the Lebewohl family, Sy Ginsberg, Ziggy Gruber, and Michel Kalifa, for allowing me to call repeatedly and answering each and every question I had about the business. Zay gezunt to you all.

I also need to thank the readers and fans of savethedeli.com, who have sustained my passion for this beyond even what I expected. You are tireless and dedicated, and that love has brought deli back from the brink. Special praise belongs to my old friend Daniel Malen, who not only designed savethedeli.com, but also the logo that adorns this book's cover. Purchase a "Pastrami Mommy" thong in his honor.

Whenever I was away from home, I was fortunate enough to have friends who lent me a hand. Foremost is Chris Farber, who not only let me live in his illegal matzo factory of a Brooklyn apartment (it's true) for a month in 2006, but who also joined me on countless deli trips around New York and Europe. I'm honored that your incredible photographs adorn the pages here. Thanks also to

Adam Caplan, who endured two years of my insanity with the utmost class.

And now, to all those whose couches I crashed on, or who gave me a hand during work on this book, let me give thanks: Asher Lack, Dara Zarnett, Jake and Joanne Bogoch, Jamie Lawson and Amy Anderson, David Katznelson, Marni Kinrys, Tom Miller, Eric Katz, David and Sara Wilson, Jems Peskin, Hugo Alconada, Ben Leszcz, Stephen Rothstein, Eiran Harris, Louis Berkowitz, Aaron Gilboe and Ariadne Siotis, Robert Gadek, Rachel Kaplan, and Clive Bettington. Your generosity made my travels an absolute pleasure. A sandwich in each of your names.

Most importantly I have to thank my family, without whom I am nothing. Mom, Dad (and Fuzz), you gave me my passion for deli from an early age, and not only taught me to love what I do, but afforded me every opportunity to do so in life with love and the utmost support.

Lauren, you and I started dating right before I ventured down this *schmaltz*-filled road, and you've somehow stuck with me every step of the way. I cannot imagine how difficult that was. You are brilliant and beautiful and a calming force. Without your love, I'm not sure I could have done this. In the sandwich of my life, you are the bread that holds me together.

Index

Illustration Credits